Women as Candidates in American Politics

Susan J. Carroll

Women as Candidates in American Politics

Indiana University Press □ Bloomington

FIRST MIDLAND BOOK EDITION 1987

Manufactured in the United States of America

Library of Congress Cataloging in Publication Data

Carroll, Susan J., 1950–
  Women as candidates in American politics.

  Bibliography: p.
  Includes index.
  1. Women in politics—United States. 2. Elections—
United States. I. Title.
HQ1391.U5C37 1985   305'3329   84-42836
ISBN 0-253-36615-1 cloth
ISBN 0-253-20425-9 Paperback

2 3 4 5 6 91 90 89 88 87

To Reo M. Christenson

Contents

TABLES

PREFACE

In the mid-1970s when I first began the research that is reported in this book, there was little public interest in, and almost no systematic information about, women candidates and their campaigns. The political arm of the women's movement was still in the early stages of its development. The "gender gap" in public opinion and voting behavior had not yet been discovered. In races for most political offices, a woman candidate was a rarity.

In 1984 as this book goes to press, systematic information about women candidates is still lacking, but interest in women candidates is at an all-time high. Although many developments over the past decades have drawn public attention to women candidates and their campaigns, none has been so dramatic in its impact as the 1984 nomination of Geraldine Ferraro as Democratic candidate for the vice-presidency of the United States.

Ferraro's candidacy was a significant breakthrough for women in American politics. On November 6, 1984, many Americans experienced their first opportunity ever to vote for a woman candidate for high-level political office. Regardless of the choice they made, the presence of a woman's name on their ballots will not seem so unusual to these Americans the next time around. Moreover, Ferraro withstood perhaps the most intense scrutiny ever received by a vice-presidential candidate and proved herself to be a most able campaigner and competitior. Her campaign probably went a long way toward alleviating fears that a woman could not handle the pressures of a major national campaign.

While Ferraro's candidacy was a great breakthrough for political women, it also vividly illustrated that women face great barriers in achieving a place in American political life truly equal to that of men. At many points in her campaign, Ferraro was treated differently because she was a woman. Ferraro was asked if she could bake blueberry muffins, called "bitchy" by her opponent's press secretary and a "four-million-dollar—I can't say it, but it rhymes with rich" by her opponent's wife, "patronized" by Vice-President George Bush before millions of viewers of the vice-presidential debate, and asked on national television if she could bring herself to push the button to fire nuclear weapons. Ferraro's campaign was hindered by relentless press attention to her and her husband's financial history, continual questions about her qualifications, and strong attacks upon her pro-choice position by the hierarchy of the Catholic Church. While these issues might have arisen regardless of Ferraro's sex, it is possible that her finances attracted more attention, her credentials received more scrutiny, and her position on abortion evoked a stronger reaction because she was a woman.

Because Ferraro's candidacy was both unique and visible, it drew public attention to the fact that women candidates confront distinctive electoral circumstances. However, Ferraro's candidacy is only the most visible manifestation of a larger phenomenon that has been evident in the American political system since the early 1970s—the movement of increasing numbers of women into politics. Ferraro is just one of many pioneers among women candidates for public office. Like Ferraro, women candidates at all levels of office are still confronting and often breaking through important barriers.

This book focuses on the broader movement of women as candidates into electoral politics in the United States. It presents the results of a systematic, nationwide study of women who seek election to congressional, statewide, and state legislative offices. The study examines various aspects of women's candidacies and campaigns including their recruitment to run for office, the reasons why they win and lose, their political ambitions, and their views toward policy issues of particular relevance to women.

I am indebted to several organizations and to many individuals for their contributions to this research. The Brookings Institution and the American Association of University Women provided major fellowships. Additional funding was furnished by the Woodrow Wilson National Fellowship Foundation, the Graduate School at Indiana University, and the Indiana University Women's Studies Program.

Three national organizations and members of their staffs gave critical assistance at various stages. Jane McMichael, former Executive Director, and Fredrica Wechsler, former Political Action Coordinator, of the National Women's Political Caucus provided the initial inspiration and encouragement to pursue this project. Various colleagues at the Center for the American Woman and Politics (CAWP) of the Eagleton Institute of Politics at Rutgers University have helped to shape my ideas about women in politics and have provided helpful suggestions on this research; they include Ruth Mandel, Marilyn Johnson, Wendy Strimling, Kathy

Stanwick, and Kathy Kleeman. I am especially grateful to the National Women's Education Fund (NWEF) for acting as a sponsoring organization and for providing me with work space while I collected data; to various staff members at the NWEF—particularly Michal Cline and Cynthia Ulman—for their help in locating and identifying women candidates; and especially to Betsey Wright, former Executive Director of the NWEF, for contributing in numerous ways to this research and to my understanding of women in politics.

Jeff Fishel, Marjorie Randon Hershey, and Leroy N. Rieselbach provided intellectual guidance, constructive criticism, and moral support. Margaret Jean Intons-Peterson and Irwin Gertzog also made useful suggestions on parts of the manuscript. Several people helped with typing at various stages, including Ginny Perrine, Martha Casisa, Mary Ahearn, and Judy Luckus.

Last, but by no means least, I owe an enormous debt to the 1,212 women candidates who took time during a busy campaign season to complete the survey that made this study possible.

Women as Candidates
in American Politics

CHAPTER ONE

■ □ □ □ □ □ □ □ □

Introduction

TRADITIONALLY, POLITICAL SCIENTISTS have overlooked questions relating to the representation of women by governing institutions. The failure to raise questions pertaining to the representation of women has stemmed, in part, from sex stereotyping. The domination of politics by men has been viewed as a natural extension of the sexual division of labor within the family. Women's preoccupation with home and family has been seen as the reason for their relative absence from political positions. Because women have been assumed to share the political views and preferences of their husbands and fathers, women's representation in the political sphere has not been viewed as an issue of major concern.[1]

However, political scientists' neglect of questions pertaining to the representation of women in American politics, while perhaps rooted in sex stereotyping, has been reinforced since the middle of this century by the changing focus of democratic theory. In "classical" democratic theory, the active participation of the citizenry was of central concern.[2] Participation was viewed as necessary to prevent leaders from pursuing their own selfish interests at the expense of the interests of the public. More importantly, for theorists such as John Stuart Mill and Jean-Jacques Rousseau, participation was assumed to enhance the self-fulfillment and development of the individual.[3]

However, for many years the dialogue in democratic theory has been dominated not by theorists in the classical democratic tradition, but by a group of revisionists, generally labeled pluralists or democratic elitists.[4] Pluralists and democratic elitists have rejected classical democratic theory

as unrealistic in light of post–World War II empirical findings. In the eyes
of these revisionists, "classical" democratic theory is inappropriate for
examining democracy in twentieth-century America because of its de-
mand that democratic citizens be interested participants, well-informed
about public affairs, and rational in their voting decisions.[5] Considerable
evidence generated in the postwar era indicated that few members of the
American public could fulfill these expectations,[6] and in light of this
evidence, the revisionists attempted to construct a contemporary theory
of democracy consistent with the findings of empirical research.[7]

The findings on the inadequacies of individual voters led the revisionists to shift the emphasis of democratic theory from a focus on the desirability of widespread participation, evident in classical theory, to a
focus on system attributes and institutional arrangements as the defining
characteristics of democracy. Attributes such as the existence of elections
and political competition became the critical criteria for judging whether
a system was democratic.[8]

Similarly, many theorists in the democratic elitist and pluralist traditions came to view elites as the guardians of democratic values and the
mass public as a potential threat to these values. Peter Bachrach has
suggested, "The relationship of elites to masses is, in a vital way, reversed
from classical theory; masses, not elites, become the potential threat to
the system, and elites, not masses, become its defender."[9] The empirical
basis and justification for this shift is evident in the post–World War II
studies of James Prothro and Charles Grigg, Samuel Stouffer, and Herbert McClosky.[10]

As portrayed by revisionists, democratic theory became largely explanatory and descriptive, unlike classical democratic theory, which had a
strong prescriptive, even utopian, emphasis.[11] Lane Davis has observed:

> Contemporary democracy is less a guide to future action than a codification of
> past accomplishments. . . . It vindicates the main features of the status quo
> and provides a model for tidying up loose ends. Democracy becomes a sys-
> tem to be preserved, not an end to be sought. Those who wish a guide to the
> future must look elsewhere.[12]

A theoretical tradition that judges democratic regimes on the basis of
system attributes and institutional arrangements rather than on the basis
of widespread participation, that views existing elites rather than ordinary
citizens as the guardians of democratic values, and that is descriptive
rather than prescriptive would not be likely to ask: Why are so few
women active participants in the policy-making process? Is there not
something wrong with a "democratic" system in which women constitute

a majority of the citizenry but an almost negligible minority of participants at the governing level?[13] Because of the basic assumptions that underlie the revisionist point of view, questions about women's participation would not, in the absence of some external provocation, be likely to occur to those working within a pluralist or democratic elitist framework.[14]

However, this is not a full explanation for why political scientists working within pluralist and democratic elitist traditions have devoted little attention to questions pertaining to the representation of women. The explanation has another critical component. In accepting elitist and pluralist conceptions of politics, most political scientists have equated interests with "the political pressure an individual or a group brings to bear on government."[15] From this perspective, there are two major means through which interests can be expressed in the political process— through voting and through interest-group activity.

The findings of early voting studies demonstrated that women divided their votes among candidates in roughly the same proportions as men.[16] No identifiable "women's vote" emerged, as some observers expected, following the extension of the suffrage in 1920. Moreover, between 1920 and the early 1960s, only two organizations—the National Woman's Party and the National Federation of Business and Professional Women's Clubs—had agendas that included a strong focus on women's rights.[17] As a result, from the perspective of contemporary theories of democracy, there was little or no visible evidence that women as a group had any distinctive interests. They voted approximately the same as men, and by and large they were not organized on behalf of any distinctive interests. Consequently, many political scientists apparently assumed, implicitly if not explicitly, that the interests of women and men in the electorate were identical.

Since women were not viewed as having distinct interests, the fact that they were represented in governing bodies by men never became an issue of concern. The equation of the interests of men and women led to the implicit assumption that male representatives would represent women in their constituencies equally as well (or as poorly) as they represented men.

Moreover, the equation of the interests of men and women meant that possible attitudinal and behavioral differences between male policymaking elites and those few females who attained positions in elites were not investigated. Susan Bourque and Jean Grossholtz have observed, "those who study elites assume that those elites will be men and seem little concerned to investigate the few women who do appear."[18] However, what has been assumed is not simply that all elites will be men but that all elites, regardless of sex, will behave similarly. Given the lack of evidence to indicate that women citizens had interests distinct from those of men, there was little reason for political scientists working within the dominant pluralist/democratic elitist framework to expect the policy-relevant attitudes and behavior of women in office to differ from those of male representatives.[19]

Major Concerns of the Study

While the dominance of pluralist and elitist conceptions of democracy may help to explain why few political scientists prior to the 1970s examined questions related to the representation of women, the research in this book is based on the premise that such questions have considerable contemporary relevance. Findings from a nationwide survey of women who ran as major party candidates for congressional, statewide, and state legislative offices in 1976 are examined in an attempt to explain the underrepresentation of women at the present time and to assess the likelihood of increased numerical representation of women in the future.[20] The possibility of a linkage between numerical representation of women and representation of the interests of women also is assessed. The emphasis is on demonstrating the importance of aspects of the political opportunity structure in impeding increases in the number of women among elective officeholders.

The major impediments to women's political participation can be grouped into two general categories: (1) limitations resulting from women's socialization and sex-role conceptions (which I refer to throughout this book as sex-role socialization variables), and (2) limitations in the structure of political opportunity (which I call political opportunity variables).

The first category consists of factors that may be societal in origin but have been incorporated into women's psychological perceptions of themselves in relation to the political world. Because these factors have been internalized by women, their importance as obstacles to women's political participation can be expected to diminish as women, either individually or collectively, alter their perceptions of sex-appropriate behavior. Examples of sex-role socialization variables that might inhibit political participation include beliefs that women traditionally have held about themselves, such as the belief that the female should bear the primary responsibility for child care and the belief that women are emotionally unsuited for politics.

The second category consists of factors external to the individual woman that exist independent of her psychological self. They are objective aspects of the political situation that a female politician confronts. Since these factors are not subject to the personal control of female politicians, their importance as obstacles to women's political participation cannot be expected to diminish as a result of alterations in women's perceptions of sex-appropriate behavior. Political opportunity variables, as defined here, would include factors such as the staying power of incumbents, voter prejudice against women candidates, and a pattern of one-party domination in a district.[21]

The key criterion for distinguishing "sex-role socialization" and "political opportunity" variables is locus of control. Sex-role socialization variables are *internal to women politicians* and through attitude change are subject to modification and alteration. In contrast, political opportunity variables are *external to individual women politicians* and, consequently, are not subject to modification or alteration by individual women.[22]

Research on politically active women has far more frequently explored and emphasized sex-role socialization variables that restrict women's participation than limitations in the political opportunity structure. Naomi Lynn has suggested, "While not questioning . . . that motivation, socialization, and stereotypic female roles are important, I suggest that more emphasis needs to be put on structural restrictions that may also have explanatory power in clarifying the relative scarcity of women political leaders."[23] This book represents an initial step toward addressing the need Lynn describes. A major theme is that political opportunity variables are critical in explaining the lack of greater numbers of women among political elites.

Using Women Candidates to Examine Representation

While some literature examining women officeholders and party elites has emerged in recent years,[24] there have been no broad-based, systematic studies of women candidates.[25] Nevertheless, studies of candidates can provide considerable insight into the factors that are responsible for the present underrepresentation of women—insight that cannot be gained through studies of officeholders or party elites.

The number of women serving in elective offices depends on two critical factors—the recruitment of women to run for office, and their rate of success in winning elections. A third factor, women's desire to remain in the offices they occupy or to seek other offices, is perhaps not as central as the other two factors but is nevertheless important.

Studies of party elites are not particularly useful in examining these three factors, largely because these elites include numerous women who have never held, and who have no interest in holding, elective office. An elite active in party affairs does not constitute a particularly good measure of a potential public officeholding elite.

Similarly, studies of current officeholders are hindered in examining the factors responsible for the numerical underrepresentation of women; they investigate only those women who have been successful in the electoral arena. Yet, much can be learned about the recruitment process and about impediments to women's success at the polls by examining women who are unsuccessful in seeking office.

In addition, while officeholders provide a base for investigating the ambition structures of those who may remain in office, women not currently serving in elective positions, who may aspire to public officeholding, are excluded. In contrast, a study of candidates allows one to examine both those who are successful in the electoral arena and those who are not. A data base of candidates includes women currently serving in office and also women who, while unsuccessful, may run again and win office in the future.

In addition to casting light on reasons for the numerical underrepresentation of women, a study of women candidates can provide insight about the relationship between the number of women serving in elective offices and the representation of women's interests.[26] While the relationship between numerical representation and representation of women's interests could be examined most directly by studying the behavior of women officeholders, this relationship has been little explored due to the small number of women serving in most offices as well as the cost and complexity of research designs that would measure behavior other than voting. Consequently, the question of whether an increase in the number of women serving in elective offices would lead to an increase in the representation of women's interests remains unresolved. A study of women candidates can provide suggestive evidence by examining whether candidates have attitudinal predispositions that would lead them to represent women's interests if elected.

The Data Base

Questionnaires were mailed to the entire population of 1,936 women who ran as major party candidates for state legislative, statewide, and congressional offices in primaries and/or general elections in 1976. Questionnaires were sent to candidates within each state shortly after the date of the primary election. A follow-up questionnaire was mailed to any candidate who did not respond to the first questionnaire within one month. A few weeks later a reminder postcard was sent to any candidate who still had not responded. Before the initial mailing, the questionnaire was pretested twice.

A total of 1,212 of the 1,936 candidates completed and returned the questionnaire, for a response rate of 62.6%. No substantial differences between respondents and the population of candidates were found for party, region, level of office, incumbency, outcome of the general election, or participation in a primary election. However, those who won contested primary elections were represented in a significantly higher proportion among respondents than among the candidate population as a whole. While 68.2% of those who won contested primaries completed and returned the questionnaire, only 55.2% of those who lost primary elections responded. Consequently, the findings of the research must be considered to be somewhat more representative of the winners of contested primaries than of the losers.

A detailed description of the data collection process and more complete statistical information on response rate are included in Appendix A. A copy of the questionnaire is included in Appendix B.

While it would have been desirable to have a sample of male candidates included in the study, this was not feasible.[27] Many of the questions addressed in this study do not require that female candidates be compared with male candidates. However, where a male-female comparison is necessary, the comparison must be based on findings from previous studies of public officials and candidates (who, for the most part, have been males). Frequently, references to earlier studies and evidence from them will be cited in notes, rather than in the text itself. Generally, this will be done when I feel the evidence fails to point conclusively to clear sex differences, or when I have strong reservations about how comparable data from previous studies are to my own. However, whenever findings from research on male candidates or officeholders, in comparison with my findings, point to a highly probable pattern of sex differences, I will make reference to the relevant studies and findings directly in the text. In this way, I will call possible sex differences to the reader's attention at several points throughout the study.

Overview of Subsequent Chapters

Chapter 2 presents arguments, rooted in democratic theory, for the contemporary relevance of questions relating to the representation of women. Recent developments in the political system and in political science suggest that the numerical underrepresentation of women and the relationship between the number of women serving in office and the representation of women's interests deserve our attention.

Chapter 3 examines the recruitment of women candidates as one factor important in explaining the current numerical underrepresentation of women among political elites. The central focus is on the extent and nature of the political parties' involvement in the recruitment of women candidates. This chapter investigates three possible patterns in the recruitment of women by party leaders: that party leaders are more active in recruiting women for low-prestige than for high-prestige offices, that they show a tendency to recruit women as "sacrificial lambs" in districts where there is little hope of general election victory, and that they recruit women disproportionately in multimember districts.

Chapters 4, 5, and 6 examine the electoral success of women candidates as a second factor having a critical effect on the numerical representation of women. Chapter 4 explores candidates' own perceptions of their major problems and assets in primary campaigns in an attempt to determine the factors candidates themselves considered critical to the outcome of their primary elections. Chapters 5 and 6 assess the empirical validity of three popular explanations for why women candidates are not more successful at the polls. These explanations focus on women candidates' lack of qualifications, their failure to employ accepted campaign techniques and practices, and handicaps related to their sex. The statistical validity of candidates' own explanations for their losses (emerging from the analysis in chapter 4) also is examined. Finally, the relative explanatory power of all of these explanations is compared with that of yet another possible explanation, based on political opportunity variables, for why women candidates do not have a higher rate of electoral success.

Chapter 7 focuses on the final factor that may influence the numerical representation of women—candidates' political ambition structures. A number of measures of ambition are examined to assess the extent to which women candidates are politically ambitious. Then, the factors that inhibit the ambitions of women candidates are explored, first by examining candidates' own explanations for their lack of ambition, and second by examining statistically whether highly ambitious and less ambitious candidates differ significantly on a number of variables generally thought to affect political aspirations.

Chapter 8 explores the possible relationship between the numerical representation of women among public officeholders and representation of the interests of women. The attitudes and behavior of women candidates are examined across a number of measures, including membership in feminist organizations, treatment of women's issues in primary campaigns, sex-role attitudes, attitude toward the women's movement, and views on various women's issues.

Finally, chapter 9 summarizes the major themes of the study, discusses the implications of the findings, and examines developments that might contribute to an increase in the number of women in elective office.

CHAPTER TWO

□ ■ □ □ □ □ □ □ □

Democratic Theory and the Representation of Women

WHILE FOR YEARS political scientists devoted very little attention to questions regarding the representation of women, such questions have considerable contemporary relevance. Recent developments both in the political system and in political science itself have made representation of women a concern for political scientists of varying theoretical persuasions.

Two developments have led to a greater concern with the numerical representation of women—the emergence of the feminist movement in the political system, and increased attention to the need for reincorporation of classical democratic ideals in political science. The recent growth of the feminist movement also has drawn attention to the importance of questions relating to the representation of the interests of women.

The Feminist Movement and Numerical Representation

Political scientists who adopt some type of democratic theoretical perspective can be arrayed along a continuum, according to their views about the desirability of greater citizen participation and involvement in the governance of society. The views of most political scientists interested in the study of American politics undoubtedly fall somewhere between the two extremes, but many lean more toward one end of the continuum than the other.

The emergence and growth of the contemporary feminist movement should lead directly to a concern with the numerical representation of women for those at one end of the continuum. These are democratic elitists who would seem content with a relatively passive role (i.e., one no more active than today) for the public. The views of individual scholars such as Thomas Dye, Joseph Schumpeter, Giovanni Sartori, and Bernard Berelson would seem to fall very near this end of the continuum.[1] Yet, perhaps the clearest embodiment of this perspective exists more as a composite caricature in the works of critics, such as Bachrach and Walker, than in the work of any single theorist. Bachrach, for example, has claimed that among democratic elitists, "the political passivity of the great majority of the people is not regarded as an element of democratic malfunctioning, but on the contrary, as a necessary condition for allowing the creative functioning of the elites."[2] Similarly, Walker has maintained that democratic elitists believe, "If the . . . masses participate in large numbers, democratic self-restraint will break down and peaceful competition among the elites, the central concern in elitist theory, will become impossible."[3]

While some might argue, as Dahl does,[4] that such beliefs are not held in extreme form by any of the theorists whom Bachrach and Walker cite, scholars who view elites as the primary guardians of democratic values, and the mass public as a potential threat to the preservation of those values, might well be concerned about the large numbers of women who have been mobilized by the feminist movement. The public is likely to remain relatively passive and to allow "business as usual" only as long as elites are able to generate widespread mass support. And the participation of thousands of women in the contemporary feminist movement can be viewed as a sign that the existing elites have failed to inspire such support. Thomas Dye has explained:

> It is essential that individuals in the masses *feel* that they have the opportunity to rise to positions in the elite. . . . A caste system which withholds any opportunity for, or erects artificial (for example, racial) barriers to, individual advancement among the masses cannot inspire mass support.[5]

Increasing the number of women among governing elites has been a major concern of many feminist organizations. It is this concern that led, in part, to the creation of the Women's Campaign Fund, a political action committee that raises and distributes money to women candidates. It is this concern that led, in part, to the formation of the National Women's Education Fund, which among other functions conducts educational programs to facilitate the entry of women into elite positions. It is this concern that has led the National Women's Political Caucus and its state and local chapters to mobilize members to work in the campaigns of women candidates, to endorse the candidacies of women, and to contribute money to their campaigns. Finally, concern for increasing the number of women among governing elites was the motivating factor that led more than fifty organizations to join together to form a Coalition for Women's Appointments in late 1976. The coalition submitted names and lobbied for the appointment of women to both the Carter and the Reagan administrations.

The slow rate of progress in achieving elective and appointive offices for women is the fuel that feeds these efforts. The few women elected or appointed to governmental positions, relative to the number qualified to hold these positions, does not lead to the feeling, critical according to Dye, that women in the general citizenry have sufficient opportunity to rise to elite positions. Feminist activists do not perceive the political system to be as open to women as it is to men.

Because of the failure of contemporary elites to provide equitable numerical representation for women, the underrepresentation of women among governing elites is an issue that should concern political scientists who are sympathetic to the democratic elitist point of view. Unless women attain a much larger proportion of elective and appointive positions, the support of active feminists is not likely to be regained. Rather, feminists are likely to continue to exert considerable pressure on, and thus to interfere with the functioning of, existing political elites.

Renewed Interest in Classical Ideals and Numerical Representation

While the growth of the feminist movement has made numerical representation of women an issue of importance to scholars who believe the public should play a limited role in the governance of society, political science itself has, in recent years, witnessed a growth in the number of theorists suggesting that classical democratic ideals be reincorporated into democratic theory. Theorists such as Peter Bachrach, Jack Walker, Carole Pateman, and those whom Dennis Thompson describes as "citizenship theorists" occupy the opposite end of the mass participation continuum since they desire a very active, participatory role on the part of the public.[6] The renewed interest of such scholars in classical democratic ideals, particularly the ideal of citizen participation, leads logically to a concern with the numerical representation of women.

Several theorists, who have advocated a reincorporation of the ideal of participation, have suggested that democratic participation be extended to the workplace and the economic sphere.[7] Although their concern with expanding the realm of democratic participation to include the private sector may be laudable, these theorists have not examined as thoroughly as they might have the inadequacy of participation within the formal political system.

Some of the best evidence for the failure of the political system to develop active qualities in its citizenry is seen in the data collected on the political orientations and participation of women.[8] Past studies have found women to be somewhat less active than men in some forms of political participation, to have lower levels of political efficacy, and to be less interested in politics.[9] While the male portion of the citizenry has fallen short of fulfilling classical democratic requirements for the ideal citizen, female citizens have fallen even shorter.

From a classical democratic perspective, this passivity of women clearly should be of concern. The greater passivity of women relative to men generally has been explained in terms of sex-role socialization.[10] If women citizens are, in fact, socialized to believe that political interest and activity are not appropriate for females, then from a classical perspective this clearly reflects a failure on the part of a democratic society.

However, the greater passivity of women may result not only from sex-role socialization, but also from the perception that opportunities to affect policy outcomes through participation are not open to women. The inhibiting effects of sex-role socialization may be reinforced by a perception that the political system discourages meaningful participation by women.

There is evidence that American women perceive that they do not have as much opportunity as men to participate in the policy-making aspects of politics. For example, the 1972 Virginia Slims Poll, conducted by Lou Harris and Associates, found 50% of American women agreed with the statement "Women are mostly given the detailed dirty work chores in politics, while men hold the real power." Only 29% of women disagreed. Furthermore, agreement was highest among those with the remaining years and knowledge necessary to make the greatest contributions to the public sector—those under forty years of age and those with a college education.[11]

One of the factors contributing to the perception that the political system discourages meaningful participation by women is the small numbers of women in visible positions of public leadership.[12] Certainly a woman who overcomes the inhibiting effects of sex-role socialization and desires to participate to her fullest capabilities must be discouraged to some extent by the knowledge that relatively few women before her have successfully attained positions of political leadership. An increase in the number of women holding public offices would serve as a visible sign that the system is open to, and encourages, women's participation.

From a classical democratic perspective, an increase in the numerical representation of women would, of course, be desirable because participation may enhance the self-development of women who attain office. However, the benefits of increased numerical representation may extend well beyond the individual women who gain political positions. By providing a visible indication that the system encourages women's participation in the policy-making process, greater numerical representation may help to stimulate greater political interest and participation among female citizens.

Theorists associated with the classical democratic perspective have outlined another argument that leads to a concern with the numerical underrepresentation of women among policy-making elites. John Stuart Mill, in his essay "The Subjection of Women," cited two reasons for an affirmative answer to the question "Would mankind be at all better off if women were free?"[13] The first benefit Mill foresaw as a consequence of greater equality for women was "the advantage of having the most universal and pervading of all human relations regulated by justice instead of injustice."[14] The second reason is of greater interest here. As Mill noted,

> The second benefit to be expected from giving women the free use of their faculties, by leaving them the free choice of their employments, and opening to them the same field of occupation and the same prizes and encouragements as to other human beings, would be that of doubling the mass of mental faculties available for higher service of humanity.[15]

While Mill was not speaking specifically of advantages that would accrue in the political sphere, his argument clearly is applicable to politics.[16] Kirsten Amundsen has echoed Mill's argument as it applies to women in contemporary American society:

> The effect of sexist ideology has been to disarm the American woman politically and also to deprive American democracy of the potentially informed and intelligent contributions of more than half of its citizenry. From the point of view of classical democratic theory, this is clearly disastrous.[17]

At the governing level, the relative absence of women indicates that the talents of many capable females are not being used to their fullest potential in public service. To scholars who have embraced the classical democratic ideal of maximum citizen participation, numerical representation is important, at least in part, because an increase in women officeholders would represent a greater use of the skills and talents available in society.[18]

Representation of the Interests of Women

The rapid growth of the contemporary feminist movement has called into question the assumption long held by political scientists that women have no policy interests distinct from those of men. During the late 1960s and throughout the 1970s, many women organized to push for concerns which had been overlooked in the political process. These concerns commonly are labeled "women's issues" and throughout this study will be referred to interchangeably as women's issues and as policy issues dealing with women. For purposes of this research, women's issues will be defined as those issues where policy consequences are likely to have a more immediate and direct impact on significantly larger numbers of women than of men.[19] This definition encompasses many, although not all, issues of concern to the feminist movement during the 1970s.[20]

Given the emergence of the feminist movement as pluralist proof that many women perceive they have interests distinct from those of men, the question of whether governing institutions have represented these interests adequately becomes important. If the political system, dominated at the elite level by men, has failed to represent the distinctive interests of women, then the question of concern becomes one of how these interests may be better represented.

To examine these questions, the meaning of "representation," "interests," and "interests of women on policy issues dealing with women" must be clarified.

Representation as an Intergroup Relationship

Kenneth Prewitt and Heinz Eulau have identified two main currents of contemporary thought regarding representational relationships. The first, or interindividual, conception focuses on the relationship between any single individual, the represented, and a second individual, the representative. Most recent empirical studies have employed this interindividual conception. Yet, as Prewitt and Eulau have noted, such research has not led to a theory that can adequately explain the functioning of contemporary representational government. They have argued:

> A viable theory of representation . . . cannot be constructed from individualistic assumptions alone. It must be constructed out of an understanding of representation as a relationship between two collectives—the representative assembly and the represented citizenry.[21]

Prewitt and Eulau, then, view representation as an intergroup relationship between a governing body and the entire community from which its members are selected.[22]

In examining the representation of women's interests, an intergroup conception of representation will be employed. For it is not the relationship between a single individual, the represented, and the representative that is of interest. Rather, the relationship of interest is that between women as a collectivity and the representative bodies which govern them.

Interests and Women's Interests

Hanna Pitkin has noted that the independence/mandate debate is "undoubtedly the central classic controversy in the literature of political representation."[23] Any discussion of the quality of representation necessarily involves an examination of this debate over whether a representative should follow the wishes of her/his constituents or be free to act according to her/his own judgment of what is best for their welfare. The independence/mandate controversy is related intrinsically to conceptions of interests. Those in the mandate tradition generally accept the Utilitarian argument that only the individual can determine what is in her/his interest. Those in the independence tradition, on the other hand, maintain that an individual's interests can be ascertained independent of the sentiments of the individual.

With reference to the mandate conception of interests, Pitkin has claimed: "Among contemporary political scientists, this view is quite common. A man's interest is equivalent to what the man wants, and the common interest of society is what the members of society want."[24] What the members of society want generally is ascertained through an examination of public policy preferences or through interest-group activity.[25]

From this perspective, women's interests can be measured through pressures women exert on government, or through the policy preferences of women. And from this perspective, the evidence indicates that predominantly male governing bodies frequently have failed to act in response to women's interests on policy issues dealing with women.

The development of several organizations within the feminist movement whose activities include lobbying and other strategies to pressure public officials is one indication that governing institutions often have not acted in response to women's interests on women's issues. Public opinion data on the public policy preferences of women provide a second indication. Unfortunately, the assumption that women had no interests distinct from those of men was pervasive throughout society for so long that there is little public opinion data on policy issues dealing with women prior to recent years. Consequently, the examples must be somewhat limited.

When women entered the work force in unprecedented numbers during World War II, an issue that gained public attention was equal pay for equal work. A 1942 Gallup poll showed women to be overwhelmingly in favor of such legislation. When asked, "If women take the place of men in industry, should they be paid the same wages as men?" 85% of females replied affirmatively.[26] The results of Gallup polls in 1945 and 1954 also showed large majorities in favor of equal pay.[27] Yet, it was not until 1963 that Congress finally passed the Equal Pay Act requiring that women and men receive equal compensation for work performed under equivalent conditions.

Similarly, the Equal Rights Amendment was first introduced into Congress in 1923 and was reintroduced in almost every subsequent legislative session. However, it was not passed by both houses in a single legislative session until 1972. A Gallup Poll taken in October 1974 showed 73% of females in favor of such an amendment.[28] Subsequent polls continued to show a plurality of women to favor the ERA.[29] Nevertheless, the amendment fell three states short of the thirty-eight necessary for ratification before the June 30, 1982 deadline.

Finally, as early as 1970, a CBS News poll found 78% of women to favor the establishment of day care centers to oversee the children of women who wished to work.[30] Yet, a program of quality child care offering services to a large proportion of working women has been provided neither by the federal government nor by state governments.

As these examples illustrate, predominantly male governing bodies frequently have not acted in response to the sentiments of their female constituents on policies dealing with women.[31] Neither, it can be argued, have they apparently responded to an objective notion of the interests of women and pursued policies to further the welfare of their female constituents.

In general, American political scientists have rejected the notion of objective, unarticulated interests as inconsistent with a democratic form of government. Implicitly at least, most seem to have accepted the logic of the argument outlined by Jeane Kirkpatrick:

> Monarchism, communism, nazism, and dictatorship in the "new" nations have all been justified by some version of the doctrine of false consciousness. . . . Doctrines that postulate the existence of abstract or objective individual interests deny the individual freedom to choose or to change his identifications. They are incompatible with the premises and practice of democratic government and constitute the epistemological and moral basis of despotism.[32]

While objective conceptions of interest have sometimes been associated with antidemocratic forms of government, it does not follow that objective conceptions are therefore incompatible with democracy, especially considering the existing evidence on the capabilities of the average citizen. Although pluralists and democratic elitists have rejected classical democratic theory's emphasis on widespread popular participation, the Utilitarian notion that a citizen is the best judge of her/his own interest has been preserved. Yet, there is a tension between viewing the citizenry as uninformed and uninterested in politics and simultaneously maintaining that individual citizens can best assess their own interests. Like the notion of a participatory citizenry, the supposition that each citizen is the best judge of her/his interest should perhaps be considered an ideal toward which a democratic society should strive.

If the notion that citizens are the best judges of their interests is viewed as an ideal, then one can argue that many citizens, at least under some conditions, may not be the best judges of their own interests. Consequently, perhaps an alternative, less subjective conception of interests should be considered.

In the case of women, there is an additional reason to consider an objective notion of interests. Gerald Berreman has observed that social ascription occurs when individuals are assigned a status on the basis of a characteristic "over which the individual generally has no control, which is determined at birth, which is crucial to social identity, and which vitally affects one's opportunities, rewards, and social roles."[33] Kate Millett has explained, "Groups who rule by birthright are fast disappearing, yet there remains one ancient and universal scheme for the domination of one birth group by another—the scheme that prevails in the area of sex."[34] Like Millett, sociologists generally recognize sex as a basis for social ascription.[35]

Sociologists also have observed that those relegated to an inferior status in society on the basis of social ascription often come to identify with, and to defend, their inferior status. It is through identity formation in the process of socialization that social ascription is effectively maintained.[36] Women have been so thoroughly socialized to accept their inferior status that the result has been what Sandra Bem and Daryl Bem have termed

a nonconscious ideology, a set of beliefs which . . . a person accepts implicitly but which remain outside his awareness because alternative conceptions of the world remain unimagined. . . . In our view, there is no ideology which better exemplifies these points than the beliefs and attitudes which most Americans hold about women. Not only do most men and women in our society hold hidden prejudices about women's "natural" role, but these nonconscious beliefs motivate a host of subtle practices that are dramatically effective at keeping her "in her place."[37]

Because of the tendency for those assigned an inferior status through social ascription to accept and to identify with their inferior status, it may be difficult for women to judge subjectively what is in their interests.[38] Dominant socialization processes would lead women to prefer inequality. For this reason, some scholars, even those who generally view opinions as valid measures of interests, might find a more objective notion of women's interests preferable to a purely subjective one.

Numerous attempts have been made to move away from the definition of interests as equivalent to policy preferences by defining interests more objectively.[39] It is not my intention to become embroiled in the dispute over which conception best defines "real" interests. Scholars who have attempted to define interests objectively generally have wanted to derive a general conceptualization that would apply to the interests of all individuals in all societies. My goal is a far less ambitious one: to specify the elements essential to an objective determination of the interests of women in American society on policy issues dealing with women.

Because social ascription limits both life's opportunities and life's rewards for women, it seems that there are at least two elements crucial to an objective determination of their distinctive interests: (1) a broadening of the range of choices or options available to females, and (2) the removal of ascriptive criteria in the allocation of rewards.

When the interests of women on policy issues dealing with women are defined objectively to include these two elements, they coincide roughly, although perhaps not perfectly, with most of the issue positions of the feminist movement. For example, passage of the ERA would both broaden the range of opportunities available to women and remove ascriptive criteria in the allocation of rights, responsibilities, and benefits. Legalized abortion provides greater choice for women either to bear or not to bear children. Provision of child care facilities would broaden opportunities by making the option of employment outside the home available to more women.

Moreover, when the interests of women on policy issues dealing with women are defined objectively, it is clear that governing bodies have not always acted in the interests of women on these issues. For example, there are still states where the husband has the right to manage and control marital property, even if the wife has purchased the property with her earnings, indicating that women and men are not equally entitled to the material benefits of a marital partnership. A comprehensive program of child care has never been instituted, thus denying many women the option to work for wages. Social security benefits for homemakers, except as a result of their status as wives, are not available, indicating that labor in the home is not rewarded equally with labor outside the home.

Thus, whether one prefers a subjective or an objective definition of interests, one arrives at the same conclusion: Women's interests on policy issues dealing with women have not been adequately represented by governing bodies.[40] In terms of the independence/mandate controversy, representatives have not acted in response to the majority sentiments of their female constituency on issues dealing with women. Nor, apparently, have they acted in accordance with an objective notion of the interests of women, as defined above, and pursued policies that would further the welfare of their female constituents.

Increasing the Representation of Women's Interests

How can more adequate representation of the interests of women on policy issues dealing with women be attained? In addition to the use of unconventional tactics such as demonstrations and boycotts, at least three conventional strategies to achieve greater representation of women's interests have been evident in the women's rights movement. The first is the use of lobbying tactics to attempt to influence representatives. It is difficult to assess the effectiveness of this strategy as employed by feminist organizations, just as it is difficult to assess the impact of any lobbying effort.[41] There is some evidence, however, that lobbying by women's organizations has had an impact on at least some issues.[42]

The second strategy focuses on organizing women to vote for representatives who will better represent women's interests. Given the influence of party identification and candidate image on voting decisions and the diversity among women, this is likely to be difficult. However, the appearance of the "gender gap" in voting in the 1980 and 1982 elections has led organizations within the women's movement to devote increased energy to mobilizing women to vote for candidates who will better represent them.[43] Future elections should help to determine whether such a strategy can be effective.

The third strategy, involving an effort to elect women to political office to represent the interests of women, is the strategy of interest in this study. This approach assumes that as more females attain political offices, they will represent the interests of women on women's issues more adequately than men have. A number of scholars have suggested that there is likely to be a relationship between the number of political positions filled by members of a group, particularly if the group is politically organized and socially conscious, and the extent to which the group's interests are recognized and acted on in the policy process.[44] If these scholars are correct, then an increase in the number of women holding elective offices should lead to greater representation of the interests of women on policy issues dealing with women. However, whether greater numerical representation of women will, in fact, lead to greater representation of the interests of women remains an empirical question that can only be answered through research.

CHAPTER THREE

□ □ ■ □ □ □ □ □ □

Political Parties and Recruitment

THE RECRUITMENT OF WOMEN to run for political office is a critical variable affecting the number of women serving as members of governing elites. As long as few women voluntarily present themselves as candidates, or are sought out and encouraged to run by various recruiting agents, numerical representation of women will remain low. Yet, as data presented in this and the next two chapters show, an increase in the number of women recruited to run for public office will not necessarily guarantee a proportionate increase in the number of women elected to office. The electoral situations female candidates confront are perhaps even more important than the number of women who seek office in determining the number of women ultimately elected.

This chapter focuses on the recruitment of women candidates by the political parties. An examination of the extent of party leaders' involvement in the recruitment process and the types of electoral situations in which party leaders recruit women to run reveals that the parties are doing very little to facilitate an increase in the numerical representation of women. In fact, the recruitment practices of political parties function as an aspect of the political opportunity structure, not subject to control by individual women candidates, that works against the rapid movement of women into political office.

The Parties' Role in Recruitment

The recruitment of women to run for office should be viewed as part of a broader process of elite circulation. Kenneth Prewitt and Alan Stone have cautioned that elite circulation should not be confused with personnel turnover. "Elite circulation is not necessarily the replacement of high officeholders by different persons; it is, instead, the replacement of officeholders by different *types* of persons."[1]

A change in the composition of elites frequently follows the emergence of new social interests or groups within a society.[2] New groups must be granted means to express their interests in the political process if the existing social order is to be maintained. To preserve stability, the existing elites frequently will attempt to assimilate leaders of the new social interests into their own ranks. If the dominant elites do not respond in this manner, they risk rebellion or even revolution.[3]

During the 1970s, women emerged as a significant political force demanding a greater voice in government. Although the circulation of women into elite positions is still in an early stage, there can be little doubt that it is taking place. One sign of this is the increase in the number of women holding elective offices; at the state legislative level, where longitudinal data are available, the proportion of women state legislators increased from 4.0% in 1969 to 13.3% in 1983.[4]

Voters may have the final say in elite circulation through their decision as to "who governs." However, they may not have the most important say. The very critical decision as to "who competes" is made earlier in the process of selecting leaders. The decision to become a candidate—to seek a major party's nomination either through a primary or through a party convention—can be primarily an individual and personal decision made by the potential candidate without the consultation of other people. Alternatively, the decision to seek a political office can involve a number of actors who attempt to persuade or dissuade potential candidates.

Among the various individuals who may play a role in persuading or dissuading prospective competitors and thus facilitating or inhibiting the circulation of women into elite positions are major party leaders, who traditionally have recruited candidates on behalf of the dominant political elites.[5] During periods when the composition of governing elites is undergoing significant change, one might expect party leaders to assume a particularly active role in the recruitment process. If continued system stability depends on the preservation of the values and rules of the game, as defined by the existing order, then party leaders, as representatives of the elite culture, have a vested interest in ensuring that any new entrants to the elite share the values prevalent among the dominant elites. For this reason, party leaders might be expected to attempt to exercise as much control as possible over the choice of the particular women who gain entry into elite positions.

However, to expect tight party control over the recruitment of women would be highly unrealistic in light of our knowledge of the ever-weakening role of state and local political parties in the candidate selection process. In most states, direct primaries have removed much of the control which party leaders exercised when candidates were selected in caucuses and conventions. Prospective candidates in primary states can circumvent party leaders, marshal their own resources, and appeal directly to voters for their support.[6]

Studies of party leaders' role in candidate recruitment have shown great interstate variation.[7] Summarizing the results of various studies of the recruitment of candidates for the state legislature, Malcolm Jewell and David Olson noted that the proportion of candidates recruited by the parties ranged from 6% among Georgia Democrats to 83% in Connecticut.[8] Perhaps Frank Sorauf's conclusion is most appropriate:

> Of the frequency of party attempts to manage or influence American primaries, it is impossible to write authoritatively. Practices vary not only from state to state but within states and descriptions of local party practice are hard to come by.[9]

One concern investigated in this chapter is the extent to which party leaders, relative to other recruiting agents, are involved in seeking out and encouraging women to run for office. The recruitment of women in 1976 took place in a national environment characterized by weakened party control over the candidate selection process and by great interstate and intrastate variations in recruitment practices. Nevertheless, because of their vested interest in ensuring that new entrants to the elite share their values, one might expect party leaders in the aggregate to have been fairly active in encouraging and dissuading prospective women candidates.

Probable Patterns in Recruitment

Although some party leaders may not have participated in the recruitment of candidates in 1976, those who were actively involved in the recruitment process probably were subject to somewhat conflicting pressures—pressures both for and against the recruitment of women candidates. The patterns of response of party leaders to these pressures and the results of those responses for the recruitment of women candidates constitute a second concern investigated in this chapter.

Pressures Favoring Recruitment of Women

Direct and indirect effects of the feminist movement, as well as women's demands for an increasing role in government, probably predisposed party leaders to consider women when recruiting candidates in 1976.

Traditionally, many men who have spent years working within the party organizations have been offered opportunities to run for political office as a reward for their service. Women who have devoted years to party service generally have not been given similar opportunities. However, as women's political consciousness developed during the 1960s and 1970s, more and more women began to insist that they deserved the same rewards as their male counterparts for loyal party service. When party leaders failed to respond to their demands for opportunities to seek public office with party support, women sometimes bucked the party, mounted independent campaigns, and occasionally won in spite of party opposition. Two very prominent cases in point are those of Margaret Heckler in Massachusetts and Martha Griffiths in Michigan, both of whom gave years of service to their parties, were denied party support for their candidacies, ran in spite of the opposition of party leadership, and won their bids for congressional seats.[10] The parties' weakening control over nominations, resulting from the proliferation of direct primaries, has increasingly made it possible for women with sufficient credibility and resources to mount such insurgent campaigns. Because victories on the part of insurgent candidates may further weaken party leaders' control over future nominations, party leaders would prefer to avoid such occurrences. Thus, one source of pressure on party leaders to consider women as candidates for office no doubt came from women themselves as they became more politically assertive during the 1970s.

Many state and local party leaders probably also felt at least some indirect pressure from the national parties to consider women as candidates for office in 1976. National party platforms and national party politics in large part define the ideas and the ideals for which the Republican and Democratic parties stand. One of the ideals, clearly espoused by both parties since 1972, is that women should be more equitably represented in party decision making. Reform commissions in both parties have recommended stronger efforts to increase the number of women delegates to national party conventions.[11] While the national parties have no jurisdiction to set guidelines for candidate selection as they do for delegate selection, their strong stand in favor of greater participation by women may have led some local and state party leaders to give more serious consideration to recruiting women candidates.

Some party leaders also may have been inclined in 1976 to back women candidates in an effort to regain voter trust in the wake of Watergate, increasing voter cynicism, and declining public confidence in government.[12] 1976 was the year of the outsider, the year in which "Jimmy Who?"—unfamiliar with and thus uncorrupted by the Washington establishment—was able to defy all odds and capture not only the Democratic nomination, but also the Presidency. Women, too, are perceived as outsiders to the political process and thus as uncorrupted by it. Voters are thought to view women as more honest, more trustworthy, and more moral than male politicians. Harriet Cipriani, former head of the women's division of the Democratic National Committee, has claimed, "Women have more credibility . . . with the voters, and can therefore attract voters from the other party more readily than a man can. A voter tends to look more at the person than at the party when a woman is running."[13] A poll, commissioned in late 1974 by the Republican National Committee, showed that only 25% of the American public trusted the Republican party and 45% of the American public trusted Democrats.[14] In an era when public confidence in parties and politicians had fallen to low levels, party leaders may well have been more inclined than in previous election years to recruit and support women candidates.

Pressures against Recruitment of Women

While the factors reviewed above may have influenced party leaders to recruit women as candidates in 1976, there were a number of factors that probably worked in the opposite direction and may have impeded the recruitment of women.

Just as there are many women who have devoted years of service to the party and deserve party endorsement in seeking office, there are numerous men who also deserve such recognition. To overlook these males in favor of women may, in fact, be a greater threat to party leaders' control over the candidate selection process than to overlook women in favor of men. Deserving men, like their female counterparts, can run insurgent campaigns by working outside the party structure. Often they can do so more effectively than women because they are more likely to be linked to business and professional networks that can provide the financial resources and expertise necessary to mount successful campaigns.

Social-psychological factors also might lead party leaders to overlook women candidates. Cynthia Fuchs Epstein has suggested, "Professions . . . tend toward homogeneity and exercise exclusionary practices which deter the participation of persons or groups who do not possess characteristics defined as appropriate."[15] This appears true for politics as well. Several scholars have noted the tendency of party leaders to recruit candidates with characteristics similar to their own.[16]

Since most party leaders are men, the tendency to recruit candidates similar to themselves may result in a reluctance to promote the candidacies of women. Such reluctance also may stem from discomfort with the idea of having a woman in a position of equal or superior status to their own. As Gunnar Myrdal has noted, "Men often dislike the very idea of having women on an equal plane as coworkers and competitors, and usually they find it even more 'unnatural' to work under women."[17]

Finally, there is evidence that male political leaders, concerned with success for their party, may sincerely believe that the public is reluctant to vote for a woman; this perception, in turn, may lead party leaders to be less than enthusiastic about recruiting women candidates. Jeane Kirkpatrick found that in every case where party leaders resisted the nomination of the women legislators she interviewed, it was on grounds that a woman could not run as well as a man.[18] Additional evidence that male political elites believe running a woman will cost the party votes comes from a nationwide study of women officeholders, conducted by the Center for the American Woman and Politics, which included a comparison sample of male officeholders. Sixty percent of the male public officials agreed that, "in general, voters are more reluctant to support women candidates"—a slightly higher proportion than among female officeholders.[19]

Hypotheses about Recruitment of Women

Party leaders actively involved in recruiting candidates in 1976, then, probably faced conflicting pressures and predispositions—some of which pushed them toward, while others worked against, the recruitment of women. One might anticipate that party leaders responded to these cross-pressures in somewhat predictable ways, resulting in patterns that would be evident in the recruitment of women nationwide. Specifically, one might expect that party leaders reacted by recruiting women disproportionately in those electoral situations where the risk incurred from doing so was minimal. In these situations, party leaders would have been freer to respond to pressures pushing them to recruit women because pressures working against the recruitment of women were greatly diminished.

As a first pattern, one would expect party leaders to have been more active in recruiting women for low-prestige than for high-prestige offices. Parties would have shown greater reluctance to seek out women as candidates for congressional and statewide offices than for state legislative offices, where the stakes were lower, where voter prejudice against women candidates was likely to be less intense,[20] and where the seats were less likely to be desired by potential male candidates.

As a second pattern, one would expect many of the women recruited by party leaders to have run in districts where the opposition party's candidate was almost certain to win. By recruiting women as "sacrificial lambs," party leaders could appear open to participation by women while incurring little or no risk. There would have been little danger of males within the party running insurgent campaigns, since such campaigns would have been futile. It would have made little difference to the final outcome if some voters were prejudiced against women, since the candidate was destined to lose anyway. And party leaders might have felt that voters' image of women as uncorrupted, honest, and trustworthy would work to the advantage of the party and lead to a better showing than with a male candidate.

As a third pattern, one would expect a sizable number of those women recruited by party leaders to have been concentrated in multimember, rather than single-member, districts. Multimember districts would have presented party leaders with the opportunity to reward a deserving woman without excluding men who also deserved such recognition. If party leaders perceived voters as reluctant to vote for a woman, they risked losing only one seat, rather than losing their "only" seat. Moreover, party leaders may have hoped that voter perceptions of women as uncorrupted, honest, and trustworthy would work to the benefit of the whole ticket by giving it a "cleaner" image.

Self-initiated Candidacies

The decision to run for office is counter to traditional conceptions of a woman's proper role in society. Kirsten Amundsen has suggested, "To run for office—to compete against a man in an arena that has for so long been a male preserve—must appear like a total improbability and an outrageous idea to the 'feminine' woman."[21] While running for office clearly is a deviant step for a woman, taking the initiative in seeking a major party nomination for office is even more incongruous with traditional conceptions of appropriate female behavior. Women are socialized to wait to be asked, rather than to take the initiative, in areas of human behavior ranging from courtship to job promotions. Because of cultural inhibitions that discourage women from initiating their own candidacies, one would expect few women candidates to be self-starters. Since men are not subject to the same inhibiting effects of sex-role socialization, one also would expect to find smaller proportions of self-starters among women than have been found for men in previous research.

Respondents in this study were asked whether anyone's persuasion or encouragement figured importantly in their decisions to run for office in 1976. Those who answered this question negatively were considered self-starters. As table 3.1 demonstrates, the proportion who claimed to be the sole initiators of their candidacies was approximately one-third for state house, state senate, and statewide candidates; at the congressional level, the proportion claiming to be self-starters increased to almost one-half.[22] Incumbents, as would be expected, disproportionately made the decision to seek re-election without encouragement or persuasion by others. When only nonincumbent office seekers were considered, the percentage of self-initiated candidacies declined somewhat for all categories of office (table 3.1).

David Leuthold, summarizing the findings of previous recruitment research, observed that the median study reported about 50% of the candidates to be self-starters.[23] While differences in findings could be the result of variations in question wording or changes over time, a comparison of the proportions of self-starters in this study with previous research suggests that somewhat fewer women are self-starters than generally has been found for male candidates.

TABLE 3.1
Self-starters among Women Candidates, 1976[a]

| | OFFICE | | | |
	Congress[b]	Statewide[c]	State Senate	State House
	%	%	%	%
Self-starters among all candidates	47.8	31.6	31.8	33.4
N =	(69)	(19)	(157)	(900)
Self-starters among nonincumbents	41.9	27.8	25.8	26.0
N =	(62)	(18)	(132)	(678)

[a]Candidates were classified as self-starters if they indicated that no one's persuasion or encouragement figured importantly in their decisions to run for office in 1976.

[b]In this and all subsequent tables, congressional candidates include both U.S. House and U.S. Senate candidates.

[c]In this and all subsequent tables, statewide candidates include only those who ran statewide for elective positions at the *state* level (e.g., governor, lieutenant governor, attorney general).

Party Leaders versus Other Recruiting Agents

Table 3.2 presents data on the types of people whom candidates spontaneously mentioned as influential in their decisions to run for office. Members of party committees and party officials appear to have influenced the decisions of more than one-third of those state legislative candidates who mentioned at least one agent as important. Party leaders were less critical to the decisions of candidates for statewide and congressional offices. The encouragement of present or former officeholders and candidates was of almost equal importance as the encouragement of party officials for candidates for all offices. Friends were listed approximately as frequently as party leaders by state legislative candidates, but much more frequently than party leaders by congressional and statewide candidates.

Particularly striking is the importance of the role played by family and relatives in encouraging women's candidacies. With the exception of candidates for the state senate, almost one-half of candidates who listed any agent cited the encouragement or persuasion of a family member. Many of these specifically mentioned the support of their husbands.

The absence in previous research of any indication that family support was critical to the initiation of candidacies suggests that family encouragement may be of greater importance to female than to male candidates.[24] Many men who run for office probably assume their families will find their aspirations acceptable. Since family support is expected, male candidates may not view it as very important in their decisions. However, because running for office is not sex-appropriate behavior for females, many aspiring women candidates may anticipate familial resistance. Moreover, most women candidates probably realize that some voters will need reassurance that they are not neglecting their families. Prospective women candidates can expect at some point in their campaigns to be asked, "Who's home with your children?" or "Who's fixing dinner for your husband?"—questions a male candidate would not be asked. Certainly, voter reservations about family neglect are more difficult for a woman candidate to counter if her spouse or other family members are not fully supportive of her candidacy. Because women candidates often may anticipate familial resistance to, and/or voter reservations about, their deviation from sex-appropriate behavior, they may perceive familial encouragement to be of great importance.[25]

Also of interest in table 3.2 is the fact that relatively few women were recruited to run for office by interest groups or organizations. Relatively few women candidates spontaneously mentioned representatives of

TABLE 3.2

Various Agents Important in Decisions to Run for Office among Women Candidates, 1976[a]

	OFFICE			
	Congress	Statewide	State Senate	State House
	%	%	%	%
Parties	17.6	16.7	40.2	35.6
Party officials or members of a party committee	17.6	16.7	39.2	34.6
Members of women's partisan club or women's division of party	0	0	1.0	1.0
Interest groups	2.9	8.3	12.7	10.4
Members of Women's Political Caucus or other feminist groups	0	8.3	5.9	4.1
Members of League of Women Voters or other traditional women's groups	0	0	2.0	1.5
Family	44.1	50.0	33.3	46.6
Husband	32.4	25.0	26.5	33.9
Present or former officeholders, candidates	20.6	16.7	33.3	30.0
Friends	58.9	58.3	41.2	32.9
Co-workers, business associates	2.9	0	5.9	3.8
Constituents, voters	5.9	0	4.9	5.8
Other	0	0	1.4	0
N^b =	(34)	(12)	(102)	(584)

[a]Candidates who replied affirmatively to a question asking if anyone else's encouragement or persuasion figured importantly in their decision to run then were asked, "Please specify each person's position or relationship to you."

[b]N's are based on those women candidates who mentioned at least one agent as important. Columns total more than 100% because respondents could give more than one response.

women's organizations, whether feminist or traditional, as influential in
their decisions to run. Similarly, women's partisan clubs and women's
divisions of the major parties apparently played little role in the recruitment of women candidates. Women's groups—whether feminist, general
social action, or partisan—maintained a very low profile in the recruitment of women candidates in 1976.

It appears, then, that encouragement for women to run for state legislative, statewide, and congressional offices came primarily from four
sources: family, personal friends, party officials, and present or former
public officeholders. Although party leaders were mentioned frequently,
there is no evidence that they dominated the recruitment process. To the
contrary, the encouragement of primary groups, including both family
and friends, was a more frequent influence on candidates' decisions.

Nevertheless, in some cases people listed by the candidates as friends
or public officials may have been party leaders as well. To obtain a more
precise overview of the major parties' role in the recruitment process,
candidates' responses to several specific questions about their interaction
with party leaders were examined.

Interaction between Party Leaders and Candidates

Respondents were asked three questions designed to ascertain the extent, direction, and nature of the interaction between women candidates
and party leaders.[26] First, candidates were asked if they had talked with
any party leaders during the early stages of deciding to run for office.
Second, they were asked whether the leaders approached them, whether
they went to the leaders, or whether some leaders approached them and
they went to others. Finally, candidates were asked about the nature of
party leaders' reactions to their proposed candidacies.

Sizable minorities of women candidates never discussed their candidacies with party leaders (table 3.3). Incumbents were less likely than
nonincumbents to talk with party leaders, probably because party leaders
and incumbents often shared the assumption that incumbents would seek
re-election. Nevertheless, even among nonincumbents, 29.7% of congressional candidates, 20.0% of statewide candidates, 19.7% of state senate candidates, and 24.9% of state house candidates reported no contact
with party leaders.[27]

Among those candidates who talked with party leaders, many did so
only at their own initiative (table 3.3). Nevertheless, party leaders did
initiate some or all contacts with candidates in one-fourth to two-thirds of
the cases.[28] Moreover, for all four types of offices, a majority of those

Table 3.3

Extent, Direction, and Nature of Interaction between Party Leaders and Women Candidates, 1976

		OFFICE		
	Congress	Statewide	State Senate	State House
	%	%	%	%
Talked with party leaders				
Yes	68.6	81.0	71.7	67.9
No	31.4	19.0	28.3	32.1
N =	(70)	(21)	(159)	(911)
Direction of interaction				
Leaders approached candidate	4.3	20.0	28.3	32.7
Candidate went to leaders	73.9	46.7	34.5	32.7
Some leaders approached candidate and candidate went to other leaders	21.7	33.3	37.2	34.6
N[a] =	(46)	(15)	(113)	(602)
Reactions of party leaders				
Encouragement	53.2	68.8	77.2	80.9
Discouragement	23.4	6.3	6.1	6.5
Mixed or neutral reactions	23.4	25.0	16.7	12.6
N[a] =	(47)	(16)	(114)	(612)

[a]N's are based on those women candidates who said they talked with party leaders.

candidates who talked with party leaders were encouraged to run (table 3.3). At the state legislative level, these majorities were large. Among candidates for offices other than the U.S. Congress, very few claimed to have been discouraged from running.[29]

Tests for Patterns in Recruitment

Overall, the parties appear to have been moderately active in recruiting those women who ran for office in 1976, although they certainly did not dominate the recruitment process. However, more than the mere amount of party activity must be examined to assess comprehensively the role of party leaders in recruitment. The types of electoral situations in which party leaders recruited women also are critically important.

Reluctance to Recruit Women for Higher Offices

Earlier it was suggested that party leaders might respond to conflicting pressures for and against the recruitment of women by seeking women to run for lower-prestige offices while showing a greater reluctance to approach women for higher-prestige offices. If this were true, then party leaders in 1976 should have been more active in approaching women to discuss possible candidacies for state legislative offices than for congressional and statewide offices.

As another look at table 3.3 reveals, the data substantiate this expectation. Roughly equal proportions of candidates for each office stated that they had talked with party leaders during the early stages of deciding to run. (In fact, candidates for statewide offices were somewhat *more* likely than candidates for less prestigious state legislative offices to discuss their candidacies with party leaders.) However, the initiators of discussions with party leaders differed markedly across offices. Among state legislative candidates who talked with party leaders, only one-third were never approached by any party representative but rather sought out the leaders. In contrast, almost one-half of statewide respondents and three-fourths of congressional respondents initiated their discussions with party leaders.

Although these differences appear to reflect a reluctance on the part of party leaders to consider women as suitable candidates for more prestigious and powerful offices, at least two alternative explanations must be considered. Perhaps party leaders *intended* to approach women candidates for statewide and congressional offices but the women went to the leaders before the leaders had a chance to approach them. Or perhaps party leaders were not recruiting candidates in these women's races, either because an incumbent from their party was seeking re-election or because party leaders customarily are not active in recruiting candidates for these congressional and statewide seats.[30]

Further examination of the data suggests the inaccuracy of part of the latter explanation. Of the thirty-four congressional candidates who sought out, but were never approached by, party officials, only one was seeking a seat filled by an incumbent of her party running for re-election. Of the seven candidates for statewide office who initiated contact with party leaders, only one was running in a primary against an incumbent. Consequently, the reluctance of party leaders to seek out women candidates for these offices rarely could have stemmed from the fact that an incumbent of their party was seeking re-election. Although these data do not rule out the possibility that party leaders simply were not active in recruiting candidates for congressional and statewide races where women ran, the fact that party leaders expressed reactions to women's candidacies (table 3.3) suggests that they were not totally uninvolved in these races.

The reactions women candidates received from party leaders strongly support the premise that party leaders were more reluctant to consider women as suitable candidates for congressional and statewide offices than for state legislative offices. As table 3.3 illustrates, congressional candidates were considerably less likely, and statewide candidates somewhat less likely, than state legislative candidates to report that party leaders encouraged their candidacies for office. Congressional candidates also were far more likely to have been discouraged by party leaders than were state legislative candidates. The relatively large proportion of congressional candidates whom party leaders did not encourage makes somewhat less credible the explanation that lack of greater party involvement in the recruitment of women for congressional races results from candidates' failure to wait for leaders to approach them. Although it is possible that these women did initiate contact with party leaders early in the recruitment process, it appears unlikely that the leaders would have come to them had they waited. Instead, it seems far more likely that the large proportion of congressional and statewide candidates who contacted party leaders and were not encouraged reflects party leaders' reluctance to consider women viable candidates for prestigious political offices.

Measures of Party Recruits

Lewis Bowman and G. R. Boynton have noted that there are two ways in which party officials may be involved in the recruitment process:

> In the first, and weaker, sense candidates may turn to local party officials seeking support before they decide whether to run and/or before they announce their decision to run. In a second, and stronger, sense the official may seek out potential candidates and ask them to run.[31]

While both types of recruitment have been considered in preceding sections, the remainder of this chapter is concerned only with those women whom parties "recruited" in the stronger sense.

Candidates are classified as "definite party recruits" if they stated that they (1) were approached by party leaders to discuss the possibility of running for office, and (2) were encouraged to run by those leaders. Thus, a definite party recruit took no initiative to seek out party officials with whom to discuss her candidacy; all party leaders with whom she spoke came to her. Candidates are classified as "likely party recruits" if they reported that they (1) were approached by some party leaders to discuss the possibility of running for office but went to talk with other party leaders as well, and (2) were encouraged to run for office. A likely party recruit differs from a definite party recruit in having sought out one or more party leaders, in addition to those who approached her. The initiator of the first contact between candidate and party leaders is unclear. While in most cases it probably was a party leader, in some cases it may have been the candidate herself. In subsequent sections of this chapter, two figures will be presented—one for "definite party recruits" and one for "total party recruits" (consisting of definite and likely party recruits combined).

Throughout the remaining analysis incumbents are excluded,[32] and only nonincumbent party recruits (table 3.4) are considered. Because so few congressional and statewide nonincumbent candidates were recruited by the parties (table 3.4), they, too, are excluded from subsequent analysis. The focus in the final sections of this chapter is on nonincumbent party recruits among candidates for the state house, and, where the number of cases will permit, nonincumbent party recruits among state senate candidates.

Recruitment of Sacrificial Lambs

In addition to seeking out women more frequently as candidates for less prestigious than for more prestigious offices, party leaders might be expected to have responded to conflicting pressures for and against the recruitment of women by recruiting females to run as "sacrificial lambs" in districts where the party's nominee had little chance of winning the general election.[33] Two factors were considered in determining whether a party recruit probably was recruited as a sacrificial lamb.

First, the incumbency status of the candidate(s) in the opposing party's primary was examined. A candidate was considered to be running in a district with no open seats when all seats were filled by incumbents of the opposing party and all of the incumbents were seeking re-election.[34] Thus, the woman candidate would oppose in the general election a full slate of incumbents and/or candidates who had defeated incumbents in primaries. As will be seen in chapter 6, the proportion of candidates winning general elections in cases where there were no open seats was extremely low, indicating that candidates seeking such seats could have had little hope of winning the general election. Because of the low probability of winning, it is reasonable to assume that many party recruits in these districts were recruited to serve as sacrificial lambs.

However, in order to ensure that only candidates whose general election prospects were particularly dismal were considered, a second

TABLE 3.4

Definite, Likely, and Total Party Recruits among Nonincumbent Women Candidates, 1976

		Percent of All Nonincumbent Respondents	Percent of Those Nonincumbent Respondents Who Talked with Party Leaders
Congress			
Definite party recruits[a]		3.0	4.4
Likely party recruits[b]		7.6	11.2
Total party recruits[c]		10.6	15.6
	N =	(66)	(45)
Statewide			
Definite party recruits		9.5	12.5
Likely party recruits		19.1	25.0
Total party recruits		28.6	37.5
	N =	(21)	(16)
State Senate			
Definite party recruits		20.3	25.5
Likely party recruits		23.3	29.2
Total party recruits		43.6	54.7
	N =	(133)	(106)
State House			
Definite party recruits		22.5	30.7
Likely party recruits		20.2	27.6
Total party recruits		42.7	58.3
	N =	(702)	(515)

[a]Definite party recruits are candidates who stated that they (1) were approached by party leaders to discuss the possibility of running for office, and (2) were encouraged to run by those party leaders.

[b]Likely party recruits are candidates who claimed that they (1) were approached by some party leaders to discuss the possibility of running for office but went to talk with other party leaders as well, and (2) were encouraged to run for office.

[c]Total party recruits = Definite party recruits + Likely party recruits.

NOTE: A state-by-state breakdown indicated that party recruits were not concentrated disproportionately in certain states. Rather, they were widely dispersed among states. Because of the disproportionate number of candidates running for the state house in New Hampshire (243 candidates, 138 respondents) relative to other states, it was numerically possible that almost one-half of the party recruits could be located in New Hampshire. However, this was not the case. For state house seats, only 26 of the 158 nonincumbent definite party recruits were in New Hampshire, with no more than 12 concentrated in any other state; 39 of the 44 states with state legislative elections in 1976 had at least one definite party recruit. Of the 300 nonincumbent total party recruits, 38 were in New Hampshire with no more than 16 in any other state; 42 of the 44 states with state legislative elections had at least two party recruits.

factor—competition—was taken into account in identifying probable sacrificial lambs. Academic observers of political campaigns frequently have noted that competition in a party's primary tends to vary with a party's prospects for general election victory.[35] If a nonincumbent is unopposed in a primary, the lack of opposition often, although not always, indicates that there is little hope of winning the general election. On the other hand, a primary with considerable competition frequently is a sign that the party's prospects for general election victory are good.

By combining information about competition in primaries with information about the incumbency status of the opposing party's candidate(s), a measure for isolating those party recruits with virtually no chance of winning the general election was derived.[36] For this measure, a party recruit was considered a sacrificial lamb if (1) she was unopposed for her party's nomination,[37] and (2) either a full slate of incumbents was running in the other party's primary (i.e., seeking re-election) and/or the number of candidates in the opposing party's primary exceeded the number of seats by two or more. Thus, a party recruit running in a single-member district was considered to be a sacrificial lamb if she was the only contender for her party's nomination and either the incumbent was running in the other party's primary and/or the number of candidates in the opposing party's primary was three or more.

Table 3.5 presents the numbers and percentages of party recruits who could be considered sacrificial lambs according to this operational definition. The proportion of sacrificial lambs among party recruits ranged from about two-fifths to one-half, depending on whether all districts or only single-member districts, and all party recruits or only definite party recruits, were considered. The proportion of sacrificial lambs increased for state house party recruits when multimember districts were eliminated and only single-member districts were considered.[38]

Party Differences in Recruitment of Sacrificial Lambs

Of the definite party recruits running for the state house,[39] 83 were recruited by the Republican party while the Democratic party recruited 75. The Republican party recruited 146 of the total party recruits in comparison with 154 recruited by the Democratic party. Apparently, then, the parties were about equally active in recruiting women to run for office. However, the similarity in absolute numbers of women recruited obscures important differences in the recruitment patterns of the two parties.

The Republican party recruited somewhat more sacrificial lambs than

Table 3.5

Sacrificial Lambs[a] among Women Candidates, 1976, Who Were Party
Recruits

	Percent of Definite Party Recruits Who Were Sacrificial Lambs	Percent of Total Party Recruits Who Were Sacrificial Lambs
Candidates in both multi- and single-member districts		
State Senate	40.0	47.2
N^b =	(25)	(53)
State House	44.2	37.6
N =	(147)	(279)
Candidates in single-member districts only		
State Senate	40.9	47.9
N =	(22)	(48)
State House	50.5	44.0
N =	(97)	(191)

[a]A party recruit was classified as a sacrificial lamb if:
(1) she was unopposed for her party's nomination, and
(2) either a full slate of incumbents was running in the other party's primary and/or the number of candidates in the opposing party's primary exceeded the number of seats by two or more.
[b]The number of cases in this table is somewhat fewer than in table 3.4 because data needed to determine whether or not a candidate was a sacrificial lamb (see "a" above) were not available in all cases.

the Democrats. For example, while the Democratic party recruited 29 definite party recruits and 41 total party recruits to run in districts where prospects for general election victory appeared slim, the Republican party recruited 37 definite party recruits and 65 total party recruits to run in similar situations. Furthermore, a greater *proportion* of Republican party recruits were recruited to run where there was little or no chance of general election victory (table 3.6). Approximately one-half of the time when Republicans sought out and encouraged women to run, they were recruiting sacrificial lambs. For Democrats, this seems to have been true only about one-fourth to two-fifths of the time. This tendency for the Republican party to recruit more sacrificial lambs than the Democratic party held true whether all districts or only single-member districts were considered (table 3.6).

TABLE 3.6

Party Differences in Sacrificial Lambs[a] among Women Candidates, 1976, Who Were Party Recruits

		Republicans		Democrats	
		Percent of Definite Party Recruits	Percent of Total Party Recruits	Percent of Definite Party Recruits	Percent of Total Party Recruits
All districts		49.3	47.8	39.7	27.7
	N =	(75)	(136)	(73)	(148)
Single-member districts only		52.9	53.1	48.5	32.9
	N =	(51)	(96)	(33)	(70)

[a]A party recruit was considered to be a sacrificial lamb if:
(1) she was unopposed for her party's nomination, and
(2) either a full slate of incumbents was running in the other party's primary and/or the number of candidates in the opposing party's primary exceeded the number of seats by two or more.

It appears, then, that the initial expectation that party leaders would respond to conflicting pressures by recruiting women in districts where there was little hope of general election victory is somewhat more valid for the Republican party than for the Democratic party.

Recruitment in Multimember Districts

Another way party leaders may have responded to conflicting pressures both for and against the recruitment of women was by recruiting women disproportionately in multimember districts. At the time of this study, approximately 36% of all state house seats nationwide were in multimember districts.[40] If the parties were no more likely to recruit women in multimember than in single-member districts, about 36% of all women recruited by the parties in 1976 would have been recruited for multimember races. However, the actual proportion was slightly larger, indicating an overall tendency for parties to recruit women somewhat disproportionately in multimember districts. Of the 158 nonincumbent definite party recruits for the state house, 71 (44.9%) were candidates in multimember districts. Similarly, of the 300 nonincumbent total party recruits, 127 (42.3%) were candidates in multimember districts.

Moreover, party leaders' recruitment of nonincumbent women candidates with a reasonable chance of general election victory seems to have been even more disproportionately concentrated in multimember districts. Of the 82 definite party recruits in races with at least one open seat (i.e., where a full slate of incumbents of the opposing party was not seeking re-election), 41 (50.0%) were in multimember districts. Of the 178 total party recruits in races with an open seat, 86 (48.3%) were in multimember districts. Thus, when women recruited to run against incumbents are eliminated from the analysis, the tendency of the parties to recruit women in multimember districts is more apparent.

Party Differences in Recruitment in
Multimember Districts

As was the case for recruitment of women as sacrificial lambs, clear-cut party differences are apparent in the recruitment of women in multimember districts. Of the 75 nonincumbent Democratic women who were definite party recruits, 41 (54.7%) were in multimember districts. In contrast, only 30 (36.1%) of the 83 nonincumbent Republican women who were definite party recruits ran in multimember districts. Similarly, of the 154 total nonincumbent Democratic party recruits, 80 (51.9%) were in multimember districts while only 47 (32.2%) of the 146 total nonincumbent Republican party recruits were in multimember districts.[41]

When those candidates recruited to run against incumbents of the opposing party are excluded and only those in districts with at least one open seat examined, party differences appear even greater. Of the 44 definite Democratic party recruits running for open seats, 27 (61.4%) were in multimember districts. Only 14 (36.8%) of the 38 definite Republican party recruits running for open seats were in multimember districts. Similarly, 60 (56.1%) of the 107 total Democratic party recruits compared with 26 (36.6%) of the 71 total Republican party recruits in races for open seats were in multimember districts.

Clearly, the finding that parties tend disproportionately to recruit women to run in multimember districts is much more valid as a description of the recruitment practices of the Democratic party than of the Republican party.

Summary and Implications

Although party leaders appear to play a moderately active role in the recruitment process, they are not thorough and careful in monitoring the recruitment of women candidates. In 1976, a significant minority of women candidates had no contact whatsoever with party leaders regarding their candidacies, and sizable proportions of those women who talked with party leaders initiated the contact themselves.

However, the lack of greater involvement in recruitment by party offi-

cials is not the only significant aspect of the relationship between women
candidates and party leaders. For even when party leaders were active in
recruiting women, they often were doing little to facilitate the movement
of women into elective positions.

Three patterns were evident in those cases where party leaders were
reported by candidates to have been involved in recruitment. As a first
pattern, party-initiated contact with women candidates was far less frequent, and the reactions of party leaders less positive, at the statewide
and congressional levels than at the state legislative level, suggesting that
party leaders less often consider women as desirable candidates for more
prestigious offices. As a second pattern, when party leaders recruited
women they often recruited them to run as sacrificial lambs in districts
where the candidate of the opposing party was almost certain to win the
general election. As a third pattern, the parties seem disproportionately
to have recruited women to run in multimember, rather than single-
member, districts. In following these practices, party leaders seem to
have employed a simple decision rule: Recruit women in those situations
where the pressures working for the recruitment of women outweigh the
pressures working against.[42]

The pattern of recruitment of women candidates for the state house
suggests that each major party had a dominant recruitment strategy.
About half of all Republican recruiting of women appears to have been
aimed at finding a sacrificial lamb, usually to run in a single-member
district. When Democrats recruited women to run in single-member
districts, one-third to one-half of their recruiting also seems to have been
aimed at finding sacrificial lambs. However, Democratic recruitment of
women appears disproportionately to have taken place in multimember
districts, with more than one-half of all Democratic recruits helping to fill
tickets in multimember districts. The Republican party much less frequently employed this practice of recruiting women to run for seats in
multimember districts.

These distinctive party strategies may well be a product of the nationwide majority/minority standing of the parties. Republicans, who occupy
a minority of seats in most states, undoubtedly must find a relatively large
number of sacrificial lambs each election year. By recruiting women as
sacrificial lambs, Republican party leaders in districts safe for the Democrats can respond to pressures to recruit women without risking the loss of
a seat. Republicans may fare better in multimember districts where
several candidates are elected than they do in many single-member districts where they clearly are the minority party. Consequently, in many

multimember districts Republican leaders may be particularly reluctant to recruit women for fear that women may not run as well as men.

The Democrats, as the majority party throughout most of the country, are less likely than the Republicans to need sacrificial lambs. Perhaps for this reason they recruit proportionately fewer women for hopeless races. However, because Democrats nationwide fare much better than Republicans in single-member races, the competition for party nominations in single-member districts may be more intense within the Democratic party. As a result, Democratic leaders may be more likely to overlook women in favor of males in these districts. In multimember districts, on the other hand, where Democrats frequently can look forward to capturing several seats, party leaders may feel that the costs of nominating a woman are lower. Regardless of whether the woman wins or loses, only one seat out of many is at stake.

These patterns apparent in the recruitment of women candidates may have wider applicability. During the early stages of the circulation of any new group into elite positions, party leaders are likely to be faced with conflicting pressures concerning the recruitment of members of that group—although the specific nature of the pressures undoubtedly would differ somewhat from group to group. Faced with such conflicting pressures, party leaders are likely to respond by recruiting members of the new social interest disproportionately in electoral situations where the pressures working against the recruitment of members of the new group, and consequently the risks incurred, are minimal. Parties are likely to respond to any emerging social interest during the early stages of elite circulation in ways similar to those found in this study.[43]

But while the patterns uncovered here may have applicability beyond the emerging social group studied, they undoubtedly have worked to inhibit an increase in the numerical representation of women among public officeholders. Perhaps the overall effect of the parties' lack of more active recruiting of women candidates and their tendency to recruit women as sacrificial lambs is best shown by extrapolation from information collected in this study. A total of 164 nonincumbent candidates for the state house and 127 nonincumbent candidates for the state senate were approached by at least one party leader and encouraged to run in a district where there was not a full slate of incumbents of the other party seeking re-election.[44] Assuming that nonincumbent candidates among nonrespondents were recruited at the same rate as respondents, a maximum of 286 nonincumbent women in the entire country were recruited by parties to run for the state house in races with at least one open seat.

Similarly, a maximum of 50 nonincumbent women nationwide were re-cruited by parties to run for state senate seats in races where at least one seat was open. This means that the two parties together recruited a max-imum of one woman who had a reasonable chance of victory for every 17 state house seats up for election in 1976. Similarly, the two parties re-cruited a maximum of one woman who had a chance of success for every 23 state senate seats.[45] While these figures are only crude estimates, they illustrate that the parties' record in recruiting women to run for office in 1976 was far from exemplary.

The parties' reluctance to approach women and to present them with the opportunity to run in races where there is at least some chance of general election victory is, then, an important feature of the political opportunity structure that inhibits substantial increases in the numerical representation of women among elective officeholders. In addition, the tendency to recruit women disproportionately in multimember districts also may be detrimental to increasing the number of women holding public office. The trend has been one of conversion of multimember to single-member districts. In the mid-1960s, 55 of 99 state legislative bod-ies in the United States had some or all members elected from multimem-ber districts; by 1975, this number had dropped to 35. Moreover, be-tween 1973 and 1976, four states eliminated multimember districts in favor of single-member districts.[46] Because of the tendency of the parties, particularly the Democratic party, to recruit women disproportionately in multimember districts, the trend toward elimination of multimember districts is another feature of the political opportunity structure that prob-ably has inhibited increases in the numerical representation of women. As multimember districts are converted to single-member districts, one can expect party leaders to show greater reluctance to recruit women to run for seats in these districts.

The attitudes and perceptions of party leaders must change before parties are likely to recruit women on a widespread basis for congressional and statewide offices, or for races in single-member state legislative dis-tricts where prospects for general election victory are good. Such changes are likely to take time and may well have to await new generations of party leaders, many of whom may themselves be women.

In the interim, the numerical representation of women will depend in part on the number of potential female candidates who are willing to run without waiting for the parties to approach and encourage them. Potential women candidates who have not been recruited by the parties may find that the proliferation of direct primaries and the weakening of party control over the candidate selection process actually work to their advantage. As a result of these developments, an ambitious woman, overlooked by party leaders, can circumvent the party and create an independent campaign organization. Although in many areas of the country it remains difficult for a candidate to capture a party's nomination if she is running without party support, increasingly there are examples of women who have done so successfully, one of the most recent being Harriett Woods of Missouri in 1982.

When Woods decided in early 1982 to run in the Democratic primary for the U.S. Senate seat held by popular Republican incumbent John Danforth, her party's leaders initially encouraged her. However, when polls showed that support for Reaganomics had made Danforth vulnerable, Democratic leaders withdrew their support from Woods and backed a newly declared male candidate, banker-lobbyist Burleigh Arnold. Nevertheless, Woods, without official party support, was able to raise more than $250,000 in four months and to defeat Arnold by a margin of more than 2 to 1.[47]

If large numbers of women are to follow Woods's example and circumvent the party in single-member state legislative districts with open seats and in statewide and congressional races, many are going to need outside encouragement to run; few women candidates appear to be self-starters. Clearly, it would seem in the interest of feminist organizations to identify and to encourage promising women candidates to run in these electoral situations. However, there is little evidence that they did so effectively in the 1970s. Only a handful of candidates in 1976 claimed that they had received important encouragement from representatives of the National Women's Political Caucus or other feminist groups. But while feminist organizations in the 1970s were not able to fill the void left by the political parties' failure to recruit women in attractive electoral situations, there are promising signs of change. Following the defeat of the Equal Rights Amendment, both the National Organization for Women and the National Women's Political Caucus announced major new initiatives aimed at recruiting more women to run for political offices—initiatives that will be discussed in the final chapter of this book. The scope and success of these efforts are likely to have important implications for the numbers of women elected to public office in the 1980s and 1990s.

CHAPTER FOUR

□ □ □ ■ □ □ □ □ □

Problems and Assets in Primary Campaigns

THROUGHOUT THE 1970s the number of women running for office increased at both state and national levels. While only 842 women were major party candidates for state legislative seats in general elections in 1972, there were 1,122 women candidates in 1974, 1,256 in 1976, 1,348 in 1978, and 1,426 in 1980. Similarly, the number of female major party nominees for congressional seats increased throughout the decade of the 70s—from 25 in 1970 to 57 in 1980.[1] Although no comparable figures are available for the number of women entering primaries, there have been notable increases in the number of female primary candidates as well.

Increases in the number of women candidates from year to year seem to follow an incremental pattern. Nevertheless, the small additional number of candidates in each election would lead to fairly substantial increases in the number of women officeholders if most women candidates won their election bids.

But women candidates are not extraordinarily successful at the polls. Neither are they especially unsuccessful. Of those women who filed for primary elections in 1976, 44.2% of congressional candidates, 45.7% of candidates for statewide offices, 67.8% of state senate candidates, and 69.0% of state house candidates survived the primaries.[2] However, many of the survivors were candidates who were unopposed in their bids for their party's nomination. Among those with primary opposition, only 22.2% of congressional candidates, 36.7% of statewide candidates, 34.7% of state senate candidates, and 42.7% of candidates for the state house won places on the general election ballot.[3]

An academic observer of women in politics has claimed, "A special frustration for women candidates is the fact that they tend to fare better in primaries than they do in the general election."[4] While women do fare better in primaries than in general elections, they do so only because so many candidates face no primary opposition. The rate of success of women candidates with primary opposition is actually lower than that for women candidates in general elections. Of the women running in general elections in 1976, 34.6% won U.S. House seats, 42.1% won statewide races, 36.7% won state senate seats, and 50.2% won seats in state assemblies.[5]

Betsey Wright, former executive director of the National Women's Education Fund, has pointed to primaries, rather than general elections, as the more critical battlegrounds for most women candidates.[6] Data from this study underscore Wright's observation. Primaries do indeed kill the election hopes of large proportions of women candidates. Of all women who declared their candidacies in 1976, 54.3% of congressional candidates, 50.0% of statewide candidates, 30.0% of state senate candidates, and 29.0% of candidates for the state house were taken out of contention by losing primary election bids. Because so many women candidates are eliminated in primaries, an understanding of the problems women candidates confront in seeking their party's nominations is critical to explaining the numerical underrepresentation of women in public office.

There are additional reasons for devoting attention to women candidates' perceptions of the factors that lead them to success or failure in primary elections—the focus of this chapter. In many locales where one party clearly is dominant over the other, the general election winner really is chosen in the primary. In these cases, a victory in the dominant party's primary virtually ensures success in the general election. Moreover, money, workers, and other forms of support often are more readily available after a woman wins her party's nomination. For many candidates, these additional resources make the road to a general election victory much easier than the path to a primary victory.

Women candidates seem to have a lower overall rate of electoral success than their male counterparts, especially in races for higher-level offices. Excluding those rare cases where a third-party candidate wins the general election, approximately 50% of all male major party candidates in general elections must emerge victorious. With the exception of candidates for state house seats, the proportion of successful female general election candidates in 1976 was significantly lower than 50% (34.6% among congressional candidates, 42.1% among statewide candidates, and 36.7% among state senate candidates).

Because the proportion of male candidates who win primary elections cannot be estimated, it is impossible to determine whether women as a group fare less well in primaries than do men.[7] Nevertheless, since the rate of electoral success among female contenders in contested primaries in 1976 was less than 37% for all offices except the state house, it is certainly possible that women candidates for higher-level offices may win contested primaries at a rate somewhat lower than that of their male counterparts.

Although a slightly greater proportion of women than men may lose elections, this chapter and the next two point to the conclusion that the electoral success rate of women candidates seems less directly related to their sex than to the structure of political opportunity and the electoral situations they confront. Winning or losing for women candidates seems affected most strongly by factors over which individual women have little or no personal control. In contrast, factors subject to the control of individual candidates exert considerably less influence on election outcomes.

Perceptions of Problems and Advantages

Candidates in contested primaries were asked to list the major problems, if any, they encountered in their primary campaigns. They then were asked to list the advantages they experienced, if any.

Of those who faced opposition in primaries only small minorities perceived no problems—14.0% of congressional candidates, 11.8% of statewide candidates, 10.7% of state senate candidates, and 20.3% of candidates for state assembly seats. Larger proportions mentioned no advantages—36.0% of congressional candidates, 23.5% of statewide candidates, 33.3% of state senate candidates, and 35.9% of state house candidates.[8]

Incumbency provides numerous benefits, such as name familiarity, visibility, access to financial resources, and opportunities to campaign throughout the officeholding term,[9] that are not often shared by nonincumbents and that frequently may be perceived by nonincumbents as disadvantages. Consequently, it is not surprising that incumbents in this study much less frequently mentioned problems than did nonincumbents.[10] However, incumbents mentioned advantages only slightly more often than did nonincumbents.[11]

Irene Diamond has argued that women are most likely to obtain legislative seats in states where the desirability of holding state assembly positions is low.[12] Where seats are highly desired, competition is likely to be great. Where seats are less desirable, competition is likely to be less. Because of stronger competition in states where seats are very desirable, candidates in these states might be expected more often to experience problems in seeking their party's nomination.

In 1970, the Citizens Conference on State Legislatures undertook a landmark study of state legislatures. Based on measures of legislative performance in nine basic areas—staffing, compensation, time, committee structure, facilities, leadership, rules and procedures, size, and ethics—the Citizens Conference on State Legislatures derived a single index (the FAIRR index) rating all fifty states on the basis of overall legislative performance.[13] For purposes of this analysis, a legislative seat was presumed to be more prestigious and desirable in a state with a strong legislative performance rating (characterized, for example, by ample and capable staffing, relatively few members, high compensation, adequate office space, orderly proceedings, and considerable power vis-à-vis the executive branch) than in a state with a weak rating (characterized, for example, by little or no professional staff, many members, low compensation, inadequate facilities, very few days in session, and little power).[14]

Based on the rankings of the Citizens Conference, states were divided into three groups, representing states with legislative seats of (1) high desirability or prestige, (2) moderate desirability or prestige, and (3) low desirability or prestige.[15] Just as nonincumbents were more likely than incumbents to report at least one problem, women who ran in states where legislative seats were highly desirable were more likely than those in states where seats were of moderate or low desirability to mention one or more problems. Proportions of state house candidates listing no problems whatsoever ranged from 10.0% in high-desirability states to 17.4% in moderate-desirability states and 33.8% in low-desirability states (tau$_c$ = .21).[16] While a larger proportion of candidates in low-desirability states were incumbents, the differences in proportions of incumbents did not account for the greater tendency of those in low-desirability states to report no problems. Rather, the proportion mentioning no problems increased as the desirability of seats decreased for both incumbents (tau$_c$ = .41) and nonincumbents (tau$_c$ = .12).

Basic Resources as Major Problems

One aspect of women's campaigns that has been subject to considerable commentary, with little or no debate, is the difficulty women candidates face in raising money. Although fund raising is a critical problem for many male candidates,[17] there are several reasons why acquiring financial re-sources may be especially problematic for women.

First, women may face greater psychological barriers than men in ask-ing for money for their candidacies. Men have a long history of asking for money for their personal use. In preparation for their roles as family breadwinners, men traditionally have been socialized to believe that requesting money in return for functions they perform is a natural part of life. As breadwinners, they have been engaged continuously in raising funds for their own use. In contrast, women, in preparation for their role in the domestic sphere, have been socialized into a different set of ex-pectations. Much, if not all, of their work is to be done without considera-tion of financial compensation; rewards for their services will come in the form of security, love, and gratitude from husbands and families. As homemakers, women's history has not been one of raising funds on their own behalf. While these socialization patterns are changing dramatically, most women who ran for office in the 1970s grew to adulthood in a society where sex roles and sex-role socialization were far less fluid than they are today. The effects of these sex-role patterns no doubt linger within those who were socialized in an earlier era and may well make it more difficult for women to solicit funds for their own candidacies.

While any difficulty women have in raising money may, in part, reflect psychological barriers, there are other reasons to anticipate that fund raising would be a particularly acute problem for *women* candidates. Most women are not well integrated into occupational and social networks that often serve as a major source of campaign funds. As a result, they may have difficulty obtaining money from sources commonly available to male candidates, who are more likely to be part of such networks. Suzanne Paizis has explained:

> Women . . . do not have the same avenues of access to money and influence as men do. They have been excluded from decision-making levels, they don't play golf or tennis with "fat cats," they don't casually drop into the bar or restaurant for social and political contacts, and they never are members of the respected "male clubs" which are frequently the first rungs on the political ladder.[18]

When women are successful in obtaining support from big donors and political action committees (PACs), they claim that they often receive less money from these sources than men do. Perhaps in part because few women are incumbents or occupy positions where they can wield political clout, even liberal PACs like the American Federation of State, County, and Municipal Employees (AFSCME) and the National Abortion Rights

Action League (NARAL) have in the past given smaller average contributions to women candidates than to men.[19]

Moreover, while other women might seem a natural fund-raising constituency, women candidates often find it difficult to attract large amounts of money from women. On the one hand, as a result of women's lesser involvement in the political sphere, women are not as accustomed as men to donating money to political causes. On the other hand, when women can be convinced to contribute, they generally give in small amounts. Paizis has observed, "While 'she' is writing a $5 check for her favorite woman candidate (and considering that a sizeable donation), 'he' is writing a $50 or a $500 check for the candidate of his choice (usually male)."[20]

Responses by candidates in this study highlight the overriding importance of fund raising as a problem for women who seek public office. Money was mentioned far more frequently than any other problem by women who ran in contested primaries for all four types of offices (table 4.1). In contrast, money was mentioned as an asset by only a very small proportion of candidates in contested primaries (table 4.2). The pattern across offices suggests that raising funds, as one might expect, is a much more frequent problem for candidates seeking higher-level offices, where the expenses of campaigning are likely to be greater, than for candidates seeking state house seats, where the amount of money needed to mount an effective campaign often is much less.

In addition to money, there are two other basic resources critical to any campaign—people and time.[21] Unlike money, there is no reason that acquiring these two resources should pose substantially greater problems for female candidates than for male candidates.[22] Nevertheless, many women candidates could be expected to perceive a lack of sufficient workers and/or sufficient time to campaign effectively.

As table 4.1 shows, these two resources were the second and third most frequently mentioned problems of women running in contested primaries in 1976.[23] In contrast, only a handful of candidates for the state house and no candidates for other offices mentioned having sufficient time as an advantage in their primary campaigns. A sizable number of respondents did, however, mention people as an asset (table 4.2).

Effects of Incumbency and Seat Desirability on Resource Problems

One might expect problems related to money, people, and time to be less severe for incumbents than for nonincumbents. Incumbency gives a candidate an advantage both in attracting publicity and in establishing seriousness. The more visible and credible the candidate, the easier it

TABLE 4.1
Problems Perceived by Women Candidates, 1976, Who Ran in Contested Primaries[a]

	Congress	Statewide	State Senate	State House
	OFFICE			
	%	%	%	%
Problems				
Resources				
Money	58.0	52.9	40.0	27.9
People	22.0	5.9	18.7	15.8
Time	16.0	11.8	16.0	15.8
Organized support				
Party	16.0	0	13.3	13.2
Organizations	0	0	2.7	5.6
Media	0	5.9	4.0	1.9
Campaign-related problems				
Visibility	10.0	11.8	4.0	3.7
Organization, planning	10.0	5.9	9.3	8.2
Dirty politics	6.0	5.9	10.7	8.4
Issue positions				
(except women's issues)	0	0	1.3	1.1
Opponents	8.0	0	10.7	10.2
Characteristics of voters or district				
Difficulty contacting voters	2.0	0	1.3	1.7
Voter apathy or distrust	6.0	5.9	10.7	5.2
District characteristics (e.g., size, area)	6.0	0	9.3	6.7
Sex-related problems				
Being a woman	2.0	17.6	13.3	8.9
Women's issues	0	5.9	8.0	1.9
Lack of support from other women	2.0	0	0	1.7
Candidate characteristics				
Name familiarity	10.0	5.9	9.3	7.1
Personality characteristics or personal problems	4.0	0	2.7	5.6
Other problems	8.0	5.9	9.3	7.1
No problems mentioned	14.0	11.8	10.7	20.3
N =	(50)	(17)	(75)	(462)

[a]Candidates were asked, "What were the major problems, if any, which you encountered in your primary campaign?" Columns total more than 100% because respondents could list more than one problem.

TABLE 4.2

Advantages Perceived by Women Candidates, 1976, Who Ran in Contested Primaries[a]

	OFFICE			
	Congress	Statewide	State Senate	State House
	%	%	%	%
Advantages				
Resources				
Money	0	0	4.0	3.2
People	2.0	5.9	20.0	10.4
Time	0	0	0	2.8
Incumbency	4.0	0	8.0	5.6
Organized support				
Party	2.0	11.8	1.3	1.9
Organizational and media endorsements	6.0	0	2.7	3.7
Officeholders, local leaders	2.0	0	5.3	2.2
Campaign-related advantages				
Weak opponents	2.0	5.9	4.0	1.1
Prior campaign experience	4.0	5.9	0	4.3
Good organization, ads, materials, etc.	2.0	5.9	1.3	4.5
Good publicity, press attention	6.0	5.9	2.7	1.9
Characteristics of voters or districts				
Voter distrust of incumbents	6.0	11.8	4.0	2.4
Support from voters generally or from segments of voters	10.0	0	6.7	4.5
Sex-related advantages				
Being a woman	10.0	5.9	12.0	7.6
Support from other women	2.0	5.9	2.7	1.5
Candidate characteristics				
Well known, good reputation	16.0	35.3	20.0	21.6
Record in politics	4.0	17.6	8.0	6.1
Knowledge	12.0	0	6.7	5.4
Personality characteristics	8.0	17.6	8.0	5.6
Training in another field	2.0	0	0	3.5
Husband/family	2.0	0	5.3	3.4
Other advantages	2.5	5.9	1.3	4.1
No advantages mentioned	36.0	33.3	35.9	23.5
N =	(50)	(17)	(75)	(462)

[a]Candidates were asked, "What advantages, if any, did you experience in your primary campaign?" Columns total more than 100% because respondents could list more than one advantage.

should be to attract funds. With added publicity and visibility, incumbents also might find it easier to attract campaign workers and staff. Moreover, the fact that incumbents can rely on their lists of workers from previous campaigns is likely to make the resource of "people" less of a problem the second, third, or fourth time around. Incumbents also might be expected to be less likely to view shortage of time as a critical problem since, in a sense, they campaign throughout their term in office. Not needing to establish visibility and name recognition as much as nonincumbents, they may need less time to campaign.[24]

Findings from this study substantiate these expectations. Money, people, and time were more frequently mentioned as problems by nonincumbent state representatives than by incumbents (table 4.3). In the case of money, the difference between nonincumbents and incumbents was sizable.[25]

Just as the three basic resources critical to campaigns pose greater problems for nonincumbents than for incumbents, resources could be expected to pose the greatest problems for candidates in states where serving in the legislature is considered most prestigious and desirable. In these states, more resources generally would be needed to wage effective campaigns.

The anticipated relationships did, in fact, exist between the desirability of legislative seats and the proportions of candidates who perceived lack of money and lack of people as major primary campaign problems (table 4.3). In the case of money, the differences between candidates in states with high and low seat desirability were substantial.

TABLE 4.3

Relationship between Perceptions of Resource-Related Problems and Incumbency, Seat Desirability for Women State House Candidates, 1976

| | Incumbency | | | Desirability of Seats | | | |
	Non-incumbents	Incumbents		High	Moderate	Low	
	%	%	$\text{tau}_b =$	%	%	%	$\text{tau}_c =$
Problem							
Money	31.1	13.4	.15	38.7	26.1	19.2	.17
People	16.8	11.0	.06	18.7	16.1	12.6	.05
Time	17.4	8.5	.09	16.7	10.6	20.5	.03
N =	(380)	(82)		(150)	(161)	(151)	

Surprisingly, however, time was mentioned as an important problem by a larger proportion of state house candidates in states with less desired seats than in states with seats of moderate or high desirability. Perhaps this finding, in part, reflects the "friends and neighbors" politics that characterize many states with less desirable seats. In these states, state house campaigns are likely to be less media-oriented, and candidates may concentrate more on direct, face-to-face communication with voters. Because canvassing and other means of direct voter contact require a great deal of time on the part of the candidate, time may be the most critical resource.

Moreover, perhaps because legislative service holds less appeal in low-desirability states, women who ran for state house seats in these states tended to make their decisions to run at a later date than did their counterparts in states with more desirable seats. While 41.2% of candidates in states with high-desirability seats and 43.1% of candidates in states with moderate-desirability seats did not make a fairly definite decision to run until the last two months before the filing deadline, this was true for an even greater proportion—53.4%—of candidates in states with seats of low desirability.[26] The larger proportion of women entering primary races at the last minute in low-desirability states also may help to account for their greater tendency to perceive lack of time as a major problem.

Lack of Party Support as a Major Problem

Based on the findings of the previous chapter, which suggested that parties seldom approached and encouraged women to run in races where they had a good chance of winning, one might expect a sizable proportion of women to mention a lack of party support (or even party opposition) as a major problem.

Table 4.1 shows that lack of party support was, in fact, the most frequently mentioned problem other than the three basic resources among candidates for all except statewide offices. In contrast to the large proportions of candidates who mentioned lack of party support as a disadvantage, candidates rarely mentioned party support as an advantage (table 4.2).

Differences between candidates of the two parties were small; 12.1% of Democratic candidates and 15.2% of Republican candidates in contested primaries for state assembly seats pointed to lack of party support as a problem (tau$_b$ = .05).[27] Party support was, however, a more frequent problem for nonincumbents than for incumbents; only 6.1% of all incumbents among state house candidates, in contrast with 14.7% of nonincumbents, cited lack of party support as problematic (tau$_b$ = .10).[28]

Gender as Problem and Advantage

Several sources of discrimination could lead women to view their gender as a specific handicap in running a primary campaign. Some voters might be resistant to the idea of a woman running for office. Party leaders might be reluctant to support female candidates as fully as they support male candidates. Contributors might be less willing to donate large sums of money to women's campaigns.

However, consistent with a major hypothesis of this chapter and the next two—that gender may pose less of a barrier for women candidates than many features of the political opportunity structure—one would expect women candidates to perceive their sex as a liability less frequently than other campaign problems such as basic resources and party support.

"Being a woman" was mentioned more frequently than most problems but less frequently than the basic resources of money, people, and time or party support (table 4.1).[29] Moreover, gender was perceived as a problem almost exclusively by nonincumbents. Among candidates in contested primaries for state assembly seats, 10.5% of nonincumbents but only 1.2% of incumbents viewed their gender as a liability in their campaigns (tau$_b$ = .13).[30] Apparently, problems accruing from gender dissipate with incumbency, just as problems with resources become less severe. Perhaps after a woman has proven herself by winning at the polls, her sex is no longer as salient a factor in her relations with other political actors.

Just as gender poses a problem for some women candidates, gender might be expected to work to the advantage of some women. In a race with several contenders, a woman's sex might set her apart from the other candidates and make her more visible. Voters might trust women candidates more, or perceive them as more honest, because of their gender. Moreover, because of cultural inhibitions, male candidates might be reluctant to attack aggressively a female opponent, and this might work to women's advantage.

Table 4.2 reveals that "being a woman" was, in fact, one of the advantages women candidates most frequently mentioned. Again, it was almost exclusively nonincumbents who perceived gender to have had an effect on their campaigns. Only 1.2% of all incumbents running in contested primaries for state house seats listed sex as an advantage, in contrast to 8.9% of all nonincumbents (tau$_b$ = .11).[31] Apparently, incumbents rarely perceive sex to have any important impact on their campaigns, either as an asset or as a liability.

Very few of the candidates who mentioned "being a woman" as a disadvantage also mentioned it as an advantage.[32] Individual women tended to view their sex as having *either* a negative *or* a positive impact on their campaigns. Nevertheless, in the aggregate, being a woman worked to the advantage and to the disadvantage of almost equal proportions of candidates. Thus, unlike money, time, and party support, which were rarely perceived as assets but frequently perceived as liabilities, the effects of gender as advantage and as disadvantage were roughly comparable across the population of women candidates.

Two other sex-related categories of answers emerged in the responses to the open-ended question asking candidates about the major problems in their primary campaigns. Unlike general references to the candidate's gender, however, these factors were cited by very few respondents. Only small proportions of candidates reported that positions on women's issues and failure to receive anticipated support from other women were major problems in their campaigns (table 4.1).

Other Major Problems

In addition to the three basic resources, party support, and gender, a few other problems were mentioned by sizable proportions of candidates (table 4.1). Since women as a group are relative newcomers to the political arena, it is not surprising that many female candidates listed problems related to name familiarity and to visibility. Disadvantages having to do with the nature of the opposing contenders for the nomination—including running against an incumbent, facing opponents who were well connected, and running against a large number of challengers—also were mentioned by a significant number of respondents. Sizable proportions of women candidates pointed to problems with their own campaign organization or planning. Perhaps most surprising in table 4.1 are the notable proportions of candidates who pointed to "dirty politics" and the use of unethical tactics as a major problem in their campaigns.[33] This finding also may reflect women's newcomer status; as newcomers to electoral politics, many women may not anticipate the kinds of unsavory practices that veteran politicians have accepted as a routine part of political life.

Differences between Primary Winners and Losers

We have seen that the five problems most frequently mentioned by women seeking party nominations in 1976 were money, people, time, party support, and gender. Since one or more of these five major problems may merely have narrowed a candidate's margin of victory, rather than causing her to lose altogether, it would be unrealistic to expect none of the winners of primary elections to have experienced these problems. Similarly, one would not expect all losers to have faced these problems, since a candidate certainly could lose for other reasons. However, if the presence of these five problems did, in fact, affect election outcomes, one would expect to find that candidates who lost their primary election bids more frequently experienced these problems than did those who won.

Table 4.4 confirms this expectation. Candidates who lost contested primaries were notably more likely than primary winners to point to money, people, time, party support, and gender as critical problems in their campaigns. While money was the problem mentioned most fre-

TABLE 4.4

Differences in Perceptions of Various Problems for Losers and Winners of Primary Elections among Women State Legislative Candidates, 1976[a]

	State Senate			State House		
	Losers	Winners		Losers	Winners	
	%	%	tau$_b$ =	%	%	tau$_b$ =
Five most frequently mentioned problems						
Money	47.7	29.0	.19	36.0	19.3	.19
People	27.3	6.5	.26	19.7	11.7	.11
Time	18.2	12.9	.07	19.7	11.7	.11
Party support	15.9	9.7	.09	19.2	6.7	.18
Being a woman	15.9	9.7	.09	15.1	2.2	.23
Other problems mentioned with significant frequency						
Name familiarity	6.8	12.9	−.10	8.8	5.4	.07
Opponents	13.6	6.5	.11	13.0	7.2	.10
Organization, planning	13.6	3.2	.18	8.3	8.1	.01
Dirty politics	13.6	6.5	.11	7.9	9.0	−.02
N =	(44)	(31)		(239)	(223)	

[a]Statewide and congressional candidates are not included in this table since the number of winning candidates in contested primaries is too small for meaningful analysis.

quently by winners as well as losers, it also was the problem for which the largest percentage difference existed between winners and losers.

For other problems mentioned with some frequency (i.e., name familiarity, nature of the opponents, campaign organization and planning, and dirty politics), the pattern generally is one of smaller and less consistent differences between primary winners and losers. Only one of these factors—the nature of the opposing contenders for the nomination—was mentioned by considerably more losers than winners among candidates for both the state house and the state senate. Name familiarity actually was mentioned more frequently as a problem by winners than by losers among state senate candidates; similarly, dirty politics was mentioned slightly more frequently by winners than by losers among state house candidates. While campaign organization and planning were mentioned much more often as a problem by losers than by winners among contenders for state senate seats, the differences between losers and winners among state house candidates were quite small.

Thus, not only were money, people, time, party support, and gender the disadvantages most frequently mentioned by women candidates, but also they were the factors most clearly perceived as more problematic by primary losers than by primary winners. Although not mentioned as frequently as a problem by candidates, the nature of the opposition also appears to have been a more severe problem for losers than for winners.

Earlier, incumbents were found less likely than nonincumbents to mention each of the five major problems as disadvantages in their primary campaigns. Incumbents also won contested primaries at a much higher rate than nonincumbents. Among candidates for the state senate running in contested primaries, 77.8% of all incumbents but only 36.4% of nonincumbents emerged victorious (tau$_b$ = .27). Among candidates for the state house, 85.4% of all incumbents who faced primary opposition won, in contrast to 40.3% of nonincumbents (tau$_b$ = .34).[34] Yet, the greater tendency for losers to mention the five major problems in their campaigns was not due merely to the concentration of incumbents among the ranks of primary victors. When incumbents were excluded and only nonincumbents considered, losers continued to mention these problems at a noticeably higher rate than victors (table 4.5).

Perhaps the difference in the degree to which winners and losers of primary elections perceived the five factors as working to their disadvantage is best illustrated by examining the proportion of winners and losers who mentioned any *one* of the five factors as problems in their campaigns. Among candidates for the state senate, 81.8% of the primary

TABLE 4.5

Differences in Perceptions of Various Problems for Losers and Winners of Primary Elections among Nonincumbent Women State Legislative Candidates, 1976

| | State Senate | | | State House | | |
	Losers	Winners		Losers	Winners	
	%	%	tau_b =	%	%	tau_b =
Problems						
Money	45.2	33.3	.12	37.4	21.6	.17
People	26.2	0	.34	18.9	13.7	.07
Time	19.0	8.3	.14	20.7	12.4	.11
Party support	16.7	12.5	.06	19.4	7.8	.16
Being a woman	16.7	12.5	.06	15.9	2.6	.21
N =	(42)	(24)		(227)	(153)	

losers, compared with only 48.4% of winning candidates, mentioned at least one of the five major problems (tau_b = .35). Similarly, among candidates for the state house, 71.1% of primary losers, but only 40.4% of primary victors, listed one or more of these five critical problems (tau_b = .31).

Candidates who lost contested primaries were not asked directly about the factors they perceived as contributing to their defeat. However, it is not unreasonable to assume that many of the losing candidates would have cited money, people, time, party support, and gender as critical factors. Moreover, to the extent that candidates' perceptions can be accepted as valid indicators of political reality, the differences between winners and losers suggest that these five factors may have had some effect on election outcomes and that they may contribute to a comprehensive assessment of the factors which led to electoral success or failure for women candidates.[35]

Major Advantages

Except for name familiarity, characteristics of the candidates themselves rarely were mentioned as problems by women in competitive primaries. However, a variety of candidate characteristics were among the advantages most frequently perceived by these women (table 4.2). The asset most often reported was being well known or having a good reputation. Sizable proportions of women candidates also cited their political records, their knowledge, and their personality characteristics (such as determination, energy, stamina, confidence, and ability to relate to voters). Only three other advantages—people, incumbency, and being a woman—were mentioned with a frequency comparable to that for these candidate characteristics. Organized support, factors related to the campaign itself, and characteristics of the voters or district generally were far less often perceived as advantages.

There were only a few notable differences between winners and losers in perceptions of advantages experienced in their campaigns (table 4.6).[36] Among candidates for both the state house and the state senate, winners were considerably more likely to mention being well known or having a good reputation. Among candidates for the state senate, winners also were much more likely than losers to mention people as an asset. However, this was not the case among state house candidates, where primary victors were no more likely than defeated candidates to view people as an advantage.

Perceptions of the effects of gender are particularly interesting. Earlier, losing candidates were found to be somewhat more likely than winning candidates to perceive gender as a disadvantage. Table 4.6 shows that among state senate candidates, winners were more likely than losers to perceive gender as an advantage; among state house candidates, there was no difference in the frequency with which victorious and defeated candidates pointed to their sex as an asset. Thus, gender seems to have operated in a double-edged fashion; losers were more likely than winners

TABLE 4.6

Differences in Perceptions of Various Advantages for Winners and Losers of Primary Elections among Women State Legislative Candidates, 1976

	State Senate			State House		
	Winners	Losers		Winners	Losers	
	%	%	$tau_b =$	%	%	$tau_b =$
Advantages						
Well known, good reputation	29.0	13.6	.19	30.0	13.8	.20
Record in politics	12.9	4.5	.15	7.6	4.6	.06
Knowledge	3.2	9.1	−.12	2.7	7.9	−.12
Personality characteristics	9.7	6.8	.05	6.3	5.0	.03
People	29.0	13.6	.19	9.4	11.3	−.03
Being a woman	19.4	6.8	.19	7.6	7.5	.00
N =	(31)	(44)		(223)	(239)	

to perceive it as a problem, while winners, at least among state senate candidates, were more likely to view it as an advantage.

Other differences between winning and losing candidates in perceptions of major advantages are small and/or not consistent for both state senate and state house candidates (table 4.6). If any of the advantages cited by women candidates affected election outcomes in contested primaries, being well known is the most likely to have had an effect.

Some Concluding Observations

Candidates perceived personal characteristics that they had worked to develop and that were subject to their own control as their strongest assets in primary races. In contrast, the factors considered to pose the greatest problems were those over which candidates could exercise little or no direct control. To some extent, party support and the basic resources of money, people, and time may be cultivated by a candidate. However, to some degree they reflect features of the structure of political opportunity that cannot be altered by those who seek public office. A candidate cannot, for example, control the number of contenders or races that compete for scarce resources in a particular election year. Neither can a candidate prevent a party favorite from entering a race and attracting the support of party influentials.

While the three basic campaign resources and party support were frequently perceived as disadvantages by candidates, they were rarely mentioned as advantages. The sizable proportions of primary losers citing these factors as critical problems suggest that these may be among the factors losing candidates viewed as responsible for their defeat at the polls. Moreover, the fact that much larger proportions of primary losers than of winners mentioned lack of money, people, time, and party support as disadvantages suggests that these factors may have had an actual impact on election outcomes—a proposition investigated further in the next chapter.

While gender was perceived as an important problem by a sizable proportion of women candidates, the overall effect of gender on women's campaigns appeared less one-sided than the effects of money, people, time, and party support. Unlike these factors, gender was mentioned as an advantage by women candidates, especially among contenders for state legislative seats, almost as frequently as it was mentioned as a disadvantage. Moreover, although losers of primary contests were more likely than winners to perceive their sex as a problem in their campaigns, winners of primary contests were just as likely, or more likely, than losers to perceive it as an asset. Thus, while gender may have worked to the advantage of some candidates and to the disadvantage of others, these findings suggest that, in the aggregate, gender probably was not a major determinant of the outcome of women's campaign efforts in 1976.

Finally, two features of the political opportunity structure not subject to alteration by individual candidates—incumbency and the desirability of legislative seats—were related both to the proportion of candidates perceiving problems and to the acquisition of critical campaign resources. Candidates who were incumbents and/or who were running in states with seats of low desirability were less likely than other candidates to report problems and to report difficulty in attracting basic campaign resources. These findings suggest that incumbency and seat desirability may be among the most important factors affecting election outcomes for women candidates—a hypothesis examined in chapter 6.

CHAPTER FIVE

□ □ □ □ ■ □ □ □ □

Qualifications, Campaigns, and Electoral Success

JUST AS CANDIDATES themselves perceived certain variables to be critical to their campaign efforts, others who have observed women's campaigns at a greater distance have drawn conclusions about why larger numbers of women are not elected to office. In the world of practical politics, there are several commonly heard explanations for women candidates' lack of greater success at the polls. Each is based on the fundamental premise that certain factors are critical to election outcomes. Because women are believed to be disadvantaged, deficient, or different from most candidates on these factors, they are thought to be less electable. This chapter and chapter 6 assess the validity of some of the most popular explanations for the lack of greater electoral success among female candidates.

This chapter focuses on two of the popular explanations for women's lack of greater electoral success—that women lack qualifications for officeholding, and that they run inadequate campaigns. Chapter 6 considers a third popular explanation—that women often lose because of factors related to their sex. Chapter 6 also explores a fourth possibility, less commonly espoused as a reason why *women* candidates lose, but a potentially powerful explanation nonetheless—that features of the political opportunity structure, such as incumbency and the presence of open seats, largely determine women's rate of success at the polls.

Each hypothesized explanation for women's lack of a higher rate of electoral success is reviewed in turn. Variables relevant to each explanation are examined in order to assess the general plausibility of the explanation as well as the extent to which the variables seem to affect election outcomes. If, for example, a lack of qualifications is a major barrier to the election of women, one would expect to find both (1) that a sizable proportion of women candidates are deficient in those qualifications deemed important for officeholding, and (2) that the qualifications of those women who win elections differ significantly from the qualifications of those who lose (i.e., that qualifications may have affected election outcomes). For each hypothesized explanation, the subset of variables that most strongly support the explanation is selected through the use of stepwise discriminant analysis. Then, at the end of chapter 6, a comparative test of all four explanations is undertaken. The four subsets of variables selected as most robust in earlier analysis are included in a final stepwise discriminant analysis to determine which factors are most useful in distinguishing winning from losing candidates and thus seem to have the greatest overall impact on election outcomes for women.

Qualifications as an Explanation

One popular explanation for the lack of women in public office focuses on previous experience and qualifications for officeholding. Political elites frequently defend an inadequate record in recruiting women by arguing that they simply cannot find sufficient numbers of "qualified" women. This, for example, was the defense used by both the Nixon and Carter administrations when challenged for not appointing larger numbers of women to major policy-making posts.[1]

In recruiting and selecting individuals to fill appointive positions in government, political leaders have good reason to be concerned with qualifications since they provide an indication of projected performance in office. Presumably, qualifications also should affect election outcomes since voters are thought to consider qualifications in judging political candidates. Kenneth Prewitt has noted:

The voter views citizens whom he respects for nonpolitical accomplishments as candidates for his respect in the political sphere. The political aspirant's success in business, military, civic, or academic endeavors is relevant to his political image, since the voter uses the candidate's past accomplishments as an indicator of his future performance.[2]

Women candidates are perceived not only to lack the nonpolitical accomplishments and credentials necessary for public officeholding, but also to lack political experience. This view has been reinforced by a well-publicized study of women who ran for statewide and congressional offices in 1976 conducted by Rothstein/Buckley, a Washington-based consulting firm, under the sponsorship of The Center for the Study of Congress. The study showed:

> Most of the women surveyed were political novices. More than half of them had never received an appointment to public office at any level.[3]

If many women candidates lack the credentials and the experience necessary for public officeholding, as is commonly believed, then the failure of women to be elected to public office in greater numbers may be attributable, in part, to their lack of qualifications.

Education and Occupation

There is general agreement that education and occupation are important qualifications for officeholding. Both demonstrate past achievement and can help to indicate the quality of an individual's probable performance in office.

Among the best-documented observations about candidates and public officials are that they are much better educated than most of the general population and that they tend to be drawn disproportionately from managerial and professional occupations. The evidence suggests that those who seek or hold more powerful offices (e.g., congressional seats) have somewhat higher educational levels and more prestigious occupations than those who seek less powerful offices. Nevertheless, previous research on mostly male samples has found that a sizable majority of state legislative candidates and officeholders are college-educated and have managerial and professional occupations.[4]

With regard to their educational backgrounds, most women candidates cannot be considered to lack the necessary qualifications for officeholding. As table 5.1 demonstrates, very large majorities had completed college. More than one-fifth of candidates for all offices had advanced degrees, and roughly another one-fifth had completed some postgraduate work. Only about one of every ten candidates had not attended college. These educational levels appear comparable to those found in previous studies of male candidates and officeholders.[5]

While women candidates as a group did not lack the educational credentials viewed as necessary for officeholding, the question of whether they lacked the occupational backgrounds generally viewed as qualifications for officeholding has a less straightforward answer.

Candidates were asked to list their occupations if they were currently employed or if they ever had worked outside the home for an extended period of time. Contrary to Jeane Kirkpatrick's assertion that women state

Table 5.1
Education of Women Candidates, 1976

	OFFICE			
	Congress	Statewide	State Senate	State House
	%	%	%	%
Education				
No college	13.6	0	9.9	14.0
Some college	23.3	20.0	22.1	27.1
College graduate	16.4	20.0	16.6	16.5
Some postgraduate work	23.3	5.0	22.7	21.5
Advanced degree	23.4	55.0	28.7	20.9
N =	(73)	(20)	(163)	(943)

legislators usually are recruited from the occupation of housewife,[6] a very large majority of candidates for all offices listed at least one occupation (table 5.2). Moreover, of those who listed an occupation, only a negligible number listed homemaker.[7]

Surprisingly, 30.1% of all candidates responding to the question on occupation listed two or more occupations, even though the question was worded in the singular. Apparently, a sizable number of women candidates perceive their careers as involving a series of two or more distinct occupations rather than a single vocation.

As has been found in previous studies of predominantly male officeholders and candidates,[8] the vast majority of female candidates have professional or managerial occupations (table 5.2). By far the largest proportions of candidates for all offices were drawn from the professional ranks.

Nevertheless, even though a majority of women candidates were professionals, very few were lawyers—the most common profession for male public officeholders.[9] Only among statewide candidates, where almost one-fourth were attorneys, did the proportion of lawyers exceed 4% (table 5.2).

The most frequent professional occupation among women candidates was elementary and secondary teaching, which provided roughly one-fifth of candidates for all offices. Significant proportions of women candidates also were employed in college teaching. This concentration of candidates in education is not surprising, since teaching is a vocation traditionally viewed as an acceptable career choice for women. Nursing

TABLE 5.2

Occupations of Women Candidates, 1976[a]

| | OFFICE | | | |
	Congress	Statewide	State Senate	State House
	%	%	%	%
Occupation				
Professional, technical				
and kindred	53.4	50.0	53.3	50.0
Lawyers	2.7	22.7	3.6	2.4
Elementary and				
secondary teachers	17.8	18.2	21.2	22.1
College teachers	6.8	4.5	9.1	3.0
Social and community				
workers	4.1	0	4.2	4.1
Editors, reporters,				
journalists	9.6	0	3.6	4.9
Nurses	1.7	0	5.5	3.6
Managers, administrators,				
and proprietors	37.0	40.9	25.5	26.6
Public officeholders or				
government administrators	20.5	22.7	5.5	9.5
Sales workers	8.2	9.1	9.1	7.6
Real estate agents	6.8	0	4.2	4.3
Clerical-secretarial				
and kindred	9.6	18.2	18.8	20.3
Farmers and farm workers	1.4	0	3.0	1.1
Students	0	0	0	1.4
Homemakers	0	0	1.2	.9
Self-employed	4.1	0	.6	.7
Other (craftswomen,				
operatives, laborers,				
except farm; service,				
except private household)	0	0	2.4	4.9
No occupation	11.0	18.2	7.9	10.1
N =	(73)	(22)	(165)	(952)

[a]Columns total more than 100% because respondents could list more than one occupation.

and social work are two other professional fields traditionally viewed as appropriate for women, and among state legislative candidates more respondents had occupations in these fields than in law. The only other profession listed by a significant number of respondents was journalism.

Like male officeholders and candidates, sizable numbers of women candidates were drawn not only from the professions but also from the ranks of managers, administrators, and proprietors (table 5.2). At the congressional and statewide levels, women candidates' managerial and administrative backgrounds were concentrated in the public, rather than in the private, sector; more than half of the candidates in this category were public officials or government administrators.

Roughly one-fifth of candidates for statewide, state senate, and state house seats and one-tenth of candidates for congressional seats listed a secretarial or clerical occupation. Past studies of predominantly male candidates and officeholders generally have found few candidates or officeholders with clerical or secretarial occupations; in fact, most studies have not reported this occupation separately but rather have placed respondents with these occupations in an "other" category. In large part, this undoubtedly reflects the fact that most secretarial and clerical work is done by females. In part, it also may reflect the fact that voters and other political actors generally consider individuals with secretarial and clerical backgrounds to lack the necessary occupational credentials for officeholding. Nevertheless, before concluding that we have located a sizable number of women candidates without the professional or managerial backgrounds considered necessary for officeholding, it is important to recall that many women candidates listed more than one vocation. As a result, one would expect that some of the candidates who listed a clerical or secretarial occupation also listed a managerial or professional one. In fact, sizable numbers did. When those who also claimed to be managers or professionals are excluded, only 5.5% of congressional candidates, 0.1% of statewide candidates, 12.1% of state senate candidates, and 12.7% of state house candidates are left among the clerical and secretarial ranks.

The same pattern is evident for those who listed an occupation in sales. While almost one of every ten candidates listed sales as an occupation, only 1.7% of congressional, no statewide, 6.0% of state senate, and 6.2% of state house candidates had an occupation in sales and no professional or managerial occupation. Moreover, the most frequent area of specialization for those in sales work was real estate, one of the more prestigious of the sales occupations and one that generally allows sufficient flexibility in work hours for pursuing political activities.

The pattern of occupational backgrounds of women candidates suggests, on the one hand, that they generally do not lack the necessary occupational qualifications for officeholding; on the other hand, they may be somewhat disadvantaged collectively with regard to occupational credentials. Like their male counterparts, women candidates are drawn largely from professional and managerial occupations. However, a pattern of sex differentiation in occupational backgrounds exists. The concentration of women candidates in traditionally female fields, such as teaching, social work, and nursing, may work to their disadvantage. To the extent that voters believe that certain types of professional credentials (e.g., law) equip one for officeholding while other types (e.g., teaching) do not, many women candidates may be perceived as lacking the necessary occupational backgrounds for officeholding despite their professional status.

Political Experience

In addition to education and occupation, another important component of a candidate's qualifications for officeholding is previous political experience. David Leuthold, reviewing the results of various surveys that asked voters about the qualities they desired in political candidates, concluded that the single quality most emphasized was experience.[10] Do women candidates lack the experience voters might consider indicative of their ability to perform the duties of the offices they seek?

There are three arenas of experience that might provide qualifications for holding office—previous elective and appointive officeholding, party activity, and organizational participation. As table 5.3 demonstrates, sizable proportions of women candidates had experience in each of these spheres.

Women candidates had least experience, not surprisingly, in elective and appointive officeholding. A majority of candidates for all offices had run for an elective office in a previous election. However, far fewer actually had been elected to some office other than the one sought in 1976. Moreover, except among statewide candidates, only slightly more than one-third of the candidates for all offices claimed to have held an appointive governmental position.[11]

The lack of larger proportions of candidates with experience in elective office is not unexpected, since only in recent years have more than a handful of women become candidates. Nevertheless, this lack of officeholding experience may disadvantage many women candidates, especially when running for higher-level offices, since the scant existing evidence suggests that male candidates in the aggregate have more officeholding experience.[12] In many states, running for a seat in the state house may be an acceptable first political step; a candidate might be viewed as qualified to hold a state house seat without previous officeholding experience. However, a candidate for state senate, statewide, or congressional office is less likely to be viewed as qualified if she lacks officeholding experience, and at these levels women may be disadvantaged by their relative lack of experience.

Although many women did lack officeholding experience, most women candidates were not deficient in partisan and organizational experience.[13] Majorities of candidates for every office claimed that they were very or somewhat active in their state and/or local party organizations and had held at least one party leadership position (table 5.3). More than one-half of state legislative candidates and two-fifths of congressional candidates had been delegates to state party conventions, although considerably fewer had been delegates to national conventions.

Women candidates also were joiners. Candidates were asked to list all organizational affiliations over a five-year period preceding their

TABLE 5.3

Political Experience of Women Candidates, 1976[a]

| | OFFICE | | | |
	Congress	Statewide	State Senate	State House
	%	%	%	%
Political Officeholding				
Had run for public office before 1976	56.9	54.5	58.0	55.1
Had held at least one previous elective office[b]	27.4	40.9	27.3	19.3
Had held at least one appointive governmental position	36.9	61.9	38.0	33.4
Party Activity				
Very or somewhat active in state and local party	73.7	77.3	78.7	77.2
Had held at least one leadership position in party	52.8	55.0	67.7	56.9
Had been delegate to state party convention	41.1	22.7	56.4	56.2
Had been delegate to national party convention	23.3	13.6	19.6	12.3
Organizational Activity				
Belonged to five or more organizations	54.8	50.1	69.7	55.0

[a]Percentages in this table are based on N's ranging from 72 to 73 for congressional candidates, 20 to 22 for statewide candidates, 162 to 165 for state senate candidates, and 931 to 952 for state house candidates. The N's vary slightly because of missing data for a few candidates.

[b]Incumbents were counted as having held a previous office only if they had been elected to an office other than the one presently occupied.

candidacies. A majority of candidates for all offices belonged to five or more organizations (table 5.3).

Overall, the political backgrounds of women candidates suggest that they accumulated experience in those spheres—partisan and organizational—most open to women and defined by society as acceptable forms of participation for members of their sex. They have not accumulated a great deal of experience in the sphere of participation—public officeholding—least accessible to women and traditionally defined by society as an inappropriate mode of participation for females.

While these generalizations characterize women candidates for all offices, there were important differences in experience across offices (table 5.3). First, the previous political experience of statewide candidates seems to have been far more heavily concentrated in public officeholding than the experience of candidates for other offices. Relatively more statewide candidates had held elective or appointive positions and relatively fewer had served as delegates to national or state party conventions. Second, congressional candidates appear to have been the least qualified candidates, relative to the prestige of the office sought, of candidates for any type of office. On every measure of party activity, except serving as a delegate to a national convention, fewer congressional candidates had experience than was true for candidates for state senate or state house positions. Similarly, a smaller proportion of congressional than other candidates belonged to more than two organizations.[14] Finally, about equal proportions of congressional candidates and state senate candidates had run for public office before 1976, had held another public office, and had served in an appointive governmental position; only slightly larger proportions of congressional than state house candidates had had these various types of officeholding experiences. Overall, then, congressional candidates appear to have been no more experienced than state legislative candidates.[15]

The Effects of Qualifications in Differentiating Winners and Losers

If women candidates fail to win at a higher rate because they lack the necessary qualifications, one would expect not only that many women candidates are deficient in credentials and political experience but also that various qualifications are critical in determining election outcomes. Specifically, one would expect to find that winners and losers can be distinguished based on their qualifications, with winners generally possessing the necessary qualifications and losers lacking them. In order to assess the possible effect of qualification variables on election outcomes, both bivariate relationships (table 5.4) and the results of a series of stepwise discriminant analyses (table 5.5) were examined.

Discriminant analysis is a multivariate technique that weighs and linearly combines the various independent variables to maximize the statistical separation of the groupings of the dependent variable (in this case, winners and losers). In order to identify the independent variables most useful in discriminating winners and losers, a stepwise procedure was used. This procedure first selects the single best-discriminating variable. It continues to select variables in the order in which they contribute, in conjunction with variables already selected, to the discrimination of the groups. Selection of variables ends when the remaining variables no longer contribute to further discrimination.[16]

Table 5.5 presents both the standardized discriminant function coefficient and the level of significance of the change in Rao's V for each variable selected by the stepwise procedure. A standardized discriminant function coefficient is somewhat analogous to a standardized regression coefficient. When the sign is ignored, a standardized discriminant function coefficient represents an estimate of the relative contribution of its associated independent variable to the discrimination of the groups. Rao's V is a measure of the overall separation of the groups. A variable that produces a sizable and positive change in Rao's V contributes to the separation of the groups and thus helps to discriminate between them. Since the change in Rao's V has a chi-square distribution with one degree of freedom, it can be tested for statistical significance.

The overall impact of qualification variables on election outcomes is assessed by examining the proportions of cases correctly classified as winners and losers (table 5.5). The discriminating variables are used as the basis for classification functions which predict general and primary election outcomes for candidates for all offices. Using these classification functions, the likely outcome (i.e., winner or loser) for each candidate running in primary and/or general elections is predicted solely from the variables included in the analysis and compared against actual electoral results. The percent correctly classified as winners or losers for primary elections and for general elections across each office is then computed.[17] The percent correctly classified is somewhat analogous to R^2 in regression analysis in that it allows the researcher to assess the adequacy of the derived discriminant functions.

While eight separate measures of qualifications were included in each of the six analyses whose results are presented in table 5.5, only those variables, as selected by the stepwise procedure, that contributed to the

TABLE 5.4

Relationships between Qualifications and Primary and General Election Outcomes for Women Candidates, 1976[a]

		Congress/Statewide[b]		State Senate		State House	
		Primary Outcomes	General Outcomes	Primary Outcomes	General Outcomes	Primary Outcomes	General Outcomes
Basic Credentials							
Education	tau_c =	-.01	.11	-.10	.07	.03	.05
Occupation[c]	tau_b =	.002	.08	-.04	.01	.01	.03
Political Officeholding							
Had held at least one previous elective office	tau_b =	.27	.13	.26	.26	.11	.11
Party Activity							
Degree of activity in state and local party	tau_c =	-.05	-.17	-.09	-.003	.15	.01
Had held at least one leadership position in party	tau_b =	.27	-.12	.03	-.003	.11	.02
Had been delegate to state party convention	tau_b =	-.06	-.002	.31	.12	.19	.03
Had been delegate to national party convention	tau_b =	.16	.04	.01	.27	.09	.15
Organizational Activity							
Number of organizational memberships	tau_c =	-.06	-.41	-.04	.10	.01	.06

[a]There were 67 congressional/statewide, 75 state senate, and 462 state house candidates in contested primaries; there were 46 congressional/statewide, 120 state senate, and 711 state house condidates in general elections.

[b]In this and subsequent tables, congressional and statewide candidates have been combined into one category in order to provide sufficient numbers of cases for meaningful analysis.

[c]Coded as a dichotomous variable: professional/managerial vs. all others.

statistical discrimination of the groups appear in this table.[18] Variables that did not help to distinguish winners from losers, in combination with previously selected variables, were excluded.

Among congressional/statewide candidates, the qualification variables that showed the strongest simple bivariate relationships to primary election outcomes were elective officeholding experience and experience in a party leadership position (table 5.4). These two variables, in combination with two others, also constituted the subset of qualification variables that best differentiated winning and losing candidates in primaries for congressional/statewide offices (table 5.5). However, if conventional standards are followed and .05 is adopted as a maximum acceptable significance level, experience in elective office is the only one of the four variables that yielded a statistically significant change in Rao's V.

The qualification variable that showed the strongest bivariate relationship to general election outcomes for congressional/statewide candidates was number of organizational memberships (table 5.4). However, contrary to expectations, those congressional candidates with more organizational memberships were more likely to lose their general election bids.[19] In combination with number of organizational memberships, elective officeholding experience and occupation also contributed to the differentiation of winning and losing congressional/statewide candidates in general elections. However, only the variable measuring the number of organizational memberships made a statistically significant contribution (table 5.5).

Among state senate candidates, the only qualification variables which showed notable bivariate relationships to election outcomes were experience in elective office, which was positively related to both primary and general election outcomes, experience as a delegate to a state party convention, which was positively related to primary election outcomes, and experience as a delegate to a national party convention, which was positively related to general election outcomes (table 5.4). The discriminant analyses also pointed to the importance of these variables relative to other qualification variables (table 5.5). Activism in the state and local party combined with elective officeholding experience and state delegate experience to constitute the subset of qualification variables that best distinguished primary winners from losers among state senate candidates. The subset of variables that best differentiated general election winners and losers included number of organizational memberships as well as elective officeholding experience and national delegate experience. How-

TABLE 5.5

Discriminant Analyses for Primary and General Election Outcomes Based on Qualification Variables for Women Candidates, 1976

	Standardized Discriminant Function Coefficient	Significance of Change in Rao's V	Cases Correctly Classified
Congressional/ Statewide Candidates[a]			
Primary Election Outcomes (N = 64)			
Had held at least one previous elective office	.56	.02	
Had held at at least one leadership position in party	.76	.11	75%
Number of organizational memberships	−.46	.14	
Degree of activity in state and local party	−.39	.22	
General Election Outcomes (N = 43)			
Number of organizational memberships	−.97	.02	
Occupation[b]	.46	.08	78%
Had held at least one previous elective office	.43	.21	
State Senate Candidates			
Primary Election Outcomes (N = 72)			
Had held at least one previous elective office	.53	.01	
Had been delegate to state party convention	.87	.02	68%
Degree of activity in state and local party	−.58	.04	

General Election Outcomes (N = 116)			
Had been delegate to national party convention	.66	.003	
Had held at least one previous elective office	.69	.005	} 71%
Number of organizational memberships	.31	.18	

Primary Election Outcomes (N = 436)			
Had been a delegate to state party convention	.74	.0001	
Had held at least one previous elective office	.37	.11	} 60%
Degree of activity in state and local party	.30	.22	

State House Candidates

General Election Outcomes (N = 682)			
Had been delegate to national party convention	.75	.001	
Had held at least one previous elective office	.52	.007	
Education	.38	.03	} 60%
Number of organizational memberships	.27	.13	

[a] In this and subsequent tables, congressional and statewide candidates had been combined into one category in order to provide sufficient numbers of cases for meaningful analysis.

[b] Coded as a dichotomous variable: professional/managerial vs. all others.

ever, number of organizational memberships did not make a statistically significant contribution to the differentiation of winners and losers.

For state house candidates, elective officeholding experience and measures of party activism again stood out as most important. Experience as a delegate to a state party convention was the variable most strongly associated with primary election outcomes for state house candidates (table 5.4), and of the three variables that helped to discriminate winning and losing primary candidates, it was the only one which made a statistically significant contribution to the discriminant function (table 5.5). The two variables that showed the strongest bivariate relationships to general election outcomes for state house candidates were experience as a delegate to a national party convention and previous experience in elective office (table 5.4). These variables also were among the four that best differentiated winning and losing general election candidates as shown by the results of the stepwise discriminant analysis (table 5.5). In addition to experience as a national party delegate and experience in elective office, the other variable that made a significant contribution to the discrimination of winning and losing candidates in state house elections was education.

The classification functions based on the discriminating variables correctly predicted primary outcomes for (i.e., correctly classified as winners and losers) 75% of congressional/statewide candidates, 68% of state senate candidates, and 60% of state house candidates (table 5.5). Seventy-three percent of congressional/statewide candidates, 59% of state senate candidates, and 52% of state house candidates actually lost their primary elections. Thus, it was possible, using the classification functions, to predict correctly the outcome for 2% more of the congressional/statewide candidates, 9% more of the state senate candidates, and 8% more of the state house candidates than would have been possible if one had simply assumed that all candidates lost.

Similarly, the classification functions led to correct predictions of general election outcomes for 78% of congressional/statewide candidates, 71% of state senate candidates, and 60% of state house candidates. Seventy-six percent of congressional/statewide candidates and 63% of state senate candidates actually lost; 51% of state house candidates won. Thus, the classification functions, based on the qualifications variables, yielded an improvement in prediction of 2% for congressional/statewide candidates, 8% for state senate candidates, and 9% for state house candidates over predictions that could have been made without knowledge of qualifications.

Improvements in prediction of 2% to 9% are not particularly impressive. While knowledge of qualifications can contribute slightly to our ability to predict election outcomes, indicating that qualifications may have some small effect on outcomes, the relatively large proportion of candidates incorrectly classified as winners or losers suggests that variables other than qualifications also are important.

Campaigns as an Explanation

The second popular explanation for why women candidates lose elections focuses on inadequacies in campaign organization and planning. There is some disagreement about how much effect campaign strategies and organization can have on election outcomes. On the one hand, some academic observers of political campaigns share Lewis Froman's view that "there is little a candidate can do that will affect the outcome of an election."[20] On the other hand, numerous practitioners operate on the premise that campaign strategies can make a considerable difference. A variety of books and campaign manuals exist to assist candidates with staffing, public relations, campaign research, voter contact, fund raising, and other aspects of campaigning. Professional consultants, fund raisers, pollsters, and advertising specialists abound. Moreover, as Dan Nimmo has suggested, "there remains the fact that a small proportion of voters (perhaps one-third of voters in national elections and far higher proportions in primary, statewide, and local contests) decide between competing candidates during the course of the campaign."[21] The presence of these undecided voters suggests that campaigns might influence a sufficient number of voters, particularly in primary elections where party identification is not a deciding factor, to affect the outcome of many races.

Few women, relative to men, have had experience in running for office. In general, women are not well integrated into business, professional, and social networks where knowledge of management principles and practices analogous to those of campaigning is acquired. As a result, observers frequently assume that women cannot, or do not, run technically sound campaigns, and that this helps to explain their relative absence from public office. There exists the stereotype of the woman political neophyte who decides to run for office only a few days before the filing deadline, who runs her campaign from her living room with herself or her husband as campaign manager, who is unfamiliar with practices such as targeting, and who never maps out a budget or formulates a coherent campaign strategy. This stereotype has been reinforced by the

Rothstein/Buckley study of women statewide and congressional candidates which found that

> many female candidates did not make full use of accepted campaign techniques. Only 44 percent based their strategies in part on polls. About 41 percent did not use demographic information to chart their strategies and only 47 percent used targeting data in their planning.[22]

An article summarizing the findings of this study concluded that "women too often fail to use sophisticated campaign techniques in seeking election."[23]

The Two Sets of Campaign Variables

Two different sets of factors related to campaigns may help to explain why women candidates are not more successful at the polls. One set has to do with the above explanation for why more women are not elected—that women candidates do not run well-planned and technically sound campaigns. The other set relates to women candidates' own perceptions (described in chapter 4) of the factors that hinder their campaigns—lack of money, people, time, and party support. If women candidates do not run technically sound campaigns, if they lack various campaign resources, and if these factors are critical to election outcomes, then such factors may explain why women are not more successful at the polls.

Campaign Organization and Planning

Robert Agranoff has noted, "Any political scientist or historian who has made an attempt to systematically study a campaign, or some aspect of campaigning, will testify that they have found a dearth of written materials from which to gather evidence."[24] The lack of systematic evidence makes it difficult to predict the specific features of campaign planning and organization, if any, which are likely to make a difference in election outcomes.

However, several features of campaign planning and organization, commonly recognized as essential ingredients of an effective campaign, were asked about in this study. Although it was not possible through a survey to assess the *quality* of a candidate's campaign organization, it was possible to ascertain whether candidates employed certain accepted practices and principles in organizing and conducting their primary campaigns.

One commonly accepted ingredient of an effective campaign is the presence of key staff personnel and advisers who can oversee the day-to-day operation of the campaign and provide the candidate with advice on critical decisions. A candidate who tries to manage her own campaign and who does not consult seasoned political advisers is likely to find herself devoting too much time to administrative details and too little time to actual campaigning; moreover, she is likely to make serious strategic mistakes. As Joseph Napolitan has noted, "The worst choice any candidate can pick for his campaign manager is himself. No one—repeat, no one—can do a competent job in a major campaign if he tries to serve both roles."[25]

In this study, candidates who ran in contested primaries were asked both if they had a manager, coordinator, or director for their primary campaign, and if they had one or more advisers who consistently played a major role in their campaign decisions. As table 5.6 shows, sizable majorities of candidates for all four types of offices had both managers and advisers.

However, women's campaign managers, by and large, were not high-salaried professionals. As table 5.7 reveals, most managers were unpaid and part-time. About one-fourth apparently had no previous campaign

TABLE 5.6

Aspects of Campaign Organization and Planning Employed by Women Candidates, 1976[a]

| | OFFICE | | | |
	Congress	Statewide	State Senate	State House
	%	%	%	%
Aspects of Campaign Organization and Planning				
Had a manager	68.0	76.5	55.4	56.2
Had one or more advisers	72.9	86.7	69.3	63.6
Had a headquarters	81.3	62.5	57.3	50.6
Had a comprehensive strategy	67.3	80.0	67.6	68.1
Had a budget	56.3	73.3	56.8	52.7
Identified undecided and/or favorable voters	71.1	58.8	71.8	76.8
Focused voter contact efforts on key voting units	67.4	62.5	80.0	71.9

[a]Percentages in this table are based on N's ranging from 45 to 50 for congressional candidates, 15 to 17 for statewide candidates, 70 to 75 for state senate candidates, and 434 to 459 for state house candidates. The N's vary slightly because of missing data for a few candidates.

experience as managers or in other roles,[26] and a sizable minority were relatives of the candidates.

Another commonly recognized prerequisite of a sound campaign organization is the existence of a campaign headquarters. Majorities of candidates for all four levels of office set up headquarters for their primary campaigns (table 5.6). However, of those who had a headquarters, 46.2% of congressional, 10.0% of statewide, 64.3% of state senate, and 67.6% of state house candidates located their headquarters in their homes.

Four other factors commonly recognized as necessary ingredients for an effective campaign are the development of a comprehensive campaign strategy, the development of an itemized projected budget, the identification of favorable and undecided voters, and the concentration of voter contact efforts in those voting units likely to yield the highest payoff. Although each of these elements was present in the campaigns of majorities, and often large majorities, of candidates for all offices, one-fifth to one-half of candidates for various offices failed to employ these commonly accepted practices (table 5.6).

Thus, the record on women's campaign organization and planning is mixed. Many women candidates across all offices employed commonly accepted principles and practices in setting up and running their campaigns, but sizable proportions of women candidates did not. Apparently,

TABLE 5.7

Characteristics of Primary Campaign Managers for Women Candidates, 1976[a]

	OFFICE			
	Congress	Statewide	State Senate	State House
	%	%	%	%
Characteristics of Campaign Managers Inexperienced in campaigning	26.7	16.7	22.0	28.2
Part-time only	33.3	61.6	77.5	66.4
Unpaid	75.8	53.9	87.5	91.0
Relative of the candidate	26.5	0	14.6	19.9

[a]Percentages are based on candidates in contested primaries who reported having a campaign manager. Because of missing data, N's range from 30 to 34 for congressional candidates, 12 to 13 for statewide candidates, 40 to 41 for state senate candidates, and 241 to 256 for state house candidates.

consistent with popular conceptions, many women who run for office do not run technically sound campaigns.

However, it is important to view this set of findings on women's campaigns in light of two critical considerations. First, while there are very few systematic data, the available evidence indicates that sizable numbers of male candidates also do not run technically sound or professional campaigns. Robert Agranoff has suggested:

> one of the most striking phenomena is that in a society priding itself on efficient management of enterprises, most American campaigns are poorly run. They lack managerial experience and ability, with low levels of reason or little application of a body of knowledge.[27]

Thus, the finding that many candidates do not run well-organized and carefully planned campaigns probably is not unique to women.

Second, as Lewis Froman has observed, "The strategics and tactics of candidates will vary a good deal depending upon the setting in which the election takes place."[28] Evidence from this study indicates that the lack of greater use of commonly recognized campaign practices was, in part, a response to the setting of the races in which women candidates ran.

Table 5.8 presents the percentage of state house candidates in contested primaries who employed various campaign practices in states with high-desirability, moderate-desirability, and low-desirability seats, as classified according to the index developed by the Citizens Conference on

Table 5.8

Aspects of Campaign Organization and Planning Employed by Women State House Candidates, 1976, in States with Seats of Varying Desirability

	Desirability of Seats in State House		
	High	Moderate	Low
	%	%	%
Aspects of Campaign Organization and Planning			
Had a manager	70.5	59.1	39.1
Had one or more advisers	71.2	69.8	49.3
Had a headquarters	71.4	47.8	32.7
Had a comprehensive strategy	76.2	73.1	54.7
Had a budget	61.6	54.2	42.2
Identified undecided and/or favorable voters	79.7	82.1	67.9
Focused voter contact efforts on key voting units	79.2	72.6	63.2
N =	(150)	(161)	(151)

State Legislatures.[29] Candidates in states with high-desirability seats were more likely to follow these practices than candidates in states with moderate-desirability seats. Moreover, candidates in states with low-desirability seats were far less likely to employ commonly accepted procedures.

Thus, even though many women candidates nationwide failed to run well-planned campaigns in 1976, many of them probably responded rationally to the demands of the settings in which they ran. When candidates ran in settings that required more-professional campaign organizations to wage successful campaigns, they employed accepted practices to a much greater extent than did candidates in settings where competition probably was less intense.

Basic Resources and Party Support

Women candidates perceived that their greatest obstacles in seeking party nominations were lack of money, lack of people, lack of time, and lack of party support. Table 5.9 suggests that the primary campaigns of many women candidates did, in fact, lack these critical resources.

Candidates were not asked directly about the total amount of money

TABLE 5.9

Campaign Resources of Women Candidates, 1976,

in Contested Primaries

	OFFICE			
Resources	Congress	Statewide	State Senate	State House
	%	%	%	%
Money				
Funds raised from large donors				
None	31.3	16.7	36.0	51.1
25% or less	53.1	58.3	44.0	32.7
26–50%	12.5	16.7	12.0	9.2
51–75%	3.1	0	0	2.2
76–100%	0	8.3	8.0	4.8
N =	(32)	(12)	(50)	(272)
Number of fund raising techniques used[a]				
0	26.0	23.5	25.3	37.9
1	18.0	17.6	33.3	26.0
2	30.0	23.5	24.0	24.0
3	18.0	23.5	13.3	9.7
4	8.0	11.8	4.0	2.4
N =	(50)	(17)	(75)	(462)

People
Number of volunteers

100 or more	28.0	56.3	21.6	14.3
50–99	16.0	12.5	24.3	18.4
10–49	28.0	18.8	33.8	36.2
Less than 10	28.0	12.5	20.3	31.2
N =	(50)	(16)	(74)	(442)

Time
Length of time before filing deadline that candidate decided to run

More than 1 year	20.0	17.6	14.7	19.7
6 months–1 year	16.0	23.5	22.7	14.3
1 month–5 months	44.0	41.2	40.0	41.0
Less than 1 month	20.0	17.6	22.7	25.0
N =	(50)	(17)	(75)	(456)

Time spent campaigning

Full-time	51.1	43.8	38.4	34.2
Full-time for part of campaign; part-time for rest of campaign	21.3	18.8	27.4	25.2
Part-time	27.7	37.5	34.2	40.7
N =	(47)	(16)	(73)	(445)

Party
Role of partisan groups in campaign

Support	22.0	11.8	16.0	11.3
Both support and opposition or neither	68.0	82.4	80.0	82.3
Opposition	10.0	5.9	4.0	6.5
N =	(50)	(17)	(75)	(462)

[a]Each of the following was counted as a separate technique: mail appeals, personal solicitation, events, sales.

raised for their campaigns, since the sum of money needed to mount a successful campaign for any given office varies greatly from one locale to another. In a state such as New Hampshire, a candidate may be able to conduct an effective campaign for a state legislative seat with only a few hundred dollars, while in California or New York campaign expenditures in state legislative races often total many thousand dollars.[30] Moreover, there are great disparities even within the same state.

Similarly, it did not seem reasonable to ask candidates if they raised more or less money than their opponents. In a primary campaign with several contenders, a candidate might not have accurate information on the amount of financial resources available to her opponents.

However, candidates were asked to indicate the percentage of the total amount of money contributed to their campaign that was obtained through large donations. A large donation was defined as a contribution of more than $100. It was assumed that the greater the percentage of funds raised from large donors, the less severe a problem money probably posed for the candidate. The candidate for whom sufficient money is available from a few sources is less likely to experience fund raising as a problem than the candidate who must raise all, or most, of her money from numerous small contributors.

Candidates also were asked about the extent to which they used four common fund-raising techniques—mail appeals, personal solicitation, events, and sales—in obtaining money to finance their campaigns. For present purposes, it was assumed that candidates who used a diversity of techniques would experience fewer problems in raising money than candidates who limited their fund-raising efforts to one or two techniques.

Table 5.9 shows that few candidates raised most of their funds from large donors. Three-fourths or more of the candidates for all offices reported that they obtained 25% or less of their funds from major contributors. Moreover, one-half of state house candidates and about one-third of congressional and state senate candidates received no money whatsoever from major donors; instead, most of the money for their campaigns was raised through contributions of $100 or less. The dependence of women candidates on small donors is illustrated by the fact that 59.4% of congressional candidates, 25.0% of statewide candidates, 50.0% of state senate candidates, and 59.5% of state house candidates reported that they raised more than 50% of the money for their campaigns in donations of less than $25. Because they infrequently obtained contributions from large donors, fund raising probably was a major problem for many women candidates.

However, part of the reason why women candidates perceived money as such an overwhelming problem in their campaigns also may have been related to their failure to employ a wide diversity of fund-raising techniques. A majority of candidates for state legislative offices and more than two-fifths of candidates for statewide and congressional offices indicated that they used none, or only one, of the four fund-raising strategies (table 5.9). Very few candidates employed all four techniques.

Table 5.9 also illustrates that the campaigns of many women candidates were characterized by small numbers of volunteer workers. Candidates were asked to estimate the total number of volunteers who gave time to their primary campaigns. A sizable minority, approaching one-third among congressional and state house candidates, had fewer than ten volunteer workers. Moreover, a majority of candidates for all offices except statewide had fewer than fifty volunteers. While ten good workers may be preferable to a hundred undependable ones, the large proportion of candidates with relatively few volunteers indicates that finding sufficient "people" probably did pose a significant problem for many women candidates.

Another critical resource that women candidates frequently mentioned as a problem in their primary campaigns was time. Table 5.9 also presents data indicating that many women candidates probably did not, in fact, have sufficient time to campaign.

About one-fifth to one-fourth of candidates for all offices did not make a fairly definite decision to run for office until less than one month before the filing deadline for the primary. Sizable majorities of candidates for all offices decided to run only five months or less before the filing deadline. Fewer than one-fifth of all candidates made a decision to run more than one year in advance of the deadline. The large proportions of candidates making late decisions about running for office suggest that many women probably did not allow themselves ample time to plan and prepare their campaigns.

Moreover, except among congressional candidates, a majority of candidates either did not or could not campaign on a full-time basis throughout the campaign. One-fourth to two-fifths of candidates for various offices did not campaign on a full-time basis for even a few weeks; rather, all their campaigning was part-time.

The final problem frequently perceived by women candidates as a disadvantage in their primary campaigns was lack of party support. Candidates were asked to list the groups and organizations that both supported and opposed them. A measure of partisan support was constructed from responses to these two questions (table 5.9). The vast majority of candidates listed partisan groups as both supporting and opposing their candidacies, or as neither supporting nor opposing their candidacies. Only very small proportions of candidates indicated unilateral support from partisan groups. These data indicate that most women candidates ran without the active support of, and occasionally in opposition to, factions within their parties.

The Effects of Campaign Variables in Differentiating Winners and Losers

Bivariate relationships between campaign variables and election outcomes were examined (table 5.10). In addition, all campaign variables were entered into a series of stepwise discriminant analyses to assess the overall utility of campaign variables in affecting electoral success and to locate the subset of campaign variables that best differentiated winners and losers of primary elections, taking into account the effects of other variables (table 5.11).

For congressional/statewide candidates, a connection between resources and election outcomes was immediately evident. All measures of resources were moderately related to primary election outcomes for candidates at these levels, and they were more strongly related to election outcomes than were the various measures of campaign organization and planning (table 5.10). Except for time spent campaigning, there was a positive association between greater availability of resources and victory. The importance of the resource variables also was apparent in the results of the stepwise discriminant analysis for congressional/statewide candidates (table 5.11). The timing of the decision to run, partisan support, the

TABLE 5.10

Relationships between Campaign Variables and Primary Election Outcomes for Women Candidates, 1976

| | | OFFICE | | |
		Congress/ Statewide	State Senate	State House
Aspects of Campaign				
Organization and Planning				
Had a manager	$tau_b =$	$-.05$	$-.15$	$-.05$
Had one or more advisers	$tau_b =$	$.26$	$.15$	$.01$
Had a headquarters	$tau_b =$	$-.17$	$-.21$	$-.08$
Had a comprehensive strategy	$tau_b =$	$.004$	$-.06$	$.12$
Had a budget	$tau_b =$	$.05$	$-.09$	$.02$
Identified undecided and/or favorable voters	$tau_b =$	$-.12$	$-.05$	$-.12$
Focused voter contact efforts on key voting units	$tau_b =$	$.03$	$-.09$	$.002$
Resources				
Length of time before filing deadline that candidate decided to run	$tau_c =$	$.32$	$.31$	$.07$
Time spent campaigning	$tau_c =$	$-.17$	$-.15$	$-.01$
Number of volunteers	$tau_c =$	$.29$	$.03$	$.06$
Percent of funds raised from large donors	$tau_c =$	$.22$	$-.04$	$-.04$
Number of fund raising techniques used	$tau_c =$	$.23$	$.04$	$-.08$
Role of partisan groups in campaign	$tau_c =$	$.27$	$.01$	$.13$

proportion of funds received from major donors, and the number of campaign volunteers were among the subset of campaign variables that best discriminated between winners and losers, and all made statistically significant contributions in discriminating between the two groups. The only other variable that produced a significant change in Rao's V for congressional/statewide candidates was the presence or absence of a campaign headquarters (table 5.11). However, contrary to expectations, candidates without headquarters more often won their primary bids (table 5.10).

The findings for state senate and state house candidates indicate that resources and primary election outcomes are not as strongly related at these levels. The only moderately strong positive relationship between a resource variable and primary election outcomes occurred for the timing of the decision to run among state senate candidates (table 5.10). As table 5.11 indicates, this was the only resource variable that, in combination with other variables, made a statistically significant contribution in differentiating winning and losing state senate candidates. Three of the variables measuring campaign planning and organization also contributed significantly to the discrimination of winners and losers at the state senate level (table 5.11). However, for two of these variables the simple bivariate relationship to primary election outcomes was contrary to expectations. Losers of primaries among state senate candidates were more likely to have headquarters and managers than were winners (table 5.10).

Among state house candidates, none of the campaign variables was even moderately related to election outcomes (table 5.10). Perhaps because no variable had a particularly strong effect, the subset of variables best distinguishing winning and losing candidates consisted of seven variables, six of which brought about a significant change in Rao's V (table 5.11). Four of the seven were resource variables and three were measures of campaign organization and planning. However, not all of these variables were related to election outcomes in the way that was anticipated. The existence of a campaign headquarters, the identification of voters who were undecided and/or favorable, the use of a greater number of fund-raising techniques, and the raising of greater proportions of funds through large donations were slightly more likely to characterize the campaigns of losing than of winning state house primary candidates (table 5.10).

The classification functions based on the discriminating variables correctly classified as primary winners or losers 85% of congressional/statewide candidates, 72% of state senate candidates, and 64% of state

TABLE 5.11

Discriminant Analyses for Primary Outcomes Based on Campaign Variables for Women Candidates, 1976

	Standardized Discriminant Function Coefficient	Significance of Change in Rao's V	Cases Correctly Classified
Congressional/ Statewide Candidates			
Primary Election Outcomes (N = 55)			
Length of time before filing deadline that candidate decided to run	.53	.003	
Role of partisan groups in campaign	.49	.004	
Percent of funds raised from large donors	.52	.02	85%
Had a headquarters	−.54	.01	
Number of volunteers	.50	.05	
Focused voter contact efforts on key voting units	−.28	.17	
State Senate Candidates			
Primary Election Outcomes (N = 66)			
Length of time before filing deadline that candidate decided to run	.66	.03	
Had a headquarters	−.50	.03	72%
Had one or more advisers	1.13	.05	
Had a manager	−1.12	.0001	
State House Candidates			
Primary Election Outcomes (N = 399)			
Role of partisan groups in campaign	.60	.0002	
Had a comprehensive strategy	.54	.003	
Indentified undecided and/or favorable voters	−.43	.004	64%
Number of volunteers	.56	.04	
Number of fund-raising techniques used	−.34	.006	
Had a headquarters	−.26	.05	
Percent of funds raised from large donors	−.21	.18	

house candidates (table 5.11). In every case, then, the predictive power of classification functions based on the campaign variables was greater than that for classification functions based on the qualifications variables. Nevertheless, the functions based on campaign variables yielded an improvement in prediction of only 12% for congressional/statewide candidates, 13% for state senate candidates, and 12% for state house candidates over a simple prediction that all candidates would be losers.

Summary and Implications

Do women candidates fail to win at a higher rate because they lack the necessary qualifications for officeholding or run poorly planned and organized campaigns? This analysis suggests that lack of qualifications and inadequacies in campaigns are of limited utility in explaining women's rate of election.

In most respects, women candidates do not lack the necessary qualifications for officeholding. They are well educated and a large majority have professional or managerial occupations—although few are lawyers. Most women candidates have party and organizational experience. Perhaps the greatest deficiency in the qualifications of women candidates is that many do not have officeholding experience.

Qualifications appear to have little effect on election outcomes. It is not the case that those who are more qualified win while those who lack qualifications lose. The only variables that seemed to discriminate between winners and losers with any consistency were some measures of party activity and former officeholding.

While party involvement may affect election outcomes, it does not follow that women candidates fail to win at a higher rate because they lack party experience; women candidates, generally speaking, have considerable party experience. It is possible, however, that part of the explanation for why women do not win at a higher rate relates to their public officeholding experience. Experience in elective office was related to election victories, and women candidates often lacked experience in officeholding. To the extent that women lose because they lack necessary qualifications, they probably do so in large part because they have not had much experience in office.

Clearly, many women candidates do not run technically sound campaigns and many lack the critical resources of money, people, time, and party support. Yet, neither women candidates' failure to employ commonly accepted campaign practices and techniques nor their lack of basic campaign resources constitutes a sufficient explanation for their failure to win primary elections at a higher rate.

As a group, campaign variables were more useful than qualifications in distinguishing winning and losing candidates. Yet, only at the highest levels of officeholding did variations in campaign resources appear important in differentiating winners from losers. Although a lack of resources may help explain why more women candidates do not win primaries for higher-level offices, the same cannot be said about primaries in state legislative races.

Most aspects of campaign planning and organization only weakly discriminated between winners and losers in primary elections, and those that did often seemed to be related to primary election outcomes in a manner contrary to expectation. Specifically, the identification of voters who were undecided and/or favorable for state house candidates, the existence of a campaign manager for state senate candidates, and the existence of a campaign headquarters for candidates for all offices seemed more often to characterize the campaigns of losing than of winning candidates. That women who did not employ these commonly accepted elements of effective campaigning won at a higher rate than those who did suggests that the failure of many women candidates to run technically sound campaigns cannot account for their lack of greater success at the polls.

CHAPTER SIX

Gender, the Political Opportunity Structure, and Electoral Success

THIS CHAPTER EXAMINES two additional possible explanations for women's rate of electoral success—that many women lose because of factors related to their sex, and that features of the political opportunity structure are critical to women's rate of election. The chapter concludes with an assessment of the relative explanatory power of all four explanations considered in this and the previous chapter.

Gender as an Explanation

One popular explanation for women candidates' lack of greater electoral success focuses on factors related to the candidate's gender. Perhaps the most frequently mentioned factor of this type is voter prejudice.[1] Many claim that it is difficult for women to win elections because a significant segment of the American public is unwilling to vote for them. Over the years, Gallup repeatedly has asked members of the American public if they would vote for a woman for president if she were nominated by the respondent's party and were qualified for the job. While the proportion answering affirmatively has increased markedly over the past four decades, by 1976 only 76% of the American public expressed support for a female presidential candidate.[2] Voter prejudice seems less severe for lower-level offices, although polls have less frequently asked questions about women candidates for such offices. A 1975 Gallup poll found that 89% of the American public would vote for a female candidate for Congress, 80% for a woman for governor, and 82% for a woman as mayor.[3]

Another sex-related factor thought to make it difficult for women to win elections is the incongruence between their sex-role socialization and the characteristics and behavior necessary to wage a successful campaign. Although socialized to exhibit values and behaviors considered appropriate for females, in running for office women enter into a sphere of life dominated by masculine values and behavior patterns. Jeane Kirkpatrick has noted:

> Campaigning requires so many types of behavior believed to be difficult, if not impossible, for women. To campaign it is necessary to put oneself forward, to "blow one's own horn," to somehow demonstrate one's superiority and dominance. What can conventionally well-behaved ladies do in such an arena?[4]

The extent to which women candidates can overcome conflict between their socialization into female behavior patterns and the need to cultivate masculine traits may affect their election outcomes.

To deal successfully with this conflict, a woman candidate may have to walk a fine line. Image is thought by many who have observed women's campaigns to be a particularly important problem for female candidates.[5] On the one hand, a woman who appears too feminine may not be perceived as strong and effective enough to handle the job. (A few males have, in fact, tried to capitalize on the incompatibility between femininity and role-behavioral expectations, campaigning on slogans such as "Elect a man to do a man's job.") On the other hand, a woman who appears too masculine in her behavior may come across as aggressive, abrasive, or pushy. Women need to strike a very delicate balance between feminine and masculine traits to convey an acceptable image. Suzanne Paizis has insightfully summarized the image dilemma:

> A woman candidate must be . . . assertive rather than aggressive, attractive without being a sexpot, self-confident but not domineering. She must neither be too pushy nor show reticence. The human qualities of compassion and sympathy must not resemble emotionality. Because society tends to label active women as pushy, aggressive, domineering or masculine, voters may be more ready to see negative traits in a woman candidate than they will in a man candidate. They may perceive determined women as shrill, strident or emotional. A woman is easily discounted by being labeled "just one of those women's libbers."[6]

A further aspect of the image problem for women candidates, and one especially related to the danger of being discounted as "just one of those women's libbers," has to do with women's issues. Women candidates, because of their sex, are identified with a social interest striving for rights and recognition in American society. As a result, women candidates, especially those who strongly emphasize women's issues, may be perceived as too narrowly concerned with the interests of women to the exclusion of the interests of their broader constituencies. This, too, may contribute to the failure of greater numbers of women candidates to wage winning campaigns.

Voter reluctance to vote for female candidates could not be measured in this study.[7] However, it was possible to measure three factors related to gender that could have an effect on election outcomes and that might help to explain why women candidates are not more successful.

Sex-Role Attitudes

Women in American society traditionally have been socialized to view different roles as appropriate and acceptable for women and men. They have been taught that a woman's place is in the home, that the man is to be the family's representative in the world outside, and that a woman should place the welfare of her husband and children above any concern she might have with career or work outside the home.

Such views are fundamentally inconsistent with active political participation by women. If women candidates maintain traditional sex-role attitudes, they are likely to experience conflict between their behavior and their perceptions of the role of women in society. This conflict might affect their ability to portray themselves as competent campaigners and potential officeholders and might help to account for their lack of a higher rate of electoral success.

Candidates were asked several questions about their attitudes toward conventional sex roles (table 6.1). Overwhelming majorities of candidates for all offices rejected sex-role stereotypes, suggesting that few women run for office unless they have overcome traditional beliefs about the roles women should play in society.

Sex-Role Identities

Sex-role attitudes and sex-role identities are both conceptually and empirically distinct. While sex-role *attitudes* are views about traditional standards of appropriate behavior for women and men, sex-role *identities* are self-evaluations in relation to traditional norms.[8]

Women traditionally have been socialized into a feminine sex-role identity—a set of personality characteristics associated with femininity, including passivity, nurturance, dependence, and empathy. Women have been discouraged from developing characteristics associated with a masculine sex-role identity—aggressiveness, dominance, ambition, and independence.

TABLE 6.1

Attitudes toward Traditional Sex-Role Stereotypes among Women Candidates, 1976

| | | OFFICE | | |
	Congress	Statewide	State Senate	State House
	%	%	%	%
Sex-Role Attitude				
It is more important for a wife to help her husband than to have a career herself				
Disagree[a]	83.1	88.9	75.2	70.5
N =	(65)	(18)	(153)	(891)
It is much better for everyone involved if the man is the achiever outside the home and the woman takes care of the home and family				
Disagree[a]	81.2	84.2	72.5	73.9
N =	(69)	(19)	(153)	(896)
A working mother can establish just as warm and secure a relationship with her children as a mother who does not work				
Agree[b]	94.0	100.0	89.2	87.6
N =	(67)	(19)	(157)	(910)

[a]Disagree responses include both those who disagreed and those who strongly disagreed.
[b]Agree responses include both those who agreed and those who strongly agreed.

Yet, campaigning is an activity that requires behavior associated far more strongly with male socialization than with female socialization. If women candidates have acquired stereotypically feminine personality characteristics without also acquiring masculine traits, they are likely to seem too weak and ineffectual, and this may help to account for their lack of greater electoral success.

However, it is probably important that a woman candidate not appear too masculine either. Candidates who come across as too masculine also might be penalized at the polls. A woman candidate must exhibit a balance of masculine and feminine traits in order to convey an "acceptable" image.

Although image could not be measured directly in this study, the concept of sex-role identity serves as a surrogate measure. A candidate with a psychologically androgynous sex-role identity would be most likely to convey an image neither too masculine nor too feminine. Sandra Bem has explained that the androgynous individual is "both masculine and feminine, both assertive and yielding, both instrumental and expressive—depending on the situational appropriateness of these various behaviors."[9] Because the androgynous individual has both feminine and masculine components of her/his personality, she/he should be able to engage in masculine behavior and feminine behavior with equal ease. Bem's research has provided evidence that androgynous individuals do, in fact, perform well under circumstances that call for both masculine and feminine behaviors; sex-typed and sex-reversed individuals do not exhibit this sex-role adaptability.[10]

Such findings suggest that androgynous women would be more effective campaigners because they would be able to respond with feminine behavior or with masculine behavior depending on the circumstances. Nonandrogynous women candidates would be less effective, responding with consistently masculine or consistently feminine behavior regardless of the situation. If few women candidates are psychologically androgynous and thus able to convey the appropriate image at various points in their campaigns, women's sex-role identities might be part of the explanation for why they do not win election at a higher rate.

However, tables 6.2 and 6.3 suggest that overwhelming proportions of women candidates are, in fact, psychologically androgynous. Sex-role identities were measured through the use of the Bem Sex Role Inventory (BSRI).[11] The BSRI includes both a masculinity scale, consisting of twenty personality characteristics judged by two samples of undergraduate students to be more desirable in American society for a male than for a female, and a femininity scale, consisting of twenty personality characteristics judged more desirable for a female. Each respondent is asked to indicate on a seven-point scale how well each characteristic describes herself. From these ratings, a masculinity score, a femininity score, and an androgyny score can be computed. All three scores have been found to have test-retest reliabilities of .90 or higher.[12]

In this study, two items (athletic and masculine) were dropped from the masculinity scale and five items (shy, flatterable, gullible, childlike, and does not use harsh language) were dropped from the femininity scale because of low inter-item correlations, indicating that the items were not reliable.[13] After these items were excluded, Cronbach's alpha reliability was .90 for the masculinity scale and .87 for the femininity scale.[14]

Two methods have been used to classify individuals as androgynous or nonandrogynous, using the BSRI. Bem's original scoring method involved computing for each individual an androgyny score, which is the student's t-ratio for a respondent's femininity and masculinity scores, standardized with respect to the means of the masculinity and femininity scores. If the t-ratio $\geq$ | 2.025 |, p < .05, the individual is classified as sex-typed or sex-reversed to indicate that masculinity and femininity scores differ significantly. Individuals with a t-ratio $\leq$ | 1.00 | are considered androgynous, because their masculinity and femininity scores differ little from each other.

Table 6.2 presents the distribution of sex-role identities for women candidates, using this classification scheme. The final column presents the distribution of sex-role identities Bem found for a sample of 290 female undergraduate students at Stanford in 1975; this serves as a basis for comparison. Most women candidates clustered near the center of the scale, indicating that the majority of candidates were androgynous or almost androgynous (i.e., either near-feminine or near-masculine). While one would expect to find a sizable proportion of individuals with feminine identifications among a sample of women, fewer than 11% of candidates for any office had feminine sex-role identities. Proportionately far fewer candidates fell on the feminine end of the scale than in Bem's sample of female undergraduates. Moreover, many fewer candidates fell on the feminine end of the scale than on the masculine end. Candidates for statewide office were especially likely to have masculine sex-role identities.

More recently another method has been developed to classify individuals based on the BSRI—a method Bem herself has accepted. Janet Spence and two associates have observed that Bem's original classification scheme considered individuals androgynous if they either scored high on both the masculine and feminine scales *or* scored low on both the masculine and feminine scales. Yet, the concept of androgyny implies the existence of both masculine and feminine traits within the same individual, not the absence of both. Consequently, Spence and her colleagues suggested that individuals who scored low on both masculine and feminine scales be considered "undifferentiated" in their sex-role identities and separated out from those individuals who scored high on both scales and

TABLE 6.2

Sex-Role Identities as Defined by the T-Ratio among Women Candidates, 1976

		OFFICE			
	Congress	Statewide	State Senate	State House	1975 Sample of Stanford Female Undergraduates
	%	%	%	%	%
Sex-Role Identity					
Masculine (t ≤ −2.025)	18.8	61.1	20.0	17.8	9
Near-masculine (−2.025 < t < −1)	17.4	16.7	18.7	18.4	13
Adrogynous (−1 ≤ t ≤ 1)	42.0	16.7	42.0	39.7	41
Near-feminine (1 < t < 2.025)	14.5	0	13.3	13.5	18
Feminine (t ≥ 2.025)	7.2	5.6	6.0	10.7	20
N =	(69)	(18)	(150)	(907)	(290)

thus were truly "androgynous." Spence's scoring procedure involves a median split—dividing the femininity scores and masculinity scores at their medians and then classifying people into four groups: masculine (high masculine, low feminine), feminine (high feminine, low masculine), undifferentiated (low masculine, low feminine), and androgynous (high masculine, high feminine).[15]

Because the evidence above indicated that women candidates may be quite atypical of the general population in their sex-role identities, it did not seem reasonable to use the medians of the distribution of their femininity and masculinity scores for the median split. Instead, medians from Bem's study of Stanford undergraduates were used as a basis for classification.[16] The distribution of candidates into various sex-role identity groups according to the median-split criterion is presented in table 6.3. Again, the distribution of sex-role identities for Bem's Stanford female undergraduate students is presented for comparison.

On the basis of this median-split classification scheme, almost all women candidates can be considered androgynous, i.e., to have both strong masculine and strong feminine attributes simultaneously. While a few seem to have masculine or feminine identities, only a negligible number have undifferentiated identities. This is not surprising, since few people who lack strong personalities are likely to run for office. The extent to which women candidates are disproportionately androgynous relative

TABLE 6.3

Sex-Role Identities as Defined by a Median Split for Women Candidates, 1976

	OFFICE				
	Congress	Statewide	State Senate	State House	1975 Sample of Stanford Female Under- graduates
	%	%	%	%	%
Sex-Role Identity					
Masculine	7.2	11.1	6.7	6.6	16
Feminine	7.2	0	5.3	9.4	34
Undifferentiated	0	0	1.3	1.5	20
Androgynous	85.5	88.9	86.7	82.5	29
N =	(69)	(18)	(150)	(907)	(290)

to other women is evident in comparing figures from this study with Bem's results. While Bem found only 29% of the undergraduate women in her study to be androgynous, more than 80% of the women who ran for office in 1976 can be so classified (table 6.3).

Thus, regardless of the method used to score the BSRI,[17] it seems unlikely that women who ran for office in 1976 failed to win at a higher rate because they lacked the mix of masculine and feminine characteristics necessary to convey the image of competent and capable contenders for office. While most women may be socialized into a predominantly feminine sex-role identity, apparently few women run for office who have not also acquired masculine traits.

Women's Issues in Primary Campaigns

The ability to convey the appropriate mixture of masculine and feminine characteristics is one image problem women candidates confront. Another, unique to women candidates, relates to treatment of "women's issues" in campaigns. Women candidates who emphasize women's issues may be stereotyped as narrowly concerned only with the interests of women to the neglect of their broader constituencies. Moreover, since single-issue constituencies have developed around a few women's issues (e.g., abortion), a candidate is almost certain to alienate some voters regardless of the position she takes. If large proportions of women who ran in 1976 did emphasize women's issues while campaigning, then this may help to explain why women candidates did not win at a higher rate.

Table 6.4 classifies candidates in contested primaries according to their strategy in dealing with women's issues. Very few candidates appear to have made women's issues, data from this study show that few women perceived a women's issues an important part of their public platforms. Only a small minority of candidates both addressed women's issues during their campaigns and initiated discussion of them on virtually every occasion when they were discussed. About one-third of the candidates chose to initiate discussion of some women's issues, while avoiding discussion of others unless specifically asked about their views. Almost one-half of congressional candidates and majorities of candidates for other offices apparently tried to avoid campaigning on women's issues altogether. Either they never discussed these issues or they discussed them only when asked.

To illustrate further that candidates did not strongly emphasize women's issues, data from this study show that few women perceived a women's issue as a central issue in their campaigns. Candidates were

TABLE 6.4

Strategies for Dealing with Women's Issues Employed by Women Candidates in Contested Primaries, 1976

	OFFICE			
	Congress	Statewide	State Senate	State House
	%	%	%	%
Strategy on Women's Issues				
Did not discuss	13.0	43.8	21.7	28.7
Discussed only when asked	34.8	12.5	31.9	31.2
Initiated discussion of some; discussed others only when asked	32.6	18.8	37.7	28.7
Initiated discussion only	19.6	25.0	8.7	11.5
N =	(46)	(16)	(69)	(436)

asked to list those issues they stressed as most important. Only 13.6% of congressional candidates, 5.9% of candidates for statewide offices, 18.8% of state senate candidates, and 10.4% of candidates for the state house mentioned a women's issue.[18]

Since large majorities of women candidates did not strongly emphasize women's issues in their public campaigns, it seems unlikely that voters could have easily stereotyped sizable numbers of women candidates as narrowly concerned with the interests of women and voted against them on this basis.

The Effects of Gender-Related Variables in Differentiating Winners and Losers

If women candidates fail to win at a higher rate because of gender, then sex-role attitudes, sex-role identities, and treatment of women's issues in their campaigns should help to differentiate those candidates who win from those who lose elections. To test for differences between winning and losing candidates, the three measures of sex-role attitudes presented in table 6.1 were combined into a single, summative measure.[19] The alpha reliability for this scale was .74. Similarly, the five categories of sex-role identities (table 6.2) were combined into three—androgynous, near-androgynous (consisting of near-masculine and near-feminine), and nonandrogynous (consisting of masculine and feminine).[20] The measure of treatment of women's issues in primary campaigns (table 6.4) was not altered.

Table 6.5 presents simple bivariate relationships between gender-related variables and election outcomes, and table 6.6 presents the results of a series of discriminant analyses based on gender-related variables. The most striking impression from these tables is the general lack of explanatory power of gender-related variables. The only moderate to strong bivariate relationships were those between sex-role attitudes and primary election outcomes for congressional/statewide and state senate candidates (table 6.5). In both cases, winners were more likely than losers to have nontraditional attitudes. Only two variables showed contributions to the discrimination of winners and losers significant at the .05 level in any of the six discriminant analyses (table 6.6). For congressional candidates, sex-role attitudes helped to differentiate winning and losing candidates in primaries. Similarly, the treatment of women's issues contributed to the differentiation of winners and losers of primary elections among state house contenders.

The classification functions based on the discriminating variables were not useful in improving ability to predict winners and losers. Using these classification functions, it was possible to correctly predict primary outcomes for only 2% more congressional/statewide candidates, 1% fewer state senate candidates, and 3% more state house candidates than would have been possible by simply predicting that all candidates lost. For general election outcomes, predictions based on the assumption that all candidates lost would have been far more accurate than predictions based on classification functions.

Overall Assessment of Gender-Related Variables

The third explanation, that women candidates fail to win at a higher rate because of gender, would appear to have little, if any, validity. The nontraditional sex-role attitudes held by most women candidates make it unlikely that many lose because conflict between nontraditional behavior and traditional views of appropriate roles for women affects their ability to portray themselves as capable campaigners and potential officeholders. Similarly, the predominance of androgynous and near-androgynous sex-role identities among women candidates suggests that it is unlikely that many women fail to win because they convey an image that is too masculine or too feminine. Finally, the fact that most women candidates did not strongly emphasize women's issues in their campaigns makes it very unlikely that large numbers of them lost because they were perceived as concerned only with the interests of women.

Since there was not great variation among candidates on sex-related variables, one would not expect these measures to be very helpful in

TABLE 6.5

Relationships between Gender-Related Variables and Primary and General Election Outcomes for Women Candidates, 1976

		Congress/Statewide		State Senate		State House	
		Primary Outcomes	General Outcomes	Primary Outcomes	General Outcomes	Primary Outcomes	General Outcomes
Sex-role attitudes	tau_c =	.50	.07	.24	.13	−.05	−.01
Sex-role identities	tau_c =	−.002	−.17	−.08	−.12	.02	.01
Treatment of women's issues in campaign	tau_c =	.05	—[a]	.14	—[a]	.15	—[a]

[a] The measure of treatment of women's issues is relevant only to the primary election campaigns, and not the general election campaigns, of women candidates.

TABLE 6.6

Discriminant Analyses for Primary and General Election Outcomes Based on Gender-Related Variables for Women Candidates, 1976

	Standardized Discriminant Function Coefficient	Significance of Change in Rao's V	Cases Correctly Classified
Congressional/ Statewide Candidates			
Primary Election Outcomes (N = 57)			
Sex-role attitudes	1.00	.0001	75%
General Election Outcomes (N = 37)			
Sex-role identities	.81	.18	30%
Sex-role attitudes	−.70	.19	
State Senate Candidates			
Primary Election Outcomes (N = 62)			
Sex-role attitudes	.89	.16	58%
Treatment of women's issues in campaign	.71	.15	
General Election Outcomes (N = 108)			
Sex-role identities	1.00	.24	34%
State House Candidates			
Primary Election Outcomes (N = 397)			
Treatment of women's issues in campaign	1.00	.005	55%
General Election Outcomes (N = 636)			
None	—	—	—

distinguishing winners from losers. In fact, they were not. Gender-related variables were less useful in differentiating winning and losing candidates than either qualification or campaign variables. Overall, gender-related variables appear to have very little explanatory power in accounting for women's rate of electoral success.

The Political Opportunity Structure
as an Explanation

With each of the three popular explanations for women's lack of greater electoral success examined in this and the previous chapter, the burden for change is placed largely on the women candidates themselves. If more of the women who run would develop the types of experience and qualifications necessary to gain election, if more would run carefully planned and technically sound campaigns, and if more could successfully overcome their sex-role socialization and deal effectively with image problems, then more women candidates would be elected. To the extent that these constitute valid explanations, women themselves must improve their preparation for officeholding, increase their political skills and knowledge, and learn to exercise greater sex-role adaptability before we can expect them to have greater success at the polls.

However, there is a fourth possible explanation 'that focuses on factors much less subject to control or modification by individual women candidates. While features of the political opportunity structure such as incumbency and the presence of open seats are perhaps less frequently mentioned as possible reasons why *women* are not more successful in winning elections, their potential importance in determining election outcomes has long been recognized by political scientists and political practitioners. Although characteristics of the political opportunity structure are not likely to affect election outcomes for individual women differently from the way they affect election outcomes for individual men, potentially they are of considerable significance in explaining the collective electoral success of women. To the extent that political opportunity variables work to the advantage of those who occupy elite positions, they may act as barriers to the circulation into elites of members of groups traditionally excluded from power (in this case, women).

This section examines the effects on election outcomes of four variables related to the structure of political opportunity: incumbency, presence of an open seat, number of seats in the district, and desirability of holding the seat.

Incumbency and Open Seats

Political scientists and political practitioners have long recognized the advantages that accrue to an incumbent in campaigning for office. In a primary race, incumbency most likely provides added resources and name recognition. In a general election, incumbency may reflect to a greater extent district patterns of voting and party dominance. Nevertheless, regardless of the nature of the particular advantages that accrue from incumbency, incumbents in the past have tended to have a very high rate of electoral success.[21]

Only small minorities of the women who sought office in 1976 were incumbents—9.6% of congressional candidates, 4.5% of statewide candidates, 19.4% of state senate candidates, and 26.3% of state house candidates among respondents in this study.[22]

Incumbency is potentially important to election outcomes not only for the candidate who may be an incumbent but also for the challenger who may face an incumbent in either the primary or the general election. For the latter, her opponent's incumbency may be a critical disadvantage.

For purposes of this analysis, a seat was considered "open" in the primary when there was at least one more seat in the district than the number of incumbents of the candidate's party seeking re-election. (Thus, for a single-member district, a seat was "open" in the primary as long as there was not an incumbent of the candidate's party in the race.) Similarly, a seat was considered "open" in the general election when there was at least one more seat in the district than the number of incumbents from the opposing party seeking re-election. Sizable proportions of women candidates in 1976 ran in races with no open seats. Of women running in contested primaries, 9.1% of congressional/statewide candidates, 23.2% of state senate candidates, and 17.5% of state house candidates were in primaries where no seats were open.[23] In general election contests, 60.0% of congressional/statewide candidates, 41.1% of state senate candidates, and 28.9% of state house candidates ran in races with no open seats.[24]

Number and Desirability of Seats

Two other political opportunity variables might affect election outcomes for state legislative candidates—whether the seat is in a multimember or a single-member district, and whether it is in a state with high-, moderate-, or low-desirability seats.

Women might be more likely to win in multimember than in single-member districts. Voters might be more likely to vote for a woman when she is one of many candidates for several seats than when she is one of very few candidates for a single seat. Women also might be more likely to win in states where seats are less desirable, and thus competition probably less severe, than in states where seats are more desirable and competition more severe.[25] Findings (from chapter 4) that candidates in states with less desirable seats were less likely to experience problems and less likely to report difficulty in attracting critical resources also suggest that women in states with less desirable seats would be more likely to win.

Eleven and one-half percent of state senate candidates and 42.5% of state house candidates ran in multimember districts; the remainder ran in single-member districts.[26] Among candidates for the state house, 31.5% ran in states with seats of high desirability, 38.2% ran in states with seats of moderate desirability, and 30.3% ran in states with seats of low desirability.[27]

The Effects of Political Opportunity Variables in Differentiating Winners and Losers

If political opportunity variables are useful in explaining why women do not win at a higher rate, then they should be related to election outcomes and should help to differentiate winning and losing candidates. Table 6.7 shows that there were, indeed, substantial bivariate relationships between each political opportunity variable and election outcomes for candidates for all offices. Overall, the relationships appeared stronger than those between election outcomes and qualification, campaign, or gender-related variables.

Both incumbency and presence of an open seat were moderately to strongly related to election outcomes for congressional/statewide, state senate, and state house candidates (table 6.7). However, the relationships in every case were much stronger for general than for contested primary election outcomes. In large part, these two variables were more strongly related to general election outcomes because many incumbents, male and female, are unopposed in bids for their party's nomination but face opposition in the general election. Greater proportions of women candidates in general elections, relative to those in contested primaries, were incumbents.[28] Also, greater proportions of candidates in general elections ran where there were no open seats because incumbents were seeking re-election.

Nevertheless, whenever incumbents ran, they almost always won, and whenever women candidates faced incumbents, they almost always lost (table 6.7). Incumbents in both primaries and general elections had much higher success rates than nonincumbents. Similarly, candidates for open

TABLE 6.7

Relationships between Political Opportunity Variables and Primary and General Election Outcomes for Women Candidates, 1976

		Congress/Statewide		State Senate		State House	
		Primary Outcomes	General Outcomes	Primary Outcomes	General Outcomes	Primary Outcomes	General Outcomes
Incumbency	$tau_b =$	.29	.82	.27	.44	.34	.52
Presence of open seats	$tau_b =$	.24	.65	.32	.46	.29	.54
Number of seats in district	$tau_b =$	—	—	.22	.10	.23	.10
Desirability of seat	$tau_c =$	—	—	—	—	-.21	-.12

seats won far more frequently than did candidates for races without open seats.

Table 6.7 also shows weak to moderate relationships between election outcomes and both number of seats in the district and desirability of seats. Women candidates were more likely to win both primaries and general elections in multimember than in single-member districts. They also were more likely to win contests for state house seats where seats were less desirable than where seats were more desirable. In contrast to the pattern for incumbency and presence of an open seat, the number of seats and the desirability of seats were more strongly related to primary than to general election outcomes.

The results of discriminant analyses based on political opportunity variables underscore the importance of political opportunity variables (table 6.8). Both incumbency and presence of an open seat contributed significantly to the differentiation of winners and losers in general elections across all offices. Incumbency seemed considerably more important than the presence of an open seat at the congressional/statewide level; the presence of an open seat was slightly more important than incumbency at the state senate and state house levels. Neither the number of seats nor the desirability of seats helped to differentiate winners and losers in general election contests at the state legislative level.

For primary election outcomes, the results were less consistent across offices (table 6.8). Among congressional/statewide candidates, incumbency was more important than presence of an open seat in differentiating winners and losers of primaries. Presence of an open seat failed to bring about a statistically significant change in Rao's V. In contrast, among state senate candidates, the presence of an open seat was more important than incumbency, with incumbency failing to make a contribution in discriminating winners and losers that was significant at the .05 level. Among state house candidates, all four political opportunity variables appeared important in helping to differentiate primary winners and losers, although incumbency and presence of an open seat were more important than the number of seats or the desirability of seats.

Classification functions based on political opportunity variables varied greatly in the degree to which they improved predictions of winners and losers (table 6.8). For general election outcomes, the classification functions based on these variables appeared quite powerful. They resulted in improvements in ability to classify winners and losers of general elections by 21% for congressional/statewide candidates, 7% for state senate candidates, and 24% for state house candidates over simple predictions that all

TABLE 6.8

Discriminant Analyses for Primary and General Election Outcomes Based on Political Opportunity Variables for Women Candidates, 1976

	Standardized Discriminant Function Coefficient	Significance of Change in Rao's V	Cases Correctly Classified
Congressional/ Statewide Candidates			
Primary Election Outcomes (N = 65)			
Incumbency	.85	.01	75%
Presence of an open seat	.52	.12	
General Election Outcomes (N = 33)			
Incumbency	.81	.0001	97%
Presence of an open seat	.59	.0001	
State Senate Candidates			
Primary Election Outcomes (N = 69)			
Presence of an open seat	.60	.03	58%
Incumbency	.46	.08	
Number of seats in district	.44	.20	
General Election Outcomes (N = 112)			
Presence of an open seat	.70	.0001	70%
Incumbency	.50	.004	
State House Candidates			
Primary Election Outcomes (N = 446)			
Incumbency	.64	.0001	69%
Presence of an open seat	.47	.0001	
Number of seats in district	.30	.0001	
Desirability of seat	.23	.03	
General Election Outcomes (N = 693)			
Presence of an open seat	.68	.0001	75%
Incumbency	.60	.0001	

congressional/statewide candidates and state senate candidates would lose and that all state house candidates would win. Moreover, it was possible using the political opportunity variables to classify correctly more statewide/congressional and state house candidates than was possible with either the qualification variables or the gender-related variables. For state senate candidates, the classification functions based on political opportunity variables yielded predictions of general election outcomes about equally as good as those based on qualification variables and better than those based on gender-related variables.

However, the predictive ability of the political opportunity variables was considerably weaker for primary outcomes. Among state house candidates, classification functions based on political opportunity variables resulted in a 17% improvement in ability to classify candidates correctly, which was better than the improvement in prediction yielded by the qualification, campaign, or gender-related variables. This was not the case, however, for primary outcomes for state senate and congressional/statewide candidates. Classification functions based on political opportunity variables yielded predictions of primary outcomes that were no better in the case of state senate candidates and congressional/statewide candidates than simple predictions that all candidates would lose.

Overall Assessment of Political Opportunity Variables

Political opportunity variables, especially incumbency and presence of an open seat, have a good deal of power in explaining why the electoral success rate of women candidates is not greater in general elections. Political opportunity variables appear somewhat less useful in explaining why women are not more successful in contested primary elections.

While the analysis presented here failed to show incumbency or the presence of an open seat to be strongly related to primary election outcomes, it is important to keep in mind that only *contested* primary election outcomes were considered. The fact that a large majority of incumbents faced no primary opposition—75.0% of congressional incumbents, 71.9% of state senate incumbents, and 67.2% of state house incumbents—suggests that incumbency may, in fact, play a very important role in determining primary election outcomes—a role that does not show up statistically in this analysis. That role is one of dissuading potential contenders from entering the primary contest in the first place.

A Comparative Test of All Four Explanations

To compare the relative effects on election outcomes of all four types of variables examined in this and the previous chapter, and thus to assess the relative validity of all four of the hypothesized explanations for why women candidates are not more successful, a final set of discriminant analyses was run. For each explanation, the subset of variables which best differentiated winners and losers of elections for each type of office was included in these final discriminant analyses.[29] The results are presented in table 6.9.

It is immediately apparent that variables of all four types, in combination with each other, contribute to the differentiation of winners and losers in both primary and general elections, suggesting that none of the hypothesized explanations for the lack of greater electoral success by women candidates is sufficient in and of itself. The reason why more women candidates do not win is more complex than any single simple explanation. Nevertheless, the alternative explanations vary in validity.

With regard to qualifications, the only variable significant in enough cases to indicate that it may have had a general impact on election outcomes was previous elective officeholding. This variable contributed significantly to the differentiation of winning and losing candidates in all cases except for general election outcomes among state senate candidates and primary election outcomes among state house candidates.

A lack of a significant relationship for state house candidates in primaries probably reflects the fact that in many areas of the country it is acceptable for a candidate to aspire to the state assembly without having previously held office. This possibility is reinforced by the low standardized discriminant function coefficient (.16) for previous officeholding experience among state house candidates in general elections, indicating that this variable, relative to other variables, contributed very little to the differentiation of winners and losers.

The standardized discriminant function coefficient for officeholding experience was small relative to that for incumbency for congressional/statewide candidates in general elections; among state senate candidates in general elections, the change in Rao's V brought about by this variable was not significant. These findings suggest that voters may rely more on officeholding experience in judging candidates in primaries than in general elections. Perhaps in general elections, where party ties become more important to voters, officeholding experience becomes less so.

Other qualification variables do not show up consistently across the six discriminant analyses. When they do appear, their standardized discriminant function coefficients are small relative to those for the other variables, suggesting that they do not make important contributions to the differentiation of winners and losers. In short, the findings here reinforce the conclusion drawn earlier when qualification variables were con-

TABLE 6.9

Discriminant Analyses for Primary and General Election Outcomes Based on Qualification, Campaign, Gender-Related, and Political Opportunity Variables for Women Candidates, 1976

	Standardized Discriminant Function Coefficient	Significance of Change in Rao's V	Cases Correctly Classified
Congressional/ Statewide Candidates			
Primary Election Outcomes (N = 52)			
Sex-role attitudes	.45	.0001	
Percent of funds raised from large donors	.59	.01	
Had held previous elective office	.43	.008	
Role of partisan groups in campaign	.41	.02	
Incumbency	.37	.01	91%
Had a headquarters	− .43	.005	
Length of time before filing deadline that candidate decided to run	.24	.12	
General Election Outcomes (N = 33)			
Incumbency	.98	.0001	
Presence of an open seat	.31	.0001	
Sex-role identities	− .38	.008	94%
Number of organizational memberships	− .44	.004	
Had held previous elective office	.35	.003	
Sex-role attitudes	.26	.01	
State Senate Candidates			
Primary Election Outcomes (N = 52)			
Length of time before filing deadline that candidate decided to run	.73	.09	
Had a manager	−1.18	.02	
Sex-role attitudes	.56	.009	
Had held previous elective office	.55	.003	87%
Had one or more advisers	.71	.005	
Degree of activity in state and local party	− .46	.12	
Had been delegate to state party convention	.37	.04	
Number of seats in district	.24	.14	

General Election Outcomes (N = 92)			
Incumbency	.63	.0001	
Presence of an open seat	.52	.0001	} 83%
Sex-role attitudes	.24	.07	
Had held previous elective office	.23	.09	
Primary Election Outcomes (N = 383)			
Incumbency	.49	.0001	
Presence of an open seat	.31	.0001	
Role of partisan groups in campaign	.27	.0004	
Had a comprehensive strategy	.36	.002	
Number of seats in district	.31	.0001	
Identified undecided and/or favorable voters	—.28	.004	} 73%
Number of volunteers	.36	.004	
Treatment of women's issues in campaign	.22	.006	
Percent of funds raised from large donors	—.18	.02	
Desirability of seat	.20	.04	
Degree of activity in state and local party	.12	.17	
General Election Outcomes (N = 676)			
Presence of an open seat	.65	.0001	
Incumbency	.58	.0001	
Had held previous elective office	.16	.003	} 79%
Education	.16	.001	
Number of organizational memberships	.07	.15	
Had been delegate to national party convention	.06	.18	

State House Candidates

sidered alone—if some women candidates lose because they lack qualifications, the single most important qualification lacking is elective
officeholding experience. Moreover, lack of officeholding experience
seems more valid a reason why women lose in races for higher, rather
than lower, offices and in primary, rather than general, elections.

The analysis of campaign variables is limited to primary elections, since
general election campaigns were not examined in this study. However,
the results of these final discriminant analyses (table 6.9) lend little support to the argument that women candidates do not win at a higher rate
because they fail to run technically sound campaigns. Only one variable
related to campaign organization and planning—the existence of a
headquarters—helped to differentiate winners and losers among
congressional/statewide candidates. However, as noted earlier, losers
more often than winners had campaign headquarters. Two variables, the
presence of a manager and the presence of advisers, contributed significantly to the differentiation of winners and losers among state senate
candidates. However, again as noted earlier, those who had managers
were more likely to lose primary elections. Similarly, while two
variables—the existence of a comprehensive campaign strategy and voter
identification efforts—distinguished winners from losers among state
house candidates, the relationship between efforts to identify favorable
and/or undecided voters and primary election outcomes was contrary to
expectations.

Thus, while some variables related to campaign organization and planning were useful in differentiating winners and losers, they often were not
directly related to election outcomes in the manner anticipated. In some
respects, those candidates whose campaigns were based on accepted
principles and practices were more likely to lose than those whose campaigns were not. Such findings cast serious doubts on any explanation that
links women's failure to win at a higher rate to their failure to run sound
campaigns.

The final set of discriminant analyses (table 6.9) suggest that women
candidates' own perceptions of the major problem they encountered, that
they lacked resources, has more validity as an explanation for their failure
to win primary elections at a higher rate. At the congressional/statewide
level, both the proportion of funds raised from major donors and support
from partisan groups contributed significantly in differentiating winning
and losing primary candidates. Among state senate candidates, the timing
of the decision to run for office contributed, although not significantly, to
the differentiation of winning and losing candidates. Three resource

variables—support from partisan groups, number of volunteers, and proportion of funds raised in large donations—helped to distinguish winners and losers among state house candidates. However, as noted earlier, the relationship between winning and raising funds from major donors was negative.

The only gender-related variable that showed up frequently enough in this final set of discriminant analyses to suggest that it may help to explain women candidates' lack of greater electoral success was sex-role attitudes. Sex-role attitudes contributed significantly to the differentiation of winners and losers among congressional/statewide candidates in both primaries and general elections and among state senate candidates in primary elections. For state senate candidates in general elections, sex-role attitudes produced a change in Rao's V which was significant at the .07 level, barely missing the acceptable .05 level. Sex-role attitudes were not important in differentiating winners and losers among state house candidates. Perhaps this pattern of findings occurs because running for higher-level offices (such as state senate, statewide office, and Congress) requires a greater deviation from acceptable sex-role behavior than running for lower-level offices. A woman with traditional sex-role attitudes may perceive less of a conflict between her beliefs and her behavior if she is running for a state house seat than if she is seeking a higher office, where male dominance is more entrenched.

Paralleling the findings of the discriminant analyses based on political opportunity variables alone, opportunity variables again appear to have been much more important in differentiating winners and losers of general than of primary elections. The only political opportunity variable that significantly distinguished winners and losers among congressional/statewide contenders in primary elections was incumbency, and the value of the standardized discriminant function coefficient for this variable suggests that it was less important than several other variables. No political opportunity variable made a significant contribution to the discrimination of winners and losers in primary elections at the state senate level. However, political opportunity variables do appear to have had more effect for state house contenders in primary elections. All four political opportunity variables contributed significantly to the differentiation of winners and losers, and incumbency had a greater impact than any other variable.

Political opportunity variables clearly were important in distinguishing winners and losers among contenders for all offices in general elections. Incumbency and presence of an open seat contributed significantly to the differentiation of winners and losers in every case. None of the other variables included in the analyses approached in magnitude the impact of incumbency at the congressional/statewide level, or of either incumbency or the presence of an open seat at the state senate and state house levels.

The importance of political opportunity variables, relative to all other variables, in differentiating winners and losers of primary contests among state house candidates, and winners and losers of general elections among candidates for all offices, is perhaps best illustrated by examining the proportion of cases correctly classified. Using classification functions based on all four types of variables, it was possible to classify correctly as winners and losers 73% of all candidates who ran in primaries for state house offices. This was only 4% better than was possible with the classification functions based on political opportunity variables alone. Similarly, using classification functions based on all types of variables, it was possible to classify correctly 94% of all congressional/statewide, 83% of state senate, and 79% of state house candidates as winners and losers in general election contests. For congressional/statewide candidates, this was fewer classified correctly than with the political opportunity variables alone. For state senate candidates, including the other variables in addition to the political opportunity variables improved the proportion correctly classified by 13%, but for state house candidates the improvement was only 4%. Clearly, it was possible, especially for congressional/ statewide and state house candidates, to do almost as well in predicting winners and losers using only political opportunity variables as it was with variables of all types. This was not true, however, for classifying congressional/statewide and state senate candidates in contested primaries; here, using all variables improved predictions considerably over predictions based on political opportunity variables alone.

Summary and Implications

When journalists, political practitioners, and political observers have addressed the question of why few women are elected to public office, they frequently have phrased explanations in terms of ways they perceive women to be different, deficient, or disadvantaged relative to men in the political arena. Women candidates generally are thought to lack the necessary qualifications for officeholding, to run campaigns that do not employ accepted principles and practices, and to be handicapped by their sex. It is for these reasons that women candidates are perceived to be less successful at the polls than they otherwise might be.

While these explanations may have some validity, the collective electoral success rate of women candidates, particularly in general elections, is better explained in terms of features of the political opportunity structure. The analysis in this chapter suggests that the single most valid explanation for women candidates' lack of greater electoral success can be summarized quite simply:

(1) While incumbents tend to win elections at a much higher rate than nonincumbents, very few women candidates are incumbents.

(2) Candidates who run against incumbents (and/or against candidates of the opposing party who have defeated incumbents in primaries) rarely win elections, and sizable numbers of women candidates run in races where they confront such situations.

In comparison to this explanation, other explanations for why women lose general elections clearly have far less explanatory power. And while political opportunity variables seemed less overpowering as determinants of outcomes in contested primaries, most incumbents do not face primary opposition and thus are not in contested primaries. Incumbency seems to have an important effect on primaries through dissuading potential opponents from entering primaries in the first place.

If women candidates are defeated largely for reasons related to the political opportunity structure, then they lose for reasons that are not subject to modification or control by the candidates themselves. Even those variables, related to the other explanations that play some role statistically in accounting for women candidates' lack of a higher rate of success, are, at least in part, beyond the control of individual candidates. Since the political system traditionally has not stimulated or encouraged women to seek public office, the failure of many women to gain officeholding experience is not entirely the fault of women candidates themselves. Similarly, as argued in chapter 4, a lack of basic campaign resources is only partly subject to the control of candidates. To some extent, women's lack of campaign resources reflects elements of the structure of political opportunity that they cannot alter.

Perhaps more women need to gain experience and develop qualifications necessary for election. Perhaps more women need to increase their use of accepted campaign practices and to improve the quality of their campaigns. And perhaps more women need to overcome their traditional sex-role socialization and to learn to exercise greater sex-role adaptability. However, this analysis suggests that these changes would have only marginal effects in improving the overall electoral success rate of women candidates. The truly critical impediments to greater success at the polls—the staying power of incumbents and the lack of larger numbers of open seats—are factors individual women can do little to change. These features of the political opportunity structure set powerful limits on the rate at which the numerical representation of women can increase.

Unless much larger proportions of incumbents begin to retire after a single term or unless the staying power of incumbents is somehow weakened, the numerical representation of women is not likely to increase by leaps and bounds, regardless of the number of women who choose to run. Reforms that would increase the number of open seats would seem to offer the greatest probability of large increases in the numerical representation of women.

Nevertheless, in 1976, and in subsequent election years, there have been races involving open seats where no contender was a woman. Since women candidates have a much higher probability of winning in such situations, efforts to stimulate more women to run in contests where incumbents are not on the ballot are likely to contribute to increasing the number of women officeholders.

Some women will continue to choose to run against incumbents, and as the data from 1976 demonstrate, in a few cases they may unseat those incumbents. The analysis in this and the previous chapter suggests that women's chances to do so will be maximized if they are not deficient or disadvantaged with regard to other factors that may affect election outcomes. A woman's chances may be improved if she has elective officeholding experience, nontraditional sex-role attitudes, and an adequate supply of money, time, and campaign workers. Nevertheless, a woman candidate stands the best chance if she also is an incumbent or is running for an open seat.

CHAPTER SEVEN

□ □ □ □ □ □ ■ □ □

Political Ambition

WHILE RECRUITMENT AND rate of electoral success are perhaps the most critical factors affecting the numerical representation of women, the political ambitions of women candidates also are important. If women who seek office lack ambition and do not plan to run again for the same office or for some other office, then large numbers of new candidates must be recruited each election year merely to maintain the size of the existing candidate pool. Moreover, the election of candidates lacking ambition can contribute only to short-term increases in the representation of women.

If, in contrast, women who seek public office are politically ambitious and intend to run again, then the recruitment of additional women in future election years is likely to enlarge the candidate pool. Moreover, the election of politically ambitious women can contribute not merely to short-term, but also to long-term, increases in the numerical representation of women.

Women candidates' ambitions have additional implications for the future of women in positions of political leadership. With the exception of judicial offices,[1] it is at the congressional level that women have continued to be most underrepresented among public officeholders. The largest number of women ever to have served in the House and in the Senate during one session was 24 in 1983. Thus, over the years, women have never held more than 4.5% of all seats in the U.S. Congress. Similarly, the proportions of women holding major statewide offices have remained low, with no more than two of the fifty state governorships ever held simultaneously by women.[2]

Joseph Schlesinger has argued that "the principle flow of public office personnel is from the state to the nation, from state office to Congress."[3] If Schlesinger is correct, prospects for increasing the proportion of women among congressional officeholders are highly dependent on the political ambitions of women who seek election to state house and state senate seats. It is from among the ranks of these women that many future female candidates for Congress are likely to come. Similarly, those women with experience as state legislators are likely to constitute an important potential pool of future candidates for governorships and other major statewide positions.

Finally, the likelihood that women officeholders will exercise greater influence in the governing bodies in which they serve is very much dependent upon the ambitions of women who seek public office. Party leadership positions, committee chairs, and frequently more informal means of influence accrue to those with seniority. If women are to capture a greater share of positions of power within legislative bodies, they must remain in office for long periods.

An Assessment of Ambition

Women who ran in 1976 were asked a series of questions about their intentions to run again for the same office, their intentions to run for political offices other than the office they sought in 1976, and the total length of time they would like to serve in elective offices of all types. Responses to these three questions are presented in table 7.1.

Schlesinger has suggested a relationship between an individual's ambitions and her/his current political situation, noting that "ambition for office . . . develops with a specific situation, that it is a response to the possibilities which lie before the politician."[4] Since candidates were surveyed in the midst of an election season, with all the uncertainty that entails, it is not surprising that many were unsure of their future intentions. More than one-fifth of candidates for all offices were unsure about running again for the same office, and even larger proportions, except among congressional candidates, expressed uncertainty over their plans to seek other offices (table 7.1).

Although sizable proportions of candidates stated that they probably or definitely would not run for the same office again, much larger proportions indicated that they probably or definitely would. The same was true for proportions expressing intentions to run for other offices. Of those candidates who responded to both of these questions, 64.4% of congressional, 60.0% of statewide, 64.6% of state senate, and 69.3% of

Table 7.1

Officeholding Ambitions of Women Candidates, 1976

| | OFFICE | | | |
	Congress	Statewide	State Senate	State House
	%	%	%	%
Plan to run again for the same office?				
Definitely or probably	43.8	47.6	55.6	61.8
Uncertain	31.5	42.9	24.7	23.5
Definitely or probably not	24.6	9.5	19.8	14.8
N =	(73)	(21)	(162)	(921)
Plan to run for another office?				
Definitely or probably	48.0	47.6	40.8	45.6
Uncertain	28.8	47.6	39.0	31.5
Definitely or probably not	23.3	4.8	20.2	22.9
N =	(73)	(21)	(164)	(941)
Length of time in future would like to serve in elective offices				
4 years or fewer	12.7	15.8	20.5	23.7
5–12 years	60.3	47.4	56.2	49.3
More than 12 years but no plans to make a career of officeholding	6.3	5.3	5.5	7.1
More than 12 years and plans to make a career of officeholding	20.6	31.6	17.8	20.0
N =	(63)	(19)	(146)	(836)

state house candidates planned to run again for the same office and/or for a different office.[5] As a group, then, women candidates showed considerable desire for future officeholding, as measured by responses to these two questions.

Nevertheless, the third measure of ambition suggests that the officeholding aspirations of women candidates are not without limits. Very large majorities of women candidates expressed a preference to remain in public office for twelve or fewer years over the remainder of their lifetimes (table 7.1). Only about one-fifth of candidates for congressional, state senate, and state house seats and a slightly higher proportion among statewide candidates stated that they intended to make a career of elective public officeholding. Sizable minorities of candidates expressed a desire to serve only for four or fewer years.

The lack of greater political ambition, as measured by projected tenure in office, was not due simply to the presence among candidates of significant numbers of officeholders who already had served long tenures in office. Women who had held office constituted only about one-third of all officeholders who expressed a desire to serve in office for a period of twelve or fewer years subsequent to 1976.[6] With those who previously had held office excluded, a large majority of the remaining candidates continued to manifest limited ambitions. Of those candidates without officeholding experience, 70.5% of congressional, 71.9% of state senate, and 71.3% of state house contenders wished to serve in public offices for no more than twelve years.[7]

Since several years of service in one office often are required to accumulate the seniority necessary to wield great influence, a period of twelve or fewer years is not likely to be sufficient to build a political career if that career involves mobility across offices. Consequently, on this measure of ambition, large numbers of women candidates can be considered to have somewhat limited ambitions.

Ultimate Officeholding Aspirations

There is another measure on which many women candidates appear to be constrained in their political aspirations. Those candidates who stated that they definitely or probably would run for another political office were asked to list all elective offices that might interest them, given the necessary political support and the right opportunities. The percentages of candidates who desired offices at various levels, expressed as proportions of all candidates who ran in 1976, are presented in table 7.2.

Of particular interest are the proportions of candidates at the state legislative level who expressed a desire to hold offices at the national level. It is from the ranks of these women, who are gaining campaign and officeholding experience as state legislators, that a significant proportion of future female candidates for Congress and statewide positions might be expected to come. Yet, overwhelming majorities of women who sought state legislative offices in 1976 expressed no long-term intentions to build political careers that would lead them to Congress (table 7.2). Rather, they more often seemed content to focus their aspirations—when they had them—on state, county, and local levels of government. Similarly, most state legislative candidates expressed no interest in statewide offices.

Table 7.2

Level of Other Elective Offices Aspired to by Women Candidates, 1976[a]

	OFFICE			
	Congress	Statewide	State Senate	State House
	%	%	%	%
Level of Office				
Local or county	9.6	0	17.1	18.0
State house	16.4	4.8	12.2	0
State senate	17.8	0	0	27.5
Minor state (e.g., public service commissioner, state board of education)	4.1	4.8	3.0	2.4
Major state (e.g., governor, state supreme court)	11.0	28.6	10.5	12.3
National (e.g., Congress, Vice-President, President)	16.4	14.3	22.0	17.9
Judgeships (other than state supreme court justice)	0	0	0	.2
Other	1.4	4.8	1.8	2.3
N =	(73)	(21)	(164)	(941)

ᵃCandidates were asked. If you had the necessary political support and the right opportunities, what other *elective* political offices at the local, state, and national levels would you
eventually like to hold? Please list *all* elective offices that might be of interest to you.

The data in table 7.2 also illustrate another important feature of the
ambition structures of women candidates. Schlesinger has developed a
typology of political ambitions consisting of three distinct types:
"discrete"—the politician desires only to hold a particular office for a
single term and then to retire from officeholding; "static"—the politician
wishes to make a long-term career out of holding a specific office; and
"progressive"—the politician wishes to attain an office more prestigious
and important than the one presently sought or held.[8] Schlesinger
assumed that a politician who did not wish either to retire from public
officeholding or to remain in a single office for the remainder of her/his
political career would desire to climb the political ladder by seeking
offices more prestigious than the one presently occupied or sought. In

other words, a politician wishing to change offices would necessarily exhibit progressive ambitions, seeking a higher, more powerful office rather
than seeking a lower, less powerful one. Heinz Eulau et al. have noted
that "there are no agreed-upon criteria by which to determine 'higher' or
'lower' office, particularly in a political system like the American with its
horizontal, federal structure cutting across vertical hierarchies."[9] While
this is certainly true, in most areas of the country a seat in a state legislature, especially a state senate seat, is more desirable and more prestigious
than many county and local elective offices. Consequently, in many in-
stances, for a state legislator or a state legislative candidate to desire a
local or county office would seem to be a step down the political ladder
rather than a step up.[10]

Yet, as table 7.2 illustrates, almost one-sixth of all state senate and state
house candidates and about one-tenth of all congressional candidates expressed an interest in holding a local or county office in the future. These
proportions are as large or almost as large as the proportions desiring to
seek major statewide or national offices. Moreover, of candidates intending to seek another office and listing at least one office of interest, 3.2% of
congressional candidates, 9.7% of state senate candidates, and 19.0% of
state house candidates listed *only* local or county offices and no offices at
any other level of government.[11] In many cases, the local and county
offices desired by these candidates were almost assuredly less prestigious
than state legislative or congressional seats. For example, among those
interested in local or county offices, 14.3% of congressional candidates,
7.1% of state senate candidates, and 21.3% of state house candidates
listed a seat on a local school board.

The tendency for many candidates to express an interest in offices that
may reflect a step down the political ladder also is seen in the desire of a
significant proportion of state senate candidates to hold seats in the lower
house of their legislatures. Approximately one-eighth of all candidates for
the state senate stated that they would like to seek state house offices in
the future.

These findings suggest that the ambition structures of candidates who
desired offices beyond the one sought in 1976 cannot in all cases be
accurately described as "progressive." A significant proportion of candidates aspired to offices less prestigious than the one sought in 1976 as well
as to more prestigious offices. In addition, a small minority of candidates
had no intention to seek offices at higher levels but rather aspired only to
offices that, in many cases, probably were lower-level offices than the
ones sought in 1976. These findings indicate that ambition structures

among women candidates are far more fluid and diverse than Schlesinger's typology would suggest.

The finding that women candidates often appeared to aspire to offices less prestigious than the ones they sought in 1976 may be a sex-related phenomenon. Barbara Farah, in a comparative study of the ambitions of male and female delegates to the 1972 national party conventions, found a distinct preference among women for offices at the lower levels of government.[12] She suggested a number of factors that might account for this preference. First, public officeholding at higher levels has been identified with men and male attributes to a greater extent than officeholding at lower levels; to aspire to a higher office requires a greater deviation from traditional sex-role expectations. Second, women may have a greater interest in local issues and may simply prefer to serve in offices that deal directly with these issues. Third, women may be more likely to aspire to those offices where they have the greatest number of role models, and female role models are more common at the local level. Another possibility, not suggested by Farah, is that women may show a preference for lower-level offices due to their role in the family, as traditionally defined by society. Because of their role as the primary nurturer, women may perceive a greater need than men to be close to home and to have time to spend with their children and spouses. Lower-level offices generally require less time and distance away from home and family than higher-level offices. Finally, women may fear that they will encounter resistance and sex discrimination in seeking higher-level offices; they may perceive various political actors as more open to their participation at local and county levels.

If any or all of these explanations are valid, then the sizable proportions of candidates aspiring to lower-level offices may be a phenomenon limited largely to *women* politicians. If so, then Schlesinger's typology may describe the ambition structures of male politicians, but may need modification to encompass the ambition structures of female politicians.

However, the finding that many women candidates for state-level offices aspire to offices at lower levels of government may stem not from the candidates' sex but rather from their status as candidates. An election campaign is a time of high uncertainty, and the lower aspirations found in this study may be a product of that uncertainty. Prospects of defeat may affect future officeholding aspirations. A candidate may see herself moving on to a higher office only if she wins her current race. However, if she loses she may focus instead on a county or local office. Candidates who listed both higher and lower offices as potentially of interest may have been responding in a manner that would allow for either possibility. Similarly, candidates with an interest only in lower offices may have been responding on the basis of an anticipated loss. They may even have entered a contest for a state legislative or congressional office in 1976 with the sole intention of gaining visibility and name recognition that would later help them wage successful campaigns for office at a lower level of government. If low aspirations among many of the individuals surveyed here are merely a response to uncertainty, then Schlesinger's classification scheme may adequately describe the ambitions of *officeholders*, but may need modification to include the full range of ambitions found among *candidates*.

Finally, the sizable proportion of women who aspired to lower-level offices may reflect neither the sex nor the candidate status of those surveyed in this study. It may be that significant numbers of politically active individuals—whether candidates or officeholders—wish to hold other offices, but their ambitions do not follow the progressive pattern Schlesinger described. If so, then his typology needs revision.

Future research will be required to determine whether those who do not exhibit strictly progressive ambitions but rather aspire to offices at lower levels of government do so for reasons related to their sex, for reasons related to their status as candidates, or for reasons that transcend both gender and electoral uncertainty. Nevertheless, the important point for this study is that a sizable block of women candidates desire other offices but do not necessarily wish to progress up the officeholding hierarchy. Their numbers will contribute to the pool of women candidates across all offices, but will not necessarily increase the number of women candidates for higher offices. That many of those women candidates who intend to seek other offices do not set their sights on higher offices, or alternatively plan to run for lower offices as well as higher offices, suggests that large increases in the number of women running for statewide and congressional offices are not likely in the near future.

Reasons for Lack of Ambition: A First Approach

Because the ambition levels of women who seek and are elected to public office may have significant implications for the numerical representation of women, it is important to examine the reasons for the low levels of ambition among those women whose aspirations were limited. Why were many women who ran in 1976 not more ambitious politically?

There are two ways to identify the factors that work to inhibit women candidates' political ambitions. The first is to examine candidates' own explanations for their lack of ambition. The second is to isolate factors suggested in previous research, as well as those that one would expect *a priori* to restrict political ambitions, and to examine whether ambitious and unambitious candidates differ significantly with respect to these factors. Both approaches will be followed in an attempt to explain why many women candidates fail to exhibit high levels of political ambition.

Those candidates who stated that they definitely or probably would not run for offices other than the one they sought in 1976 were asked to list the major reasons why. Their reasons, presented in table 7.3, provide some insight into the factors candidates themselves perceived as restricting their ambitions.

Most researchers noting a lack of political ambition among women have offered explanations focusing on sex-role socialization and sex-role prescriptions.[13] The data in table 7.3 provide some support for explanations of this type. Perhaps the reason most clearly related to sex-role factors is that the time, energy, and travel involved in serving in office would take women away from other responsibilities—most frequently their families. This was the third most frequently mentioned reason among state legislative candidates. One of the other two reasons mentioned by even larger proportions of candidates—a simple lack of higher aspiration—may also be related to sex-role socialization, since women are not socialized to be strongly oriented toward achievement outside the home.[14] Those who disliked politics, who felt they could serve the public better in some other capacity, who found the pressures of campaigning too severe, or who seemed to lack confidence in their own abilities as politicians perhaps did so in part because of sex-role socialization. All of these reasons reflect a basic distaste for politics and/or a perceived lack of political competence that could stem from the fact that women are not socialized to view themselves as political animals. Politics may be too male in its values, and too severe in its demands, for many women's liking.

Many of the other reasons for lack of greater ambition do not lend themselves as readily to sex-role related explanations. Various personal reasons given by some candidates seem largely independent of sex roles. The most important of these is age, the single most frequent reason given for a lack of greater ambition by women candidates for congressional, state senate, and state house seats.[15] Significant proportions of candidates also cited having "served long enough."

Of particular interest are those reasons linked to the political opportunity structure. One-fourth of congressional candidates and smaller, but significant, proportions of state legislative candidates pointed to a lack of

TABLE 7.3

Reasons Why Candidates Did Not Intend to Run for Other Offices for
Women Candidates, 1976, Expressing at Least One Reason[a]

	OFFICE			
	Congress	Statewide	State Senate	State House
	%	%	%	%
Reasons linked to the political opportunity structure				
Lack of political opportunity	25.0	—	7.7	13.3
Financial cost of campaigning	18.8	33.3	10.3	11.6
Opposition to women	18.8	—	—	1.7
Voter apathy or lack of attention to issues	—	—	—	2.5
Reasons possibly linked to sex-role socialization				
Time, energy, or distance required takes her away from other roles	—	—	15.4	14.1
Dislike of, frustration with, politics	12.5	—	10.3	7.9
Pure lack of higher aspiration, satisfaction with present position	18.8	—	20.5	27.0
Belief that she can serve the public better in some other capacity	—	33.3	—	1.2
Pressures of campaigning	—	66.7	5.1	7.9
Lack of self-confidence	6.3	—	7.7	5.4
Personal reasons				
Age	31.3	—	30.8	20.3
Professional reasons	—	—	2.6	3.7
Other personal reasons	—	—	—	3.3
Other reasons				
Belief that she has served long enough, fulfilled her civic duty	6.3	—	12.8	7.1
Lack of support from other women	—	—	—	.4
Miscellaneous	—	—	2.6	1.2
N =	(16)	(3)	(39)	(241)

[a]Candidates who did not intend to seek other offices were asked: Please explain the major reasons why you do not think you will run for any other political office. Columns total more than 100% because candidates could list more than one reason.

political opportunity in their districts or areas (e.g., the conservative political climate of the district, or the domination of the district by voters of the opposing party) as a reason for not seeking future offices. In addition, notable proportions of candidates cited the high financial costs of campaigning. Finally, a few candidates for congressional and state house offices mentioned another aspect of the political opportunity structure women candidates must confront—opposition to women.

The data in table 7.3, then, suggest that women in this study were not more ambitious politically for a wide diversity of reasons. While some of these reasons may be linked to socialization patterns and sex-role behavioral prescriptions, factors related to the political opportunity structure also are important in restricting political ambition.

Reasons for Lack of Ambition: A Second Approach

An examination of differences between ambitious and less ambitious women candidates on a number of background and attitudinal variables also yields insight into the factors that restrict women's political ambitions.

One variable measured in this study and found strongly related to political ambition in a number of previous studies is age, with increasing age having a depressing effect on expectations of holding higher levels of office.[16] Education also has been found to be related to political ambition, perhaps because it increases efficacy or perhaps because it provides credentials that make higher aspirations more realizable.[17]

Experience in party leadership positions or in public office might result in increased officeholding ambitions. Such experiences can lead to the acquisition of important political skills, the development of political contacts, and an increase in political confidence, which may, in turn, enhance ambition.[18]

Similarly, incumbency might be related to ambition, since political success might enhance self-confidence and stimulate a desire for greater success. Just as election to office might heighten ambition, a series of defeats might dampen aspirations; if so, political ambition might be inversely related to the net number of election losses minus victories a politician has experienced.

Two other variables which might affect the political ambitions of politicians regardless of their gender are ideology and party affiliation. Some research has found only a weak relationship between ideology and political ambition.[19] However, other research has found liberalism related to greater ambition among both male and female officeholders. Marilyn

Johnson and Susan Carroll have suggested, "Perhaps both political ambition and ideology are related to a more general psychological predisposition that enables an individual to cope with change, and even to desire it—whether it be change at the societal level, as is the case with liberalism, or change at the personal level, as is the case with officeholding ambitions."[20] Farah has noted that party affiliation might lead to differences in ambition for either attitudinal or structural reasons.[21] Attitudinally, for many politicians party affiliation may reflect an ideological preference. For this reason, liberals cluster in the Democratic party, while conservatives are found more frequently in the Republican ranks. Structurally, however, party affiliation might exert an independent effect on ambition, over and beyond any relationship between ideological orientation and ambition. As the majority party nationwide, the Democratic party may be perceived as providing more political opportunities than the Republican party. Because of the greater opportunities available, ambitious candidates may more frequently be Democrats than Republicans.

The variables discussed above might affect the political ambitions of both sexes. However, there also are sex-role socialization and sex-role behavioral variables that might influence the ambitions of women but not of men.

One such variable is sex-role attitudes, or views about traditional standards of appropriate behavior for women and men. A woman with more traditional sex-role attitudes, who believes, for example, that a woman's place is in the home and that her roles as wife and mother are far more important than interests outside the home, probably would be less likely to have far-reaching political ambitions than a woman who has less traditional attitudes.

Similarly, sex-role identities, or self-evaluations in relation to traditional norms, might well affect political ambitions. To the extent that personality characteristics influence ambition, masculine characteristics, such as independence, assertiveness, forcefulness, competitiveness, willingness to take risks, and aggressiveness, should promote the development of political ambition as politics is presently defined. Stereotypically feminine characteristics, such as sensitivity to the needs of others, soft-spokenness, gentleness, and willingness to yield to others, in the absence of masculine characteristics, should inhibit the development of political ambition. As a result, one might expect to find ambitious women more likely than less-ambitious women to have either masculine or androgynous sex-role identities, wherein masculine characteristics are

strongly developed. Similarly, less-ambitious women might be more likely than ambitious women to have either feminine sex-role identities,
where feminine characteristics are developed but masculine characteristics are not, or undifferentiated sex-role identities, where neither feminine nor masculine characteristics are strongly developed.[22]

Sympathy with the feminist movement and its goals also might affect
political ambition. The feminist movement has resocialized many women,
encouraging them to move into nontraditional vocational fields and to
break through barriers that previously barred them from achievement.
For some, it has provided support to aspire to levels of achievement
inconceivable without the stimulus provided by the movement. In this
way, the feminist movement may have served as a catalyst that enhanced
the political aspirations of women who, if untouched and unaffected by
the movement, would have been satisfied with much less. There also is a
purposive component to feminism which may motivate women to aspire
to higher offices and to longer political careers. Women who feel strongly
about achieving feminist goals and eliminating the inequities women face
may feel a personal responsibility to contribute to the achievement of
these goals. This feeling of commitment might motivate some women to
aspire to higher offices, or to longer tenure, in order to obtain positions
where they could try to eliminate various inequities.

A final variable related to sex-role behavioral prescriptions that might
affect political ambitions is the presence or absence of young children at
home. Since many women still bear the primary responsibility for child-
rearing, young children might dampen their ambitions by making them
reluctant to consider offices that are time-consuming in their responsibilities or necessitate extensive time away from home.

To examine differences between ambitious and less-ambitious women
on all these variables, state legislative candidates who were the most
ambitious both in terms of desire to achieve higher office and in terms of
projected tenure in political offices were separated from all other state
legislative candidates. "Ambitious" state legislative candidates were those
who desired to run for a major statewide or national office and who hoped
to remain in public office for twelve years or more. All other candidates
were classified as "less ambitious."[23] If the variables above do, in fact,
affect ambition, then the women who were most ambitious should differ
significantly from other candidates on these measures.

Table 7.4 presents measures of association between this dichotomized
measure of ambition and the various independent variables. None of the
relationships were strong, but several of the independent variables did

show at least weak relationships to ambition. Ambitious candidates were notably younger than other candidates. While 22.9% of all ambitious candidates were thirty or younger, only 9.1% of the less-ambitious candidates fell in this age group. At the other extreme, 0.7% of ambitious candidates but 9.6% of other candidates were over sixty.

Party affiliation also was weakly related to ambition, with 77.8% of ambitious candidates, compared to 56.3% of other candidates, running under the Democratic label. Ambitious candidates also tended to be slightly more liberal; 57.4% of all ambitious candidates, compared with 40.9% of other candidates, identified as liberals.

All four variables related to sex-role socialization showed weak relationships to ambition, although one seemed to operate contrary to expectations. Ambitious women candidates were more likely than other women candidates to have nontraditional sex-role attitudes, to have masculine or androgynous sex-role identities, and to express positive senti-

TABLE 7.4

Relationships between Ambition[a] and Measures Hypothesized to Be Related to Ambition for Women State Legislative Candidates, 1976

Variable	Tau_b or Tau_c =
Age	.24[b]
Education	.05
Experience in party leadership position	.04
Prior elective officeholding experience[c]	−.04
Incumbency	−.01
Net number of previous losses over wins	.01
Party affiliation	.15
Ideology	.10
Sex-role attitudes[d]	.19
Sex-role identities[e]	.09
Attitude toward women's movement	.11
Children 12 or under at home	−.10

[a]Ambition as measured here was a dichotomous variable. "Ambitious" candidates (N = 144) were those who desired to run for a major statewide or national office and who hoped to remain in public office for twelve years or more. All other candidates were classified as "less ambitious" (N = 973).

[b]This coefficient is the value for Pearson's r, rather than tau.

[c]This measure is independent of incumbency. Incumbents were classified as having held a previous elective office only if they had held another office in addition to the one in which they were serving in 1976.

[d]Three sex-role attitude items were combined into a single, summative measure. See chapter 6 for a description of this scale.

[e]This is a dichotomized measure of those with and without androgynous sex-role identities.

ments toward the women's movement. However, ambitious candidates were somewhat *more* likely than others to have children age twelve or under. This negative relationship reflected, in large part, the tendency for ambitious women candidates to be disproportionately in the younger age-groups. When age was controlled, the relationship virtually disappeared.[24]

The other variables hypothesized to have an impact on political ambition showed no notable relationships to ambition. Ambitious candidates differed very little from their less-ambitious counterparts in educational attainment, experience in a party leadership position, experience in elective offices, incumbency, or net losses over wins in previous election bids.

To assess the relative importance of the independent variables in differentiating ambitious candidates from their less-ambitious counterparts, and to determine the overall utility of these variables in explaining why more women are not more politically ambitious, all twelve variables hypothesized to affect ambition were entered into a stepwise discriminant analysis[25] (table 7.5). Nine of the twelve variables, in combination with the other variables, contributed to the discrimination of ambitious and less-ambitious women candidates, but only four led to a change in Rao's V that was statistically significant at the .05 level. These four were age, sex-role attitudes, party identification, and sex-role identities. Of these, age clearly was the most robust, with a standardized discriminant function coefficient much larger than that for the other three variables.

The classification function based on the discriminating variables correctly classified 86% of all state legislative candidates as ambitious or less ambitious.[26] On first glance, this may appear to be a relatively high proportion. However, only 13% of all state legislative candidates met the two criteria necessary to be considered "ambitious" (i.e., aspiring to a major statewide or national office, and intending to spend more than twelve years in public office), while 87% did not. Consequently, by simply predicting that no women candidates were ambitious, one could correctly classify more candidates than with the classification function. This suggests that even those variables which contributed to the discrimination of ambitious and less-ambitious candidates are limited in their utility.

This analysis included four potentially powerful measures of sex-role socialization and sex-role behavioral prescriptions, and the lack of greater explanatory power for these variables, individually and in combination with other variables, suggests that sex-role socialization may not play as deterministic a role in limiting women's political ambitions as previous research has suggested. Similarly, most of the major variables unrelated

TABLE 7.5

Discriminant Analysis for Ambitious and Less-Ambitious Women State Legislative Candidates, 1976

Variable	Standardized Discriminant Function Coefficient	Significance of Change in Rao's V	Cases Correctly Classified
Age	.76	.0001	
Sex-role attitudes	.23	.0001	
Party identification	.25	.01	
Sex-role identities	.23	.04	
Incumbency	.19	.06	
Attitude toward women's movement	.22	.09	86%
Net number of previous losses over wins	−.13	.17	
Experience in party leadership position	.13	.22	
Previous elective officeholding experience	.12	.25	

to gender which previous literature has suggested to be likely to exert an important influence on political ambition, with the possible exception of age, are not particularly useful in explaining the presence or absence of ambition.

If sex-role socialization variables are of limited utility in explaining differences in ambition levels, and if other commonly investigated variables have little explanatory power, what additional variables could contribute to differences in ambition? Several variables that could not be measured in this study would seem to have the greatest potential explanatory power. These include various aspects of the structure of political opportunity that lie before the candidates—for example, the political composition of the constituencies of offices candidates might seek in the future, the costs of campaigning for these seats, the degree to which political influentials are willing to support women candidates for these offices, and the rate of turnover in these seats. Part of the explanation as to why so many women candidates are not more politically ambitious may well lie in these unmeasured aspects of the political opportunity structure.

Summary and Implications

While political ambitions are fluid and likely to change over time, this chapter has provided a glimpse of how women candidates viewed their political futures in 1976. With respect to their desire to run again for the same or for another office, women candidates appeared relatively ambitious. Most expressed an intention to run again. However, with regard to the offices to which they aspired and their projected tenure in office, the ambitions of women candidates appeared far more constrained. Only small minorities of state legislative candidates aspired to statewide and congressional offices, and fewer candidates at any level viewed public officeholding as a long-term career choice.

Women candidates may well be no less ambitious than their male counterparts. While there are no nationwide data on the ambitions of male candidates or officeholders, the results of the few small-scale studies that do exist suggest that most men also are not particularly ambitious.[27] However, because far fewer women than men are candidates and officeholders, far more female than male candidates and officeholders must be politically ambitious if women in elective office are to achieve numerical parity with men. Unless the ambitions of women who seek office change substantially over the next several years, findings from this analysis suggest that equitable numerical representation of women at statewide and congressional levels may be slow in coming. Similarly, we are unlikely to see large numbers of women accumulate the tenure and seniority necessary to capture formal or informal leadership positions within legislative bodies in the near future.

There appears to be no single, simple explanation for candidates' lack of greater ambition. While some candidates explained their lack of political aspirations as due to factors related to sex-role socialization, a sizable number gave reasons related to the political opportunity structure. Similarly, an analysis of the extent to which various variables were useful in differentiating the most ambitious candidates from all others did not point to a clear explanation for variations in ambition. One conclusion emerging from this analysis was that variables other than those measured in this study probably are of considerable importance. These variables may not be limited to, but are likely to include, various aspects of the political opportunity structure that women candidates confront.

CHAPTER EIGHT

□ □ □ □ □ □ □ ■ □

Representation of the Interests of Women

HISTORICALLY, AMERICAN GOVERNING institutions have not adequately represented women's interests on policy issues dealing with women. Many feminist activists hope to obtain better representation of the interests of women through electing more women to public office. These activists assume, as do some scholars, that there is a relationship between the number of political positions members of a particular group hold and the extent to which that group's interests are recognized and acted on in the policy process. If these activists and scholars are correct, an increase in the number of women holding elective public offices should lead to greater representation of the interests of women on policy issues dealing with women.[1]

However, for an increase in the numerical representation of women to result in an increase in the representation of the interests of women, women elected to office must exercise an influence on public policy significantly different from that of their male counterparts. And to date, we lack empirical evidence which would provide a definitive answer as to whether women officeholders differ from their male counterparts in their impact on legislation related to women's interests. To conduct a definitive test for sex differences in impact on legislation involving women's issues would require comparative data for a highly representative and broad-based sample of male and female officeholders. The study would have to examine not only voting records, as some past research has done on a

A modified version of this chapter appeared in *The Western Political Quarterly*, Vol. 37, No. 2 (June 1984), pp 307–323.

limited scale,[2] but also behavior related to the development of legislation, the direction and nature of influence among colleagues, and coalition building. For a multitude of reasons, including the complexity of the design required, the small proportion of women currently holding public offices, and the costs of such a study, we presently lack the data necessary to examine whether women differ from men in their impact on legislation concerning women's issues.

However, data from this study make it possible to assess the logically prior question: Are women who seek and win public office attitudinal and behavioral feminists?[3] If large proportions of women candidates and officeholders are not, the argument that an increase in the numerical representation of women will lead to increased representation of the interests of women would seem to have little merit. However, if large proportions of women candidates and officeholders are found to be attitudinal and behavioral feminists, then the argument that an increase in number of women holding public office will lead to increased legislative attention to women's issues, and to more favorable action on such issues, should be taken seriously and investigated in future research.

This chapter examines whether women candidates exhibit the characteristics of attitudinal and behavioral feminists. As will become apparent, the evidence on this question is conflicting. Women candidates simultaneously manifest both distinctly feminist and distinctly nonfeminist tendencies. An explanation for these apparent inconsistencies is offered and the implications of the findings for increased representation of women's interests are discussed.

Defining Attitudinal and Behavioral Feminism

Any attempt to define "attitudinal and behavioral feminism" precisely is likely to be both difficult and inadequate. Feminism is a diverse political ideology with numerous variants. Alison Jaggar has noted:

> Within the women's liberation movement, several distinct ideologies can be discerned. All believe that justice requires freedom and equality for women, but they differ on such basic philosophical questions as the proper account of freedom and equality, the functions of the state, and the notion of what constitutes human, and especially female, nature.[4]

Jaggar has identified and outlined differences among three well-established strains of feminist thought—liberal feminism, classical Marxist feminism, and radical feminism—as well as two variants that have emerged more recently—lesbian separatism and socialist feminism.[5] Because of the diversity apparent within the contemporary women's movement, it would be misleading and inappropriate to put forward a single definition of feminism to represent the beliefs of all feminists. No simple definition can possibly portray the complexity, richness, and diversity of feminist ideology.

Nevertheless, for present purposes a definition of feminism consistent with the "liberal feminist" perspective will be employed. Jo Freeman has perhaps best summarized the components of such a definition:

> The [liberal] feminist perspective looks at the many similarities between the sexes and concludes that women and men have equal potential for individual development. Differences in the realization of that potential, therefore, must result from externally imposed restraints, from the influence of social institutions and values. The feminist view holds that so long as society prescribes sex roles and social penalties for those who deviate from them, no meaningful choice exists for members of either sex.[6]

From this perspective, then, an individual is an attitudinal feminist if she favors the elimination of societally prescribed sex roles and the removal of any legal constraints that prohibit women from pursuing their potential for individual development just as fully as men do.[7] An individual is a behavioral feminist if she engages in behavioral acts that reflect such beliefs—for example, joining organizations that espouse these beliefs, publicly advocating measures consistent with these beliefs, developing legislation or projects as an extension of these beliefs. All measures examined in this chapter as evidence of feminist attitudes and/or behavior are consistent with this definition.

There are several reasons for adopting a definition of feminism phrased in terms of liberal feminist beliefs. First, as the ideology of the National Organization for Women, the National Women's Political Caucus, and other major national feminist organizations, liberal feminism has become the dominant strain of feminism in this country.[8] Second, because liberal feminism is the most moderate feminist ideology, adherence to its basic principles serves as a minimal criterion to assess whether an individual is a feminist. While feminists of other persuasions are likely to view the goals of liberal feminists as too limited and/or less significant than goals more central to their ideologies, in most cases they would not oppose most of the issue positions favored by liberal feminists.[9]

However, the most important reason why a definition phrased in terms of liberal feminism seems appropriate is that it coincides closely with the definition of women's interests set forth in chapter 2. As suggested there, two elements are critical to an objective definition of the interests of women on policy issues dealing with women: (1) a broadening of the range of choices or options available to women, and (2) the removal of ascriptive criteria in the allocation of rewards. When the interests of women are defined objectively to include these elements, they coincide with most of the issue positions of the contemporary feminist movement—a movement dominated by a liberal feminist ideology. The use of measures congruent with a liberal feminist perspective allows a direct examination of the predispositions most relevant to assessing whether women candidates, if elected, might bring about greater representation of the interests of women.

Behavioral Measures: Women Candidates as Nonfeminists

On two measures of reported behavior, most women candidates for public office failed to exhibit strong feminist tendencies. Judging from these measures, one would conclude that most women candidates in 1976 could be characterized as nonfeminists.

Organizational Memberships

Candidates were asked to list all organizations to which they belonged in the five years preceding 1976. A large majority, 79.5% of the respondents, did not list membership in a single organization whose primary purpose is the improvement of women's status in society through the elimination of inequities between women and men.[10] This proportion did not vary greatly by office, although candidates for statewide office were somewhat more likely, and candidates for state house seats somewhat less likely, than congressional and state senate candidates to belong to "feminist" groups.[11]

An even larger majority of women candidates across all offices, 98.8%, were not identified with "antifeminist" groups, which seek to maintain social and legal differentiations between the sexes.[12] Only 5.5% of congressional candidates, no statewide candidates, 2.4% of candidates for the state senate, and 0.7% of candidates for the state house reported membership in an antifeminist organization.

To the extent that belonging to an organization serves as a measure of identification with the goals of that organization, women candidates in 1976, by and large, could not be considered to have had a strong feminist or antifeminist commitment. Rather, on this measure, the great majority of women candidates seem most appropriately characterized as nonfeminists.

Women's Issues in Primary Campaigns

Data on the role women's issues played in the primary campaigns of women candidates in 1976 also suggest that the behavior of most women candidates can most appropriately be described as nonfeminist. Of those women who were opposed in bids for their party's nominations, sizable proportions—13.0% of congressional candidates, 43.8% of statewide candidates, 21.7% of state senate candidates, and 28.7% of state house candidates—reported that they never discussed a single women's issue at any time during their campaigns. Even larger proportions at most levels of office—34.8% of congressional candidates, 12.5% of statewide candidates, 31.9% of state senate candidates, and 31.2% of state house candidates—discussed women's issues only when asked by others for their positions on these issues.[13] Thus, a near-majority of congressional candidates and majorities of candidates for other offices who ran in contested primaries did not initiate discussion of women's issues at any point during their campaigns.[14]

Even among those women candidates who initiated discussion of women's issues during their primary campaigns, few listed a women's issue as one of the leading issues in their campaigns.[15] Only 13.6% of congressional candidates, 5.9% of candidates for statewide office, 18.8% of state senate candidates, and 10.4% of candidates for the state house who ran in contested primaries reported the ERA, abortion, or another women's issue among the concerns they emphasized as most important.[16]

Attitudinal Measures: Women Candidates as Feminists

The previous sections demonstrated that most women candidates did not belong to feminist organizations and did not strongly emphasize women's issues in their primary campaigns. On these behavioral measures, most women candidates cannot be considered to have exhibited feminist tendencies and might most appropriately be characterized as nonfeminists. However, across a series of attitudinal measures, women who ran for office showed strong feminist leanings.

Sex-Role Attitudes

Candidates were asked several questions designed to measure their attitudes toward conventional sex roles in American society. Since a major goal of the feminist movement is to free both women and men from restricting sex-role stereotypes, candidates' attitudes on these items serve as one indicator of the degree to which the candidates manifested a feminist consciousness. A sizable majority of candidates running for all levels of office rejected the roles traditionally defined as appropriate for women and men and endorsed the feminist position on three sex-role attitudinal items (table 8.1).

One might expect to find differences in levels of support between

TABLE 8.1

Attitudes toward Traditional Sex-Role Stereotypes among Women Candidates, 1976

	Percent Who Gave Feminist Responses on All 3 Items[a]	N =	Tau$_c$ =
Congressional Candidates			
All	69.1	68	
Democrats	75.6	45	.19
Republicans	56.5	23	
Statewide Candidates			
All	72.2	18	
Democrats	62.5	8	−.26
Republicans	88.9	9	
State Senate Candidates			
All	62.8	156	
Democrats	65.6	93	.14
Republicans	55.2	58	
State House Candidates			
All	58.3	892	
Democrats	66.2	533	.23
Republicans	46.5	359	

[a]The three agree/disagree items were as follows:
(1) It is much better for everyone involved if the man is the achiever outside the home and the woman takes care of the home and family.
(2) It is more important for a wife to help her husband than to have a career herself.
(3) A working mother can establish just as warm and secure a relationship with her children as a mother who does not work.
Feminist responses were considered to be "strongly disagree" or "disagree" for items 1–2 and "strongly agree" or "agree" for item 3.

Democratic and Republican candidates on these, and on other feminist attitudinal items. Jeff Fishel has explained, "Contrary to repeated efforts at stigmatizing the major parties as 'two empty bottles, into which the same liquid is poured,' virtually every study of those who are most active in party politics, from precinct worker to Presidents, has shown that the national parties differ on many important issues of public policy—and have done so for as long as systematic research has been collected."[17] Although the concerns of the women's movement cut across the broad coalitions of demographic groups that form the bases of support for the two major parties, one might expect that the Democrats' historic concern for the socially disadvantaged and their greater support for government activism in solving social and economic problems would make them more favorable to feminist goals.[18]

The data in table 8.1 confirm this expectation. Republicans were somewhat less likely than Democrats to endorse the feminist position on the three items, except among statewide candidates. Nevertheless, even among Republicans a near-majority of candidates for the state house and majorities of candidates for other offices sided with the feminist position on all three measures, indicating rejection of roles traditionally prescribed for women and men.

Attitudes toward the Women's Movement

Earlier studies found lack of support for, and even opposition to, the women's movement among politically active women.[19] In contrast, women who ran for office in 1976 were overwhelmingly favorable toward the feminist movement (table 8.2).

Party differences in attitudes toward the women's movement closely parallel those found for sex-role attitudes. With the exception of candidates for statewide offices, where both parties' candidates were 100% supportive, Democrats were more favorable toward the feminist movement than were Republicans. Nevertheless, large majorities of Republican as well as Democratic candidates for all offices expressed positive sentiments toward the women's movement (table 8.2).

Attitudes toward Women's Issues

In order to determine whether candidates' positive views of the women's movement translated into supportive positions on some of the specific issues of concern to the movement, candidates were asked to respond on a five-point, agree/disagree scale to a number of items on policy issues relating to women and women's rights, including three items dealing with various child care alternatives, three focusing on abortion, and two about the Equal Rights Amendment. The other items covered issues such as social security benefits for homemakers, equal rights regarding credit, and compensation for working women who take time off for childbirth.

Table 8.3 presents the proportions of women candidates who gave feminist responses to six of the women's issue items. The particular child care and abortion items which showed the lowest levels of support for feminist positions were chosen in order to provide the most conservative estimate of levels of attitudinal feminism.[20] Nevertheless, on *every* issue a majority of candidates for every office expressed attitudes congruent with the feminist movement's position. On the items dealing with the ERA,

TABLE 8.2

Attitudes toward the Women's Movement among Women Candidates, 1976

	Percent with Positive Attitudes toward Women's Movement[a]	N =	Tau$_c$ =
Congressional Candidates			
All	83.6	73	.40
Democrats	93.8	48	
Republicans	64.0	25	
Statewide Candidates			
All	100.0	20	−.09
Democrats	100.0	10	
Republicans	100.0	9	
State Senate Candidates			
All	88.2	162	.31
Democrats	94.8	96	
Republicans	78.7	61	
State House Candidates			
All	84.5	927	.33
Democrats	92.3	554	
Republicans	73.0	373	

[a]The question was worded as follows:
Overall how do you feel about the "women's movement" and its major goals?
——— Very positive   ——— Somewhat positive   ———Neutral
——— Somewhat negative   ——— Very negative
Those who checked "very" or "somewhat" positive were considered to have positive attitudes.

abortion, social security coverage for homemakers, and equal credit, the majorities were large, with about two-thirds or more supporting the feminist position. Moreover, sizable proportions of women candidates, ranging from about one-fifth on the child care item to more than one-half on the ERA and equal credit, gave the most feminist response (either "strongly agree" or "strongly disagree"), indicating that they held feminist views with some intensity.

Among women who ran for office in 1976, Democratic candidates outnumbered Republican candidates by a ratio of approximately 3 to 2.[21] However, attitudinal feminism on women's issues was not limited to Democrats (table 8.4). Although the relationship between party affiliation and issue positions was generally moderate across the various levels of

TABLE 8.3

Attitudes on Women's Issues among Women Candidates, 1976

	Percent Who Gave Feminist Response[a]	Percent Who Gave Most Intense Feminist Response[b]	N =
ERA			
I favor ratification of the Equal Rights Amendment.			
Congress	78.9	59.2	71
Statewide	94.8	63.2	19
State Senate	82.8	66.9	157
State House	79.1	58.1	897
Abortion			
I would oppose a constitutional amendment which would prohibit abortion in all or almost all circumstances.			
Congress	61.2	44.8	67
Statewide	77.8	55.6	18
State Senate	66.0	51.9	156
State House	65.9	45.2	898
Child Care			
The national and/or state government should provide child care services to all parents who desire them with fees charged for those services according to ability to pay.			
Congress	63.2	19.1	68
Statewide	55.6	27.8	18
State Senate	52.6	19.3	150
State House	53.8	19.1	880
Social Security for Homemakers			
Social security coverage should be extended to homemakers.			
Congress	79.5	36.6	63
Statewide	75.0	37.5	16
State Senate	73.6	36.1	144
State House	70.4	32.7	826
Equal Credit			
A married woman should be able to obtain credit without the consent of her husband.			
Congress	91.5	54.9	71
Statewide	100.0	78.9	19
State Senate	91.7	54.8	157
State House	92.6	54.7	914

Pregnancy Disability Benefits
Working women who choose to bear children should not
receive compensation for workdays missed during childbirth and recovery

Congress	64.1	32.8	67
Statewide	70.6	41.2	17
State Senate	59.7	30.5	154
State House	56.4	25.4	874

[a]Feminist responses were considered to be "agree" or "strongly agree" on the items focusing on abortion, the ERA, child care, social security benefits for homemakers, and equal credit. Feminist responses were considered to be "disagree" or "strongly disagree" on the items dealing with pregnancy disability benefits.

[b]The most intense feminist response was considered to be "strongly agree" on the items focusing on the ERA, abortion, child care, social security benefits for homemakers, and equal credit. The most intense feminist response was considered to be "strongly disagree" on the item dealing with pregnancy disability benefits.

office, majorities or near-majorities of Republican candidates at most levels of office expressed feminist views on five of the six issues. The sole item that failed to elicit strong support among Republicans was the one focusing on universally available child care; on this item, support for the feminist position among Republican state legislative and congressional candidates dipped to about one-third. Among Democrats, large majorities at every level of office expressed positions congruent with those espoused by the feminist movement on child care and all other issues.

Just as attitudinal feminism on women's issues was not limited to Democratic candidates, it also was not limited to those who identified themselves as liberals (table 8.5).[22] Like party affiliation, ideology was moderately related to issue positions. Liberals and moderates greatly outnumbered conservatives, and on most issues a very large majority of liberals and a smaller majority (or a near-majority) of moderates expressed feminist views.[23] With few exceptions, support for feminist positions dropped below 50% only among conservatives.

However, even among conservatives support for feminist positions fluctuated between one-third and one-half on four of the six issue statements. As was the case for party differences in support, the single item on which support for the feminist position among conservatives was lowest was the one focusing on government provision of universally available child care. On this item, fewer than one-third of conservatives agreed with the feminist position. However, at the other extreme, three-fourths

TABLE 8.4

Partisan Differences in Support for Women's Issues among Women Candidates, 1976[a]

	Percent Who Gave Feminist Responses		
	Democrats	Republicans	Tau$_c$ =
ERA			
Favor ratification of the ERA[b]			
Congress	89.3	58.3	.34
Statewide	100.0	88.9	.15
State Senate	94.6	64.4	.37
State House	91.2	60.4	.41
Abortion			
Oppose constitutional amendment to prohibit abortion			
Congress	71.1	40.9	.34
Statewide	100.0	66.6	.39
State Senate	72.5	58.4	.21
State House	68.8	61.6	.15
Child Care			
Government should provide child care for all who desire it			
Congress	80.0	30.4	.54
Statewide	62.5	55.6	.54
State Senate	69.4	31.7	.47
State House	68.9	32.5	.45
Social Security for Homemakers			
Social security coverage should be extended to homemakers.			
Congress	88.4	60.0	.29
Statewide	87.5	57.2	.36
State Senate	82.9	59.6	.30
State House	80.4	57.9	.28
Equal Credit			
Married woman should be able to obtain equal credit			
Congress	93.6	87.5	.14
Statewide	100.0	100.0	.22[c]
State Senate	95.6	87.0	.21
State House	94.9	89.1	.20
Pregnancy Disability Benefits			
Working women should not receive compensation for childbirth			
Congress	68.9	54.5	.10
Statewide	85.7	66.6	.45
State Senate	69.7	46.6	.31
State House	67.2	40.3	.34

[a]Among respondents, there were 48 Democratic and 25 Republican candidates for Congress; 11 Democratic and 10 Republican candidates for statewide offices; 97 Democratic and 63 Republican candidates for the state senate; 560 Democratic and 392 Republican candidates for the state house.

[b]See table 8.3 for the exact wording of each of the issue items.

[c]tau$_b$

TABLE 8.5

Ideological Differences in Support for Women's Issues among Women Candidates, 1976[a]

| | Percent Who Gave Feminist Responses | | | |
	Liberals	Moderates	Conservatives	Tau$_c$ =
ERA				
Favor ratification of the ERA[b]				
Congress	92.6	92.3	31.3	.39
State Senate	100.0	83.6	36.3	.45
State House	96.6	77.8	44.8	.48
Abortion				
Oppose constitutional amendment to prohibit abortion				
Congress	85.2	38.5	42.9	.43
State Senate	78.7	68.5	33.3	.31
State House	74.2	61.3	54.1	.22
Child Care				
Government should provide child care for all who desire it				
Congress	92.3	66.6	18.8	.56
State Senate	85.0	30.7	25.0	.55
State House	75.8	41.5	30.4	.42
Social Security for Homemakers				
Social security coverage should be extended to homemakers				
Congress	96.0	83.4	38.5	.43
State Senate	86.4	73.9	45.5	.38
State House	88.5	64.3	49.7	.36
Equal Credit				
Married women should be able to obtain equal credit				
Congress	100.0	92.4	81.3	.18
State Senate	96.7	92.9	75.0	.22
State House	96.7	92.0	85.5	.26
Pregnancy Disability Benefits				
Working women should not receive compensation for childbirth				
Congress	72.0	61.6	42.9	.12
State Senate	75.8	50.0	47.8	.32
State House	77.9	45.5	32.9	.40

[a]Among respondents, there were 28 liberal, 14 moderate, and 16 conservative candidates for Congress; 63 liberal, 58 moderate, and 25 conservative candidates for the state senate; 364 liberal, 263 moderate, and 219 conservative candidates for the state house. Figures are not presented for statewide candidates because the number of cases was too small for meaningful analysis (5 liberals, 10 moderates, 3 conservatives).

[b]See table 8.3 for the exact wording of each of the issue items.

or more of self-identified conservatives believed that married women should be able to obtain credit without the consent of their husbands.

Support for Women's Issues among Candidates Elected to Office

The findings of high levels of support for feminist positions on women's issues among candidates in 1976 describe the views of women elected to office as well. The issue positions of women who won their general election bids were compared with candidates defeated in either primaries or general elections. There was an absence of even weak relationships between winning the general election and attitudes on the various women's issues for state senate and state house candidates.[24] Overall, defeated women candidates and general election victors were very much alike in their fairly strong support for feminist positions.

Attitudes toward Women's Issues in Unratified States

If there are certain areas of the country less conducive to the development of feminist political views than others, these areas probably are those states that failed to ratify the ERA. Many legislators in these states, mostly men, demonstrated their lack of support for the ERA by voting against the amendment. Because women candidates and officeholders in these states are products of the same political environment, one also might expect that they would show a lack of support for feminist positions on the ERA and other issues of concern to the women's movement.

The views of women candidates for the state senate and the state house in the fifteen states that failed to ratify the ERA and Indiana (which had not ratified at the time of the 1976 elections) were examined (table 8.6).[25] More than 50% of the candidates for the state legislatures in unratified states expressed attitudes congruent with the feminist movement's position on all six issue statements. On most issues, the proportion was well over 50%. Thus, even in these states where the greatest opposition to the ERA has been concentrated, women candidates in 1976 were disproportionately feminist in their views.

Particularly noteworthy was the strong support for the ERA in these states. Approximately three-fourths of candidates for both the state house and the state senate supported the ERA. More importantly, almost all of the supporters of the ERA seemed to hold their views intensely. Among candidates for the state senate, 68.8% *strongly* agreed that they favored ratification. Among candidates for the state house, the corresponding figure was 60.8%.

Of course, many of the respondents from the unratified states were not elected to office. When the final ballots were tallied in November, only

TABLE 8.6

Attitudes on Women's Issues among Women State Legislative Candidates in Unratified States, 1976[a]

	Percent Who Gave Feminist Responses	
	State Senate	State House
ERA		
Favor ratification of the ERA[b]	77.1	75.7
Abortion		
Oppose constitutional amendment to prohibit abortion	70.8	69.5
Child Care		
Government should provide child care for all who desire it	56.6	53.4
Social Security for Homemakers		
Social security coverage should be extended to homemakers	71.7	70.0
Equal Credit		
Married women should be able to obtain equal credit	92.0	93.9
Pregnancy Disability Benefits		
Working women should not receive compensation for childbirth	54.2	57.6

[a]There were 51 respondents who ran for the state senate and 202 respondents who ran for the state house in unratified states.

[b]See table 8.3 for the exact wording of each of the issue items.

27.5% of the respondents who ran for state senate seats had been elected. Candidates for the state house fared better; 41.6% were elected.[26] Nevertheless, like the candidate population as a whole, the victors were feminist in their attitudes toward the ERA. A total of 83.3% of the newly elected state senators favored ratification of the ERA—all of them intensely. Similarly, 72.8% of the newly elected state representatives favored the ERA—64.2% of them intensely.

It is possible, although perhaps unlikely, that male candidates and officeholders in the unratified states supported the ERA attitudinally at levels comparable to the levels of support found among female candidates in these states. Without comparative male-female data, it is impossible to determine conclusively that female candidates and representatives in the unratified states were more feminist in their support of the ERA than were their male counterparts. Nevertheless, the high level and intensity of support for the ERA found among women candidates in these states suggests that the fate of the ERA might have been different if women had held one-half of the state legislative seats in states that failed to ratify the amendment.

Intersection of Attitudinal and Behavioral Feminism

As one might expect, there was considerable overlap among those who could be classified as attitudinal feminists on the three measures examined in this study (sex-role attitudes, evaluation of the women's movement, and attitudes on women's issues). Almost one-half of women candidates at all levels of office appeared strongly feminist on all three attitudinal measures (table 8.7).[27]

Significant proportions—about one-fifth to one-third—of women candidates were both strong attitudinal *and* behavioral feminists. However, proportions equally as large were strong attitudinal feminists whose behavior on the measures examined in this study did not reflect their strong feminist sentiments (table 8.7). Because of the discrepancy between their attitudes and their behavior, these women might most appropriately be described as "closet feminists."

Summary and Implications

High levels of attitudinal feminism exist among women candidates and are related to party affiliation, but are characteristic of many Republicans as well as most Democrats. Considerably fewer women candidates report feminist behavior in terms of joining feminist organizations or initiating discussion of women's issues in campaigns. In fact, if one looked only at the reported behavior of women candidates, one probably would conclude that they are predominantly nonfeminist. The gap between the number of women candidates who show strong signs of attitudinal feminism and the much smaller number of women who translate these attitudes into behavior is due to the existence of those who might be characterized as "closet feminists." These women are committed to women's issues and to the goals of the feminist movement, but in large part their feminism remains hidden from public view—at least during the campaign stage of their public careers.

A sizable number of women candidates are both attitudinal and behavioral feminists who, if elected to office, are likely to work to pass legislation that would bring about greater equality between women and men. However, the question of whether increased numerical representa-

TABLE 8.7

Intersection of Attitudinal and Behavioral Feminism among Women Candidates, 1976

	Percent Who Were Strong Attitudinal Feminists[a]	N =	Percent Who Were Strong Attitudinal Feminists but Did Not Belong to a Feminist Organization	Closet Feminists		
				N =	Percent Who Were Strong Attitudinal Feminists but Did Not Initiate Discussion of Women's Issues in Primary Campaign	N =[b]
Congressional Candidates	48.6	64	28.6	55	20.7	43
Statewide Candidates	46.7	15	11.0	14	21.7	12
State Senate Candidates	51.4	142	30.8	131	22.8	63
State House Candidates	44.5	812	25.6	725	20.9	375

[a]Strong attitudinal feminists were those who:
(1) expressed feminist positions on all three sex-role items in table 8.1,
(2) evaluated the women's movement positively, and
(3) expressed feminist positions on at least four of the six issue statements in table 8.3.
[b]N's vary because of missing data. Also, in this case, only candidates who were opposed in their primary election bids were examined.

tion of women will lead to increased representation of the interests of women will depend as well on the behavior of those women who have been characterized in this study as "closet feminists."

There may be at least two reasons why the feminism of many women candidates remained largely hidden from public view before and during their 1976 primary campaigns. Some may have concealed their feminism intentionally because they feared that they would be stereotyped as concerned *only* with women's rights. Too much emphasis on women's issues in a campaign might lead to speculation that the candidate is narrow in her interests and would not adequately represent all the people. Candidates who perceive a danger in being so stereotyped may intentionally relegate women's issues to a secondary role, or, alternatively, may ignore them altogether.[28]

A second reason the feminism of many women candidates remained largely hidden from public view during their 1976 primary campaigns may be that remnants of the old "I'm not a Women's Libber but . . ." syndrome persist for many candidates. While most candidates support feminist concerns, many may not recognize and accept the degree to which their attitudes and concerns coincide with those of the feminist movement. They may not consciously perceive or identify themselves as feminists. As a result, their feminist attitudes remain latent and unactivated, and do not translate into feminist behavioral acts. The low level of membership in feminist organizations among women candidates in 1976 may be one manifestation of this latency. While many women candidates held beliefs congruent with the goals of many feminist groups, few had chosen to translate these beliefs into an organizational and behavioral commitment.

It is not surprising that past research has found women officeholders vote disproportionately in favor of the ERA.[29] To the extent that personal attitudes affect voting behavior,[30] women officeholders are likely to demonstrate support for feminist positions in voting, especially as long as those women who run for and are elected to public office continue to be disproportionately Democratic and liberal/moderate. Moreover, to the extent that male officeholders and candidates lack the strong feminist attitudinal support found among their female counterparts, an increase in the numerical representation of women should increase the representation of the interests of women in legislative voting.

However, if women officeholders are to represent the distinctive interests of women in ways that go beyond mere voting, we might expect them to do more than simply cast feminist votes on women's issues. We also might expect them to take leadership roles in developing legislation on women's issues and in paving the way for its passage. If many women candidates and officeholders are "closet feminists," the extent to which women take the lead in initiating legislation, influencing colleagues, and building coalitions will be determined largely by characteristics of the political environment in which they operate.

Previous research on women officeholders has found few listed projects related to women as among those of most concern to them, and few conferred frequently with their female colleagues about women's issues.[31] The suggested causes of closet feminism—fear of being stereotyped as narrowly concerned only with women's issues, and lack of conscious recognition and acceptance of feminist predispositions—could lead to these outcomes, especially in an environment not conducive to the open expression of feminism. If officeholders fear being stereotyped as too narrow, they are not likely to devote a large part of their time and effort to projects related to women. Similarly, women whose latent feminist attitudes have never been activated are not likely either to take the initiative in making a women's project one of their main concerns or to confer frequently with other women about women's issues.

If women officeholders are to improve the representation of the interests of women through becoming the prime movers of legislation to improve the status of women, conditions conducive to mobilizing the vast reservoir of latent feminist attitudinal support among women officials must be created. Removing the fear of being stereotyped as narrowly concerned with women's issues is likely to be difficult. Not only must the perceptions of women officeholders change, but also the attitudes of voters and other political actors must change. This change is likely to come about only gradually, as more women hold office and demonstrate that they can be concerned with women's rights and simultaneously serve the interests of their broader constituencies.

Efforts are underway which may succeed in mobilizing many of the women who have not consciously recognized and accepted their feminism. Perhaps the most important factor in activating the latent feminist support among female candidates and officeholders is a supportive network of other women who share feminist sentiments on women's issues and who can activate and sustain these sentiments. Such networks of women, focusing on mutual concerns, have been developing in recent years—for example, the Congressional Caucus on Women's Issues,[32] state associations of women public officials, and women's caucuses among state legislators in Connecticut, Illinois, Maryland, Massachusetts, Oregon, and Washington bring elected women together with one another and with other women to focus on mutual interests. Conferences of women officeholders and candidates, sponsored by organizations such as the National Women's Education Fund and the Center for the American Woman and Politics, also may help to activate latent feminist support. While the formal agenda of these conferences may focus on topics such as management skills, much sharing of other concerns and experiences takes place. Frequently, informal, supportive networks evolve from such gatherings.

If these efforts to link women officeholders into supportive networks of feminist women are successful in mobilizing the vast reservoir of latent feminist support, women officeholders may well exercise considerable impact in the area of legislation on women's issues. An increase in their numbers may well lead to a significant increase in the representation of the interests of women.[33] More and more women may take the lead in developing legislation, influencing colleagues, and building coalitions on policy issues of particular concern to women.

An overwhelming majority of women candidates, and of those elected, feel that they can do a better job of representing women's interests than their male counterparts. Of the women surveyed in this study, 90.4% of congressional candidates, 94.7% of statewide candidates, 85.9% of state senate candidates, and 77.7% of state house candidates believed that they would be more sensitive to the interests of women than would a typical male candidate.[34] Whether these women will, in fact, translate their attitudinal feminism into behavioral acts and thereby bring about better representation of women's interests can only be answered through future research. Nevertheless, the strong levels of attitudinal support for feminist concerns found among women candidates and recently developing efforts to mobilize this support should encourage those who hope that the election of larger numbers of women will lead to increased representation of the interests of women.

CHAPTER NINE

□ □ □ □ □ □ □ ■

Conclusion

THE NUMBER OF WOMEN among elective officeholders has been kept low partly, and perhaps primarily, by systemic limitations in the structure of political opportunity. In contrast to other research, which has emphasized sex-role socialization and thus women's own attitudes as explanations for women's relative absence from the political arena, this study has called attention to the ways in which political opportunity variables—objective aspects of the political situation not subject to direct control by the individual politician—function as impediments to increasing the numbers of women holding public office. Barriers in the political opportunity structure affect the recruitment of women candidates, reduce their probability of winning election, and constrain their future officeholding aspirations.

Some features of the political opportunity structure that help to keep the numbers of women officeholders low, such as access to financial resources and the advantage added by previous elective officeholding experience, probably pose greater problems for female candidates than for male candidates. However, other features of the political opportunity structure probably do not affect individual women much differently than they affect individual men. The power of incumbency and the paucity of open seats pose barriers for the male challenger just as they do for the female challenger. Proportionately as many men as women may be recruited by party leaders to run as sacrificial lambs in hopeless contests.

Nevertheless, the fact that individual men as well as individual women confront barriers in the structure of political opportunity does not negate the importance of these barriers to women as a group. The absence of a differential, sex-related impact at the individual level does not mean that a sex-related bias is absent in the aggregate. Barriers in the existing political opportunity structure work to keep outsiders out, regardless of sex, and to perpetuate the power of those who hold political positions. Since those who are in power are disproportionately men, the present structure of political opportunity helps to maintain the power of those men. Because far fewer women than men presently hold elective office, the barriers in the political opportunity structure work against women as a group to a far greater extent than they work against men.

This concluding chapter examines both possible reforms and actual developments that might help increase the number of women in elective office. Two distinct, although not incompatible, means for helping women to counteract the adverse effects of the political opportunity structure and capture a greater share of elective positions are considered. The first would involve direct and systematic efforts to alter those features of the political opportunity structure that work against women. Although such efforts potentially could lead to large gains in the number of women officeholders, reforms in the political opportunity structure have received little attention from those interested in increasing the numbers of women in elective office. A second possible means for counteracting and over-coming barriers posed by the political opportunity structure involves the mobilization of women in support of women candidates. Proponents of increased numerical representation have focused attention on this strat-egy. There is evidence of the development of an increasingly conscious relationship between women candidates and other women (and women's organizations), with women providing an added base of support that can help individual women candidates compensate for and overcome the adverse effects of the political opportunity structure. Although both structural reforms and the mobilization of women in support of women's candidacies offer potential for greater increases in the number of women officeholders, a strategy that includes both components holds the greatest hope for achieving parity in numerical representation between women and men in the short term.

Possible Reforms in the Opportunity Structure

Several possible reforms might make our electoral system more perme-able, thereby increasing the probability that larger numbers of women and members of other presently underrepresented social interests would be elected to office. One such reform is the setting of an upper limit on the number of terms incumbents can serve in high-level offices, such as the U.S. Senate and the U.S. House, now characterized by relatively low turnover. This step is not unprecedented in American politics, since U.S. presidents, as well as governors in more than one-half of the states, presently face constitutional restrictions on the number of consecutive terms they can serve.[1] Moreover, a rotational system for selecting representatives, limiting tenure in Congress to one or two terms, was adopted and implemented in many congressional districts during the nineteenth century.[2] Contemporary proposals to limit the number of terms of service often are opposed on the basis of loss of expertise, the lack of accountability during the final term, and shifts in the balance of power between executive and legislative branches of government. While these are legitimate concerns, the benefits of a well-conceived proposal in creating more open seats and perhaps thereby promoting better representation in the intergroup sense (see chapter 2) might outweigh the costs.

Another way in which our electoral system might be made more permeable to women and other underrepresented social interests is through stricter curbs on, and/or more careful monitoring of, officeholders' use of franking privileges, office staff, and travel at public expense during campaign seasons. For incumbents, there is a fine line between using the resources of office to perform officeholding duties and using those resources to further re-election bids. Although mailings to constituents and trips to one's constituency are desirable because they facilitate representation, these often become more frequent as an election draws near. Any reform that would discourage or prohibit incumbents from using the resources of their offices for campaign purposes might work to the advantage of women and other underrepresented groups who most frequently run as challengers.[3]

Some types of campaign finance reform also would work to increase the representation of women and other underrepresented social interests by offsetting the advantages of incumbency. Gary Jacobson's work is particularly informative in this regard. Jacobson's analysis of campaign spending in congressional elections shows that some types of reform, specifically limits on campaign contributions and ceilings on spending by candidates, actually lessen competition and work to the advantage of incumbents. As Jacobson has explained:

> Even though incumbents raise money more easily from all sources, limits on campaign contributions will not help challengers because the problem is *not* equalizing spending between candidates but rather simply getting more money to challengers so that they can mount competitive races. Anything that makes it harder to raise campaign funds is to their detriment.[4]

Challengers would be most advantaged by substantial public subsidies or any other policy change which would increase the amount of money they have available, even if the reform also channels more money to incumbents.

Few advocates of campaign finance reform would favor a proposal for public financing with no ceiling on overall spending, since such a proposal would not reduce, and might even increase, the influence of special-interest money. However, a campaign finance reform package, combining public subsidies with a high enough limit on spending to allow challengers to compete effectively with incumbents, might facilitate increased movement of women and other underrepresented groups into elected office.

No reform can mandate changes in the attitudes of local and state party leaders who overlook women when recruiting candidates for winnable races. However, the heightened involvement of women at the national level within the parties' structures, especially in the Democratic party, which has required that one-half of all elected delegates to national conventions must be women, may over time have an impact on the recruitment practices of state and local leaders. As women become more involved in party affairs, they may themselves become formal or informal party leaders. Alternatively, they may have an influence on men who are in state and local party leadership positions. If these female party activists are more concerned with women's advancement in the political arena than party leaders have been in the past, their presence may lead to more party recruitment of women in situations where they can win.

Until the attitudes of state and local party leaders change, women stand a better chance of being recruited by party leaders for winnable races in multimember than in single-member districts. As a result, the trend toward the conversion of multimember state legislative districts to single-member districts should concern those who desire an increase in the number of women officeholders. In the absence of major changes in the attitudes of party leaders, the conversion of multimember to single-member districts, if unchecked, may well work against increased numerical representation of women.

The Effect of the Gender Gap in Expanding Political Opportunities

Reforms in the political opportunity structure along the lines suggested in the previous section would go a long way toward bringing about parity in the numerical representation of women and men. However, just as the payoffs from changes in the political opportunity structure potentially are great, so too are the obstacles to the enactment of such reforms. One of the most obvious and important obstacles is the fact that reforms must be enacted by the beneficiaries of the existing system. And those who hold office are not likely to be predisposed to pass reforms that will work to the advantage of those who might challenge them.

Changes in the political opportunity structure rarely are easily attained, and under usual circumstances they could be expected to come about only through the mobilization of large numbers of people and considerable resources. However, the development in the early 1980s of a "gender gap" in public opinion and voting behavior, which initially emerged without specific organized efforts to mobilize it, seems to have brought about at least temporary changes in one component of the political opportunity structure—the attitudes of party leaders toward women candidates.

In the 1980 presidential election, men voted overwhelmingly for Ronald Reagan while women split their votes almost evenly between Reagan and Jimmy Carter. After the election, women and men continued to diverge in their attitudes toward Reagan, with women more likely to disapprove of Reagan's performance as president. A difference in party identification between women and men also developed after the election, with women more likely to identify with the Democratic party. In the 1982 elections, this so-called "gender gap" was again apparent in voting. Women more often than men voted Democratic in U.S. House elections, and notable sex differences in candidate preferences were apparent in several U.S. Senate and gubernatorial contests. In a few cases, such as those of Governor Mario Cuomo in New York and Governor James Blanchard in Michigan, the votes of women provided the margin of victory to the Democratic candidate. Although sex differences in voting and opinion have appeared before, never before have they been so deep and so sustained. Nor have such differences ever been the subject of so much attention from the media and politicians.[5]

The existence of this gender gap in evaluations of political phenomena has created political opportunities for women which might not have existed in the absence of such a gap. Perhaps Ronald Reagan appointed Sandra Day O'Connor to the Supreme Court because of a desire to bring an end to women's exclusion from that deliberative body, but many viewed O'Connor's appointment as an attempt to woo women voters. Similarly, the midterm appointments of Margaret Heckler as Secretary of

Health and Human Services and Elizabeth Dole as Secretary of Transportation were seen by some as attempts to counter Reagan's "problem" with women.

Just as the gender gap may have provided opportunities for women in terms of these very visible appointments, it appears to have affected the national parties' attitudes toward women candidates. Both national parties, apparently convinced that female candidates have become assets rather than liabilities, began making greater efforts to support women candidates in the early 1980s than they had in the 1970s.

In 1982 the Democratic party, which has had less money to give to candidates than the Republican party, established the Eleanor Roosevelt Fund to raise money specifically for women candidates. In 1982, this fund gave $50,000 to 267 candidates.[6] Democrats also claimed that they were looking for capable women candidates, and they included special components for women candidates in party-sponsored candidate training sessions.[7]

The Republican party, concerned with bridging the gender gap by appealing to women voters, also began voicing support for women's candidacies. Party influentials hoped that women candidates could attract the votes of women who otherwise might vote Democratic. As Richard Lugar, chairman of the Republican Senate Campaign Committee, noted, "If there is a national difference in support for the Republican Party between men and women, it behooves the party to take a look at how the gap might be closed in a hurry."[8] Lugar found what he thought might be one way to close the gap. He announced that the Senatorial Compaign Committee would provide the maximum legal financial support to any woman nominated by the Republican party for a U.S. Senate seat in 1984, regardless of her prospects for victory. Although the committee normally does not get involved in primaries, Lugar claimed that he also would consider providing assistance to women candidates prior to their nomination.

If the gender gap in political attitudes and behavior (or its perceived importance) fades in the mid to late 1980s, so too may the national parties' newly found commitment to supporting women candidates for congressional offices. The change in this feature of the political opportunity structure—party leaders' attitudes—may prove to be only temporary. Alternatively, however, the parties may, in fact, discover that women make good candidates. Moreover, the national parties' commitment to supporting women candidates may spill over to affect the recruitment practices of state and local party leaders and a more permanent change in the political opportunity structure may result. More permanent change is most likely if women's movement organizations succeed in organizing and sustaining the gender gap. Regardless of how long the increased level of national party support for women candidates lasts, the gender gap has created a climate of support for women candidates that is more favorable than that which women faced in the 1970s. Women candidates in the early 1980s are perceived as likely to pull in extra votes, and this perception provides women with clout and opportunities they previously lacked. If women are able to capitalize upon this climate of support, some significant short-term gains in numerical representation may be possible.

The Mobilization of Women to Support Women Candidates

Aside from the apparent change in party leaders' attitudes toward women candidates brought about by the gender gap, few efforts are underway that are likely to lead to fundamental alterations in the political opportunity structure and accompanying significant increases in political opportunities for women. However, there have been promising developments on another front. The efforts of feminist organizations and evidence from women's campaigns suggest the development of an increasingly conscious relationship between women candidates and other women. In races where aspects of the political opportunity structure work against women candidates, the support of women and women's groups can help women run competitively and contribute to a victory. A discussion of recent efforts of feminist groups and some specific examples of how women candidates appealed to, and received support from, other women in the 1982 elections serve to illustrate the developing relationship between women who seek office and other women.

Feminist Organizations and Support for Women Candidates
Since its founding in 1971, the National Women's Political Caucus (NWPC) has had as one of its primary goals the election of more women to public office.[9] As early as 1974, the NWPC developed its first "Win With Women" program to encourage and support women running for office, and the Caucus has had a "Win With Women" campaign in every subsequent major election. However, much of the NWPC's energy and resources, like those of NOW, were channeled before 1982 into the drive to ratify the ERA. Although the Caucus has always been concerned with electing more women to office, a large proportion of the NWPC's electoral involvement during the late 1970s and early 1980s focused on electing and defeating legislators in unratified states, many of whom were men.

Since the battle for ratification of the ERA ended, the Caucus has focused its efforts more directly on the election of women to public office. Under the leadership of Kathy Wilson, who became chair of the NWPC in 1981, the Caucus renewed its commitment to electing large numbers of women, especially to state legislatures. The battle for the ERA led Wilson and others in the Caucus to the conclusion that the future of the ERA, if passed by Congress a second time and sent to the states for ratification, may well depend on the election of larger numbers of women state representatives. As Wilson noted in her speech at the NWPC's biennial convention in San Antonio in July 1983:

> We lost the Equal Rights Amendment, not because we failed to win the hearts and minds of the American public—we did that—but because we are not yet sufficiently represented in those institutions which govern our lives. . . . That's why, right now, right here, we affirm our commitment to recruiting, training, financing and electing women to political office. This has been, and will continue to be, our primary agenda.[10]

The other major feminist membership organization, the National Organization for Women (NOW), reached a similar conclusion and began to channel resources in the same direction. While the commitment to the election of more women to office was for the NWPC a return to one of the organization's original goals, such a commitment represented a step in a new direction for NOW. NOW, which in the early 1970s was not oriented toward electoral activity, became increasingly involved in electoral politics as the struggle for the ERA waged on. However, its efforts were concentrated largely on key legislative races in unratified states. Since the June 1982 deadline for ERA ratification, NOW, like the NWPC, has turned more of its attention (and its much larger pool of resources) to electing women to public office. One reporter had this to say about NOW's annual conference held in Washington, D.C., in early October 1983:

> Although the visits by NOW's male presidential suitors grabbed most of the headlines, more conference time was actually spent discussing women's candidacies, from local office to the vice-presidency. NOW is developing into a quasi-women's party of late, taking the lead in finding, grooming and supporting women candidates around the country.[11]

A fund-raising letter from NOW President Judy Goldsmith sent to the organization's members shortly after NOW's 1983 convention announced the initiation of a "Women's Political Development Campaign" aimed at electing more women to office at every level of government. Components of this campaign include research to identify districts where women have the best chance of defeating incumbents with poor records on women's rights, recruitment of women candidates, and candidate training seminars.

In addition to the new initiatives on the part of NOW and the NWPC, other support services for women candidates have been in place for some time. The National Women's Education Fund (NWEF), a nonprofit educational organization founded in 1972, has a history of offering campaign training and resource materials to potential women candidates. The Women's Campaign Fund (WCF), a national political action committee for women candidates, founded in 1974, gave $270,000 in cash and in-kind contributions to federal and state candidates in 1982.[12] The WCF also assists candidates in raising money by providing them with contacts with other political action committees. At the national level, NOW has the NOW/PAC, which contributes to federal races, and the NOW/EQUALITY/PAC, which focuses on state and local contests. NOW's PACs contributed about $1.5 million to candidates in 1982. Like NOW, the NWPC also has a federal political action committee, the Campaign Support Committee, and a PAC that donates to state legislative candidates, the Win With Women Fund. The NWPC's PACs gave about $50,000 to congressional candidates and $500,000 to candidates in various states in 1982.[13] Several small, state-based PACs, unaffiliated with NOW or the NWPC, also have sprung up in recent years.[14]

The new initiatives on the part of NOW and the NWPC, combined with existing programs of women's movement organizations to assist women candidates, suggest the beginnings of what may evolve into a comprehensive strategy for identifying and recruiting women candidates in winnable electoral situations and supporting their candidacies. For perhaps the first time in history, the potential and the commitment exist for developing a mechanism that can do for women candidates what political parties, in areas of the country where parties are strong, traditionally have done for male candidates. Although it is too early to assess the impact of this growing commitment to recruit and support women candidates, the potential, if fully realized, could have a significant effect in helping women overcome the obstacles posed by the structure of political opportunity.

Women's Support for Women Candidates in the 1982 Elections

The more elements of the political opportunity structure work against a woman candidate, the more she is likely to need "extra" support that can help her overcome the barriers which stand in the way of victory. The support of women and women's organizations can be especially critical to women candidates who confront adverse electoral situations. Such support may be less necessary or critical when most features of the political opportunity structure work to the advantage of, or at least not against, a woman candidate. Some specific examples from the 1982 elections help to illustrate this relationship between the impact of the political opportunity structure and the importance of the support of women and women's organizations.

In situations where elements of the political opportunity structure do not work against a woman candidate, she can in many cases run competitively despite a lack of strong support from women and women's organizations. A case in point is Nancy Johnson, a Republican elected in 1982 to Congress from Connecticut's Sixth District. Johnson ran for an open seat vacated when Toby Moffett chose to run for the U.S. Senate. Johnson had considerable political experience. She had long been active in community affairs, ran unsuccessfully for the city council in 1975, was elected in 1976 to the state senate, where she served three terms, and co-chaired Ronald Reagan's 1980 primary campaign in Connecticut.

When Moffett decided to run for the Senate, Johnson quickly jumped into the race for the vacated seat. Within a short time, she obtained the backing of the Republican party establishment. She easily won the endorsement of the party nominating convention in her district, although her opponent, conservative Nicholas Schaus, attracted enough votes to force a primary election, which Johnson won with 70% of the vote. Johnson, who represented a Democratic district in the state senate, went on to defeat her liberal Democratic opponent, State Senator William Curry, Jr., and to become one of the few Republicans elected in 1982 to succeed a Democrat in Congress.

Johnson outspent her opponent, with expenditures for her campaign totaling almost $500,000. She received substantial financial support both from her party and from the business community.

Running for an open seat in a competitive district, with strong support from her party and substantial financial backing, Johnson was able to win without strong and uniform support from women and feminist groups. She did receive some support from women; for example, she was backed by the Women's Campaign Fund in the primary, and both Senator Nancy Kassebaum and former First Lady Betty Ford came to Connecticut to campaign on her behalf. However, NOW endorsed her Democratic opponent, while the NWPC endorsed neither candidate. Johnson supported many of the issues of concern to feminists, including the ERA, a woman's right to choose abortion, Medicaid funding for abortions, and joint state and federal funding of child care centers. In the Connecticut senate, she sponsored bills to establish shelters for battered women and to provide tax incentives for businesses which establish day care facilities for their employees. Nevertheless, many women and women's groups did not throw their support strongly behind Johnson, because her Democratic opponent, Curry, also was a strong supporter of women's rights who, in addition, campaigned against many of the policies of the Reagan administration which they viewed as harmful to women.[15]

More typical than candidates like Johnson who run with most elements of the political opportunity structure operating in their favor are women who run in situations where at least some features of the political opportunity structure work to their disadvantage. In these cases, the support of women and/or women's organizations can give their campaigns the extra boost necessary to help offset disadvantages stemming from the political opportunity structure.

Two cases in point from the 1982 elections are those of Harriett Woods from Missouri and Gloria Molina from California. As mentioned in chapter 3, Democratic party leaders in Missouri were initially supportive of Harriett Woods's decision to seek the Democratic nomination for the U.S. Senate because they thought Republican incumbent John Danforth was unbeatable. However, when polls began to show that Republicans in general, and Danforth in particular, might be vulnerable in 1982, party leaders changed their minds and threw their support behind Burleigh Arnold, a banker and a major fundraiser for the Democratic party. Party leaders argued that Woods was too progressive to capture the necessary votes in the rural part of the state and that a woman could never attract the money necessary to run competitively against Danforth.

Woods, a two-term state senator who had never lost an election in twenty years of public service, was not deterred. Having introduced the ERA in the Missouri legislature and having then led the statewide drive for ratification, she had fought uphill battles previously. Woods defeated Arnold by a margin of two-to-one in the primary and came within two percentage points of defeating Danforth. Although she lost the general election, the fact that she came so close to defeating a fairly popular incumbent was a great accomplishment. As she explained, "To understand the full impact of what we did, you must understand where we started: without money, without traditional political support, without any statewide organization, and with very few people believing that a female state senator could mount an effective challenge against a well-financed, well-entrenched incumbent senator of the President's party."[16]

Woods was able to raise $250,000 in four months and $1.25 million over the course of the entire campaign, although Danforth still outspent her two-to-one. While much of her money came from traditional sources, she made specific appeals to women in an attempt to raise funds. According to Woods, many women who had never given to a political candidate before contributed to her campaign. She established the "100 Women Fund" with the goal of getting 100 women to contribute $1,000 each. While this goal was not reached, 49 women did write $1,000 checks to her campaign. Several women prominent in the women's movement and feminist community wrote fund-raising letters on her behalf.

Woods appealed to, and was helped by, women in other ways. The National Women's Political Caucus, the National Organization for Women, and the National Abortion Rights Action League endorsed her campaign. Woods campaigned hard against "Reaganomics" and Danforth's support for Reaganomics. In addition to her support for the ERA, she was openly pro-choice on the abortion issue. She favored a verifiable nuclear freeze. Perhaps in part because of these issue positions, polls taken during the campaign showed women voters supported her candidacy to a much greater extent than did men.

Woods blended an appeal to the traditional Democratic coalition—labor, the elderly, and minorities—with a special appeal to women. Running against a powerful incumbent and initially without party support, she needed something "extra" to make her campaign competitive. And in Woods's case, the "extra" came in large part from other women who responded to her appeals for assistance.[17]

Another candidate in 1982 whose candidacy was helped by strong support from women and women's groups was Gloria Molina, who in 1982 became the first Hispanic woman elected to the California legislature. Molina's campaign differed from Woods's in many respects. Because Woods was running statewide, most of her campaign expenditures went to buy media time. Molina, on the other hand, spent about four-fifths of her funds on mailings and ran a rigorous, door-knocking, grass-roots campaign. Although state legislative races in California are more expensive than in most other states, Molina had to raise much less money than Woods in order to run a competitive race. Molina made a bid for an open seat while Woods challenged an incumbent. Because Molina as a Democrat ran in a district that is about 80% Democratic, she, unlike Woods, had strong opposition only in the primary. While Woods and Danforth disagreed on almost every issue, Molina and chief opponent Democrat Richard Polanco agreed on most issues.

Despite these differences, the similarities between Molina's campaign and Woods's campaign are striking. Like Woods, Molina was a well-qualified candidate with a great deal of political experience. At the time she ran, she was chief deputy to California Assembly Speaker Willie Brown and had served as a deputy in the Office of Presidential Personnel in the Carter White House. She later was appointed to be Regional Director of Intergovernmental and Congressional Affairs for the U.S. Department of Health and Human Services. She also had worked as chief administrative assistant for the legislator who preceded her in California's 56th district.

Like Woods, Molina was not supported in the primary by the "power brokers"—in this case, the Hispanic leadership of Los Angeles. When the city's Latino leaders got together to decide who should run in the predominantly Hispanic legislative districts, Molina was overlooked in favor of Richard Polanco, her primary opponent. As was the case for Woods, those who opposed Molina's candidacy expressed doubts that a woman could be elected to office in her district.

Molina, like Woods, had a broad coalition of supporters and ran a strong campaign despite having less money than her primary opponent. And like Woods, she made a strong appeal to, and had strong backing from, women. In combination with her experience, a well-run campaign, and some aid from traditional Democratic bases of support such as labor, Molina's support from women enabled her to win 52% of the vote to defeat Polanco in a close primary and 83% of the vote to defeat her Republican opponent, Donald Hyde, in the general election. A core group of friends from the Comision Feminil of Los Angeles, a Chicana feminist organization of which Molina had been president, was important in encouraging Molina to run for office. Moreover, 75% of the $175,000 Molina raised came from women, women's networks, and women's political action committees. Molina's first $5,000 contribution came from California Assemblywoman Maxine Waters. Several other women in the California Assembly contributed to her campaign, and Los Angeles Councilwoman Joy Picus also helped Molina raise money.[18]

Conclusion

The lack of open seats, the advantages of incumbency, the accelerating costs of campaigning, and the reluctance of party leaders to recruit women for winnable seats pose formidable obstacles to increasing the numerical representation of women. By impeding the entry of women into elective office, they also have helped to impede representation of women's interests.

Any attempt to increase the numerical representation of women, if it is to be effective, must work either to change or to compensate for the effects of those elements of the political opportunity structure that work against women. If enacted, reforms that would directly alter barriers to women's movement into office imposed by the political opportunity structure could have high payoffs. Although proponents of increased numerical representation of women have not focused their attention on such reforms, direct reforms in the political opportunity structure are one direction for possible change that might merit more attention in the future.

The developing relationship between women candidates and other women (including women's organizations) is another possible avenue for change. In the absence of structural reforms, this relationship would seem to offer the greatest possibility for notable increases in the number of elected women officeholders.

In cases like those of Harriett Woods and Gloria Molina, where support from the parties and the traditional bases is not readily available, the extra boost of support from women and women's groups may help to make women's campaigns successful. The examples of Woods and Molina suggest that women candidates are realizing the competitive edge that such added support can provide, and women and women's groups show an increasing willingness to supply such support. As in the case of Woods, the added boost of strong support from women and women's groups may help candidates run competitively where features of the political opportunity structure converge to make the situation particularly adverse (e.g., running against an incumbent, without party support, and with little money). In other cases, strong support from women may help female candidates capitalize on situations where at least some elements of the political opportunity structure (e.g., the presence of an open seat) are less adverse, as in Molina's case.

If, in the future, more and more women are elected to office in part because women and women's organizations have mobilized to support them, the apparent relationship between numerical representation and representation of women's interests on policy issues dealing with women may become even stronger. The numbers of women candidates and officeholders who are "closet feminists" may decrease while the numbers who are behavioral as well as attitudinal feminists may increase. For as women candidates receive more support for their campaigns from women, they will be less likely to shy away from explicit identification with the interests of those women.

In the early 1980s, there were signs that the attitudes of women candidates on policy issues dealing with women were at least as strongly feminist as they were in 1976. The National Women's Political Caucus through state and local chapters collected data on the issue positions of women candidates in thirty-four of the forty-six states holding state legislative elections in 1982. They found that 78% of women candidates favored the Equal Rights Amendment and 60% supported both the ERA and a woman's right to choose an abortion. The proportions were slightly larger among those who were elected to office.[19] Similarly, a study of women holding elective office in 1981, conducted by the Center for the American Woman and Politics, found substantial support for feminist positions on women's issues among female state legislators, with notably lower levels of support among male legislators. For example, 77% of women state legislators, compared with 49% of their male colleagues, favored the ERA.[20] The growing relationship between women candidates and other women, and the increasing commitment of feminist organizations to recruiting and supporting candidates, suggest that strong attitudinal support for feminist concerns is not likely to diminish and may grow.

Not withstanding substantial barriers posed by the political opportunity structure, there are signs of change and reasons for optimism on the part of those who are concerned with increasing the number of women holding public office. The growing relationship between women candidates, women's organizations, and other women, based on an evolving awareness of what they have to gain from each other, is likely to decrease the length of time we must wait before parity in numerical representation and adequate representation of women's interests are achieved. If more effort also is directed toward political reforms which may lessen the adverse effects of the political opportunity structure, the goals of parity in numbers and adequate representation of interests may be achieved that much sooner.

APPENDIX A
Data Collection and Response Rate

This appendix discusses the pretests, the compilation of the names and addresses of candidates, the timing of mailings, the decision regarding organizational backing, and the representativeness of respondents.

The Pretest

An initial pretest of the questionnaire was conducted in May 1976 with fourteen women who had run in recent primaries for local or county offices in Bloomington and Monroe County, Indiana. Because the entire population of female candidates for statewide, state legislative, and congressional offices was to be included in the study, candidates for these offices could not be used for the pretest. Instead, the pretest was administered to candidates at local and county levels who had run recently enough to provide thoughtful and meaningful responses.

Based on the initial pretest, a number of changes were made in the questionnaire. These modifications seemed sufficiently significant to merit additional pretesting. As a result, a second pretest was conducted in early July 1976 with ten women who had run for local or county offices in the suburban areas of Maryland and Virginia surrounding Washington, D.C. The results of this pretest were very promising, and few additional changes were made in the measuring instrument.

Compilation of the Names and Addresses
of Candidates

The names and addresses of all women candidates across the country were compiled through a cooperative effort with the staff of the National

Women's Education Fund (NWEF). To obtain the names and addresses of candidates, letters requesting official filing lists for the primary were mailed to the secretary of state and/or the election commissioner, as well as to the major parties' headquarters, in each state. For most states, a list of all candidates who filed for the primary was obtained from one or more of these sources. (Where possible we obtained lists from multiple sources to cross-check names to ascertain that all candidates were included.) However, a few states did not compile official lists at the state level. In these cases, lists of women candidates were obtained from other sources. These sources included both feminist organizations and government employees, who either compiled lists for our use or had access to lists compiled for other purposes. In only one state, Vermont, were we unable to locate an individual or an organization who had compiled a list of candidates or was willing to do so. For this state, we wrote to every state legislative district clerk and every state senate district clerk requesting the names and addresses of candidates in their districts. Through follow-up letters and phone calls, we eventually obtained the names and addresses of all candidates in the state.

All names on filing lists that could not immediately be identified as male or female (e.g., Chris, Terry, Lynn, Shirley) were checked for gender by calling congressional offices in Washington, D.C., or, in some cases, by calling congressional district offices directly. Questionnaires were mistakenly mailed to a few male candidates because congressional offices occasionally provided incorrect information on the sex of candidates and because initially I naïvely assumed that names such as Kay, Connie, Junie, and Molly belonged to women when, in fact, they belonged to men. A few women with names such as Leon or A. J. also were initially excluded, but were sent questionnaires when the mistakes were discovered.

Despite problems with sex clarification, I am confident that the final list of 1,936 names represents the total population of women candidates within a very small margin of error for the following reasons:

1. There were several points during the course of data collection when mistakes in the list of candidates would have been discovered. First, following the primary in each state, we either placed a call or sent a list to a knowledgeable politico in the state to obtain primary results. (These results were later verified by obtaining official state lists of candidates for the general election.) These state contacts pointed out women who had been

excluded, or men who had been included, on our list. Similarly, our lists of candidates in the general election were sent to state contacts for verification or correction. In addition, information and materials on women candidates across the country were continually flowing into the NWEF and these, too, served as a check.

2. While all candidates who listed two initials rather than a first name were assumed to be men, this seems to have been a reasonable assumption. Through the series of checks described above, we discovered only one woman in the entire country who used a two-initial listing.

3. Of the few males discovered through our series of checks who were mistakenly sent questionnaires, most wrote back to explain that an error had been made. After being contacted as many as three times and asked to participate in a study of *women* candidates, most men seem to have been sufficiently offended or amused to inform me of their true sex.

The Timing of Mailings

Mailings of the questionnaire were staggered throughout the summer and fall of 1976. Primaries in the fifty states ranged from late April to early October. Many questions on the questionnaire dealt with the primary campaigns of the candidates. To permit candidates to reflect on the entire course of their primary campaigns, an initial copy of the questionnaire was mailed to each candidate shortly after the primary election in her state. For candidates in states with primaries before the end of July, initial copies of the questionnaire were mailed in late July. For candidates in states with primaries in August, September, and October, initial copies of the questionnaire were mailed during the week following the primary. For candidates in states where general election contenders were nominated through some means other than a primary, initial copies of the questionnaire were mailed shortly after a list of party nominees was received.

Approximately three weeks after the first mailing, a second copy of the questionnaire, with a second cover letter, was sent to any candidate who had not responded to the initial questionnaire. (The second cover letter included a handwritten P.S., thanking candidates for their assistance and asking them to complete as much of the questionnaire as possible, even if some questions were not applicable in their specific cases.) A reminder postcard was then mailed to candidates who had not responded after an additional two weeks had passed.

There was one major deviation from this pattern. For candidates with primaries in the early fall, the final mailing of reminder postcards should have taken place a week or two before the general election. However, to improve the response rate, the mailing to women who won fall primaries was delayed until after the general election. Candidates who lost fall primaries received reminder postcards on schedule.

The Decision Regarding Organizational Backing

Questionnaires were mailed from, and returned to, the office of the National Women's Education Fund in Washington, D.C. The cover letters for the initial and first follow-up mailing also were drafted on the letterhead of this organization. However, the cover letter made clear that it was an individual's study conducted for academic purposes.

An organizational backing for the study was considered desirable to add credibility to the study and to increase response rate. While I wanted backing by a women's organization to appeal to candidates' identification as women, I chose to avoid explicit identification with a feminist group because I feared that such an endorsement might introduce a feminist and/or liberal bias to the response rate. The NWEF is a nonprofit, nonmembership, research and education organization, rather than an activist membership group like the National Women's Political Caucus or the National Organization for Women. For this reason, and because of the nonfeminist nature of the organization's name, the NWEF seemed an ideal choice for organizational backing.

Representativeness of Respondents

To check for biases in response rate, I collected information for the entire candidate population, including nonrespondents as well as respondents, across a number of variables. This information was gathered from sources independent of the survey instrument itself. Information such as state and party identification was extracted from state filing lists. Incumbents were identified through sources such as *The Almanac of American Politics* and *The Book of the States*. Winners and losers of primary and general elections were ascertained in most cases by examining lists of general election candidates and/or newly elected officeholders supplied by the various state governments and/or parties.

The data below show the proportions of respondents and members of the candidate population included in each category of variables examined in testing for representativeness of respondents. In every case, except for the winners and losers of contested primary elections, the difference between the proportion of respondents and the proportion of all candidates in each category is less than 2%. Thus, these data suggest that, except for a slight underrepresentation of those who lost primary elections, respondents are highly representative of the candidate population as a whole.

Variable	Percent of Respondents	Percent of Total Candidate Population
Party		
Republican	40.6	41.4
Democratic	59.4	58.6
Level of Office		
Congressional	6.0	5.9
State Legislative	92.2	92.2
Statewide	1.8	1.9
Incumbency		
Incumbents	23.9	24.1
Nonincumbents	76.1	75.9
Region*		
New England	26.6	25.7
Middle Atlantic	8.6	6.9
East North Central	11.6	10.8
West North Central	14.3	16.2
Border States	5.0	4.7
Solid South	10.6	10.3
Mountain States	12.9	14.1
Pacific States	8.5	9.3
Noncontinental States	2.0	2.0
Participation in Primary		
Nominated by some means other than primary	6.0	6.4
Participated in primary	94.0	93.6
Contested Primary Outcome		
Won	45.0	39.9
Lost	55.0	60.1
General Election Outcome		
Won	48.0	47.6
Lost	52.0	52.4

*The regional groupings of states presented here are the standard categories used by the Center for Political Studies of the Inter-University Consortium for Political and Social Research. For a listing of the states within these regions, see, for example, the following codebook: ICPSR, *The CPS 1976 American National Election Study: Volume II*, pp. 610–612.

APPENDIX B
Questionnaire

SURVEY OF CANDIDATES FOR PUBLIC OFFICE

IN ANSWERING THE QUESTIONS BELOW, PLEASE CHECK THE APPROPRIATE RESPONSES OR FILL
IN THE BLANKS PROVIDED. THE NUMBER IN THE RIGHT HAND CORNER ABOVE WILL BE USED
ONLY TO CHECK RATE OF RESPONSE AND WILL NOT BE ASSOCIATED WITH YOUR NAME. ALL
RESPONSES WILL BE CONFIDENTIAL.

FIRST WE WOULD LIKE TO ASK SOME QUESTIONS ABOUT YOUR POLITICAL ACTIVITY.

1. What office did you run for in the 1976 primary? _____-

2. Which party's nomination were you seeking?

    ____ Republican   ____ Other party (PLEASE SPECIFY) _____
    ____ Democratic   ____ Independent

3. Were you opposed in your bid for your party's nomination?   ___Yes   ___No

4. Are you the incumbent of the office?   ___Yes   ___No
    If NO: Was the incumbent opposing you for the nomination?   ___Yes   ___No

5. Did you win or lose your 1976 primary election?   ___Won   ___Lost

6. Did anyone else's encouragement or persuasion figure importantly in your
    decision to run in the 1976 primary?

    ____ Yes (PLEASE SPECIFY EACH PERSON'S POSITION OR RELATIONSHIP TO YOU)

        _____

    ____ No _____

7. In the early stages of deciding to run for the office you sought in the 1976
    primary, did you talk with any party leader(s) about the possibility that you
    might run for this office?

    ____ Yes   ____ No
    If NO: Please skip to Question 11.

8. What positions or offices in the party did each of these people hold?

    _____

    _____

9. Did these party leaders initially approach you to talk about the possibility
    of running, or did you go to them?

    ____ The leader(s) approached me.
    ____ I went to the leader(s).
    ____ Some leaders approached me and I went to others.

10. Overall, how would you describe the reactions of these leaders to the possibility that you might run for this office?

_____ They encouraged me to run.
_____ They discouraged me from running.
_____ They neither encouraged me to run nor discouraged me from running.
_____ Other (PLEASE SPECIFY) _____

_____

11. Regardless of the outcome of your primary and/or general election this year, at some time in the future do you think you will run again for the office you were seeking in 1976?

_____ Definitely   _____ Probably   _____ Probably not

_____ Definitely not   _____ Don't know

12. Do you think you will ever run for any political office other than the one you ran for in 1976?

_____ Definitely   _____ Probably   _____ Probably not

_____ Definitely not   _____ Don't know

If DEFINITELY or PROBABLY: If you had the necessary political support and the right opportunities, what other elective political offices at the local, state, and national levels would you eventually like to hold? Please list all elective offices that might be of interest to you. _____

_____

_____

If DEFINITELY NOT or PROBABLY NOT: Please explain the major reasons why you do not think you will run for any other political office.

_____

_____

_____

_____

13. Which statement best characterizes the total length of time in the future that you would like to serve in elective political offices of all types?

_____ I would like to serve in elective political offices for a total of 4 years or less.
_____ I would like to serve in elective political offices for a total of 5 to 12 years.
_____ I would like to serve in elective political offices for a total of more than 12 years but do not plan to make a career out of elective public service.
_____ I would like to serve in elective political offices for a total of more than 12 years and hope to make a career out of elective public service.

14. Prior to 1976, did you ever run for public office in a primary, general, or any other type of election?

_____ Yes   _____ No

If YES: What public offices have you run for in:

(a) past <u>primary</u> elections?

Office	Level (local, county, state, or national)	Year(s) in which you ran in a primary for this office	Year(s) in which you won the primary for this office
_____	_____	19__,__,__,__	19__,__,__,__
_____	_____	19__,__,__,__	19__,__,__,__
_____	_____	19__,__,__,__	19__,__,__,__

(b) past <u>general</u>, <u>special</u>, or <u>nonpartisan</u> elections?

Office	Level (local, county, state, or national)	Type of election (general, special, or nonpartisan)	Year(s) in which you ran	Year(s) in which you won
_____	_____	_____	19__,__,__,__	19__,__,__,__,__
_____	_____	_____	19__,__,__,__	19__,__,__,__,__
_____	_____	_____	19__,__,__,__	19__,__,__,__,__
_____	_____	_____	19__,__,__,__	19__,__,__,__,__
_____	_____	_____	19__,__,__,__	19__,__,__,__,__

15. Were you ever <u>appointed to an elective public office</u> to fill an unexpired term?

_____ Yes   _____ No

If YES: Please list office(s) and year(s) of appointment. _____

_____

16. Have you ever held any <u>appointive governmental</u> positions?   _____Yes   _____No

If YES: Please list all appointive governmental positions you have held.

Position	Level (local, county, state, or national)	Years in which you held this position
_____	_____	From 19__ to 19__
_____	_____	From 19__ to 19__
_____	_____	From 19__ to 19__
_____	_____	From 19__ to 19__

17. Were you ever a delegate to a state and/or national political convention?

_____ Yes, state. When? 19__,__,__,__
_____ Yes, national. When? 19__,__,__,__
_____ No

18. How active are you in your state and/or local party organization?

_____ Very active   _____ Somewhat active   _____ Not very active

19. Have you ever held any elective or appointive positions <u>within your party</u>?

____ Yes   ____ No

<u>If YES</u>: Please list all party positions, both elective and appointive, which
you have held.

Position	Elected or appointed?	Level (local, county, state, or national)	Years in which you held this position
_____	_____	_____	From 19__ to 19__
_____	_____	_____	From 19__ to 19__
_____	_____	_____	From 19__ to 19__
_____	_____	_____	From 19__ to 19__

20. In the blanks provided below, please list all organizations (professional,
civic, social, political, etc.) in which you have been a member at some time
<u>during the past five years</u>. Then, in the parentheses to the right of the name
of the organization, place <u>all</u> of the following numbers that describe your
participation in the organization during this time.

1 = Held office or chaired a committee   2 = Participated on a committee
3 = Attended most meetings   4 = Attended some meetings   5 = Not active

_____ ( )   _____ ( )
_____ ( )   _____ ( )
_____ ( )   _____ ( )
_____ ( )   _____ ( )
_____ ( )   _____ ( )
_____ ( )   _____ ( )
_____ ( )   _____ ( )
_____ ( )   _____ ( )
_____ ( )   _____ ( )

NEXT WE WOULD LIKE TO ASK YOUR OPINIONS ON A FEW ISSUES.

1. Overall, how do you feel about the "women's movement" and its major goals?

____ Very positive   ____ Somewhat positive   ____ Neutral

____ Somewhat negative   ____ Very negative

2. Generally speaking, if you were elected do you think you would be more, about
equally, or less sensitive to the interests of women than a typical male
candidate?

____ More sensitive   ____ Less sensitive
____ About equally sensitive   ____ Don't know

3. On most contemporary issues, do you generally think of yourself as:

____ Very conservative   ____ Liberal
____ Conservative   ____ Very liberal
____ Middle-of-the-road   ____ Other (PLEASE SPECIFY) _____

4. Please indicate your degree of agreement or disagreement with each of the following statements by placing a number from 1 to 6 in the blank provided.

1 = Strongly agree   3 = Neutral   5 = Strongly disagree
2 = Agree   4 = Disagree   6 = Don't know

_____ a. The best way to handle the crime problem is to make punishments more severe.

_____ b. I oppose federal income tax deductions for child care services.

_____ c. It is more important for a wife to help her husband than to have a career herself.

_____ d. The defense budget should be reduced.

_____ e. I would oppose a constitutional amendment which would prohibit abortion under all or almost all circumstances.

_____ f. A woman can live a full and happy life without marrying.

_____ g. I would work actively to defeat the Equal Rights Amendment.

_____ h. Social security coverage should be extended to homemakers.

_____ i. In the long run, busing school children to promote racial balance will prove to be a good thing for the country.

_____ j. Women working in industry often need protective legislation beyond that which exists for men working in industry.

_____ k. The national and/or state government should provide child care services to all parents who desire them with fees charged for those services according to ability to pay.

_____ l. A married woman should be able to obtain credit without the consent of her husband.

_____ m. A working mother can establish just as warm and secure a relationship with her children as a mother who does not work.

_____ n. In rape cases, the burden of proof should lie with the victim.

_____ o. A man can live a full and happy life without marrying.

_____ p. I would favor a constitutional amendment which would return the authority to legislate abortion to the states.

_____ q. If a wife earns more than her husband, the marriage is headed for trouble.

_____ r. I favor the ratification of the Equal Rights Amendment.

_____ s. Working women who choose to bear children should not receive compensation for workdays missed during childbirth and recovery.

_____ t. It is much better for everyone involved if the man is the achiever outside the home and the woman takes care of the home and family.

_____ u. If a woman wants to have an abortion that is a matter for her and her doctor to decide, and the government should have nothing to do with it.

_____ v. The national and/or state government should provide child care services for those low income families in need of such services.

_____ w. Women who volunteer for active duty in the armed forces should be exempted from combat duty.

_____ x. Generally speaking, any able-bodied person who really wants to work in this country can find a job and earn a living.

BELOW ARE LISTED A NUMBER OF PERSONALITY CHARACTERISTICS. PLEASE INDICATE, ON
A SCALE FROM 1 TO 7, HOW TRUE OF YOU EACH OF THESE CHARACTERISTICS IS. PLEASE DO
NOT LEAVE ANY CHARACTERISTIC UNMARKED.

1	2	3	4	5	6	7
NEVER OR ALMOST NEVER TRUE	USUALLY NOT TRUE	SOMETIMES BUT INFREQUENTLY TRUE	OCCASIONALLY TRUE	OFTEN TRUE	USUALLY TRUE	ALWAYS OR ALMOST ALWAYS TRUE

No.	Characteristic		No.	Characteristic	
1	Self-reliant		21	Makes decisions easily	
2	Yielding		22	Compassionate	
3	Defends own beliefs		23	Self-sufficient	
4	Cheerful		24	Eager to soothe hurt feelings	
5	Independent		25	Dominant	
6	Shy		26	Soft-spoken	
7	Athletic		27	Masculine	
8	Affectionate		28	Warm	
9	Assertive		29	Willing to take a stand	
10	Flatterable		30	Tender	
11	Strong personality		31	Aggressive	
12	Loyal		32	Gullible	
13	Forceful		33	Acts as a leader	
14	Feminine		34	Childlike	
15	Analytical		35	Individualistic	
16	Sympathetic		36	Does not use harsh language	
17	Has leadership abilities		37	Competitive	
18	Sensitive to the needs of others		38	Loves children	
19	Willing to take risks		39	Ambitious	
20	Understanding		40	Gentle	

THE NEXT SET OF QUESTIONS DEALS WITH YOUR 1976 <u>PRIMARY</u> CAMPAIGN.

1. Would you say that the single most important objective of your 1976 primary campaign was to win your party's nomination for office, or was it something else?

____ To win the nomination
____ Something else (PLEASE SPECIFY) _____

_____

2. Approximately how long before the filing deadline did you make a <u>fairly definite</u> decision that you would run for office in 1976?

____ More than 1 year   ____ 6 months to 1 year   ____ 3 to 5 months
                ____ 1 to 2 months   ____ Less than 1 month

3. Did you have a campaign manager, coordinator, or director for your primary campaign?

____ Yes   ____ No

If YES: a. Was your campaign manager, coordinator, or director:
                ____ full-time, paid   ____ full-time, volunteer
                ____ part-time, paid   ____ part-time, volunteer

         b. Was this person one of your relatives?
                ____ Yes (PLEASE SPECIFY RELATIONSHIP) _____
                ____ No

         c. What previous campaign experience, if any, did this person have?

                _____

                _____

4. Did you have any <u>full-time</u> staff members? ___No ___Yes (HOW MANY?)_____

5. Did you have any <u>paid</u> staff members? ___No ___Yes (HOW MANY?)_____

6. What would you estimate to be the <u>total</u> number of volunteers who worked in your primary campaign?

____ Fewer than 10   ____ 25 to 49   ____ 75 to 99
____ 10 to 24   ____ 50 to 74   ____ 100 or more (HOW MANY?)_____

7. Approximately how many volunteers worked in your campaign on a <u>regular</u> <u>and</u> <u>continual</u> <u>basis</u>?

____ Fewer than 10   ____ 25 to 49   ____ 75 to 99
____ 10 to 24   ____ 50 to 74   ____ 100 or more (HOW MANY?)_____

8. Please <u>check</u> <u>all</u> of the following which were sources of volunteers for your primary campaign. Then <u>circle</u> <u>the</u> <u>one</u> from which you obtained the greatest amount of volunteer assistance.

____ Political party   ____ Friends of other family members
____ Family and relatives   ____ Organizations in which you <u>are</u> a member
____ Personal friends   ____ Organizations in which you <u>are</u> <u>not</u> a member
        ____ Other (PLEASE SPECIFY) _____

9. Did you personally campaign:

_____ on a __full-time__ basis throughout the campaign
_____ on a __part-time__ basis throughout the campaign
_____ on a __part-time__ basis during some of the campaign and on a
__full-time__ basis during the remainder of the campaign

10. Did you have one or more advisers who consistently played a major role in your primary campaign decisions?

_____ Yes _____ No

11. Did you have a comprehensive campaign strategy which was developed early in your primary campaign?

_____ Yes _____ No

If YES: Did you follow this strategy throughout the campaign?

_____ Yes, mostly _____ Yes, partly _____ No

12. Did you develop an itemized, projected budget early in your campaign?

_____ Yes _____ No

If YES: In retrospect, was this budget realistic? _____ Yes _____ No

13. Did you hire professionals to help with any aspect of your campaign (e.g., design of materials, management, advertising, polling)?

_____ Yes _____ No

If YES: What aspect(s) of your campaign did these professionals help with?

_____

14. Did you have a primary campaign headquarters? _____ Yes _____ No

If YES: Where was this campaign headquarters located (e.g., in your home, in a rented office, etc.)?

_____

15. Please list below any groups, organizations, and media that supported your candidacy, whether formally or informally. Also indicate the kinds of support they gave you.

Organization	Endorsement	Money	Campaign Workers	Other Support (PLEASE SPECIFY)
_____	____	____	____	_____
_____	____	____	____	_____
_____	____	____	____	_____
_____	____	____	____	_____
_____	____	____	____	_____
_____	____	____	____	_____
_____	____	____	____	_____

16. Which groups, organizations, and/or media, if any, opposed your candidacy?

_____

17. What were the major problems, if any, which you encountered in your primary campaign?

 (1) _____

 (2) _____

 (3) _____

 (4) _____

18. What advantages, if any, did you experience in your primary campaign?

 (1) _____

 (2) _____

 (3) _____

19. Approximately what <u>percentage</u> of the total amount of money contributed to your primary campaign was given by small, medium, and larger donors?

	None	25% or less	26-50%	51-75%	76-100%
Small donors (under $25)	___	___	___	___	___
Medium donors ($25-100)	___	___	___	___	___
Larger donors (over $100)	___	___	___	___	___

20. Approximately what <u>percentage</u> of all the money raised for your primary campaign was obtained through the use of each of the following strategies?

	None	25% or less	26-50%	51-75%	76-100%
Mail appeals	___	___	___	___	___
Personal solicitation	___	___	___	___	___
Events (meals, parties, concerts, etc.)	___	___	___	___	___
Sales (merchandise, bake sales, etc.)	___	___	___	___	___

21. In deciding <u>how to raise funds</u> for your campaign, did you get ideas from:

 (a) other people?   ___Yes   ___No

  If YES: Please specify the positions of these people or their relationship to you. _____

  _____

 (b) campaign manuals or other printed materials?   ___Yes   ___No

  If YES: Please list the manuals and/or printed materials you consulted. _____

  _____

 (c) your experience from a previous campaign in which you ran?   ___Yes   ___No

 (d) your experience from a previous campaign in which you worked for someone else?   ___Yes   ___No

22. During your primary campaign, how much did you use each of the following methods for contacting voters?

	Used a great deal	Used some	Used a little	Didn't use
Door-to-door contact by candidate	___	___	___	___
Door-to-door contact by campaign workers	___	___	___	___
Telephone contact by candidate	___	___	___	___
Telephone contact by campaign workers	___	___	___	___
Contact at public places (factories, shopping centers, etc.)	___	___	___	___
Appearances before groups of people (meetings, cocktail parties, etc.)	___	___	___	___
Door-to-door distribution of literature	___	___	___	___
Mailings to voters	___	___	___	___
Mass media advertising	___	___	___	___

23. In deciding which methods to use in contacting voters, did you get ideas from:

(a) other people? ___Yes ___No

   If YES: Please specify the positions of these people or their
   relationship to you. _____

   _____

(b) campaign manuals or other printed materials? ___Yes ___No

   If YES: Please list the manuals and/or printed materials you
   consulted. _____

   _____

(c) your experience from a previous campaign in which you ran? ___Yes ___No

(d) your experience from a previous campaign in which you worked for someone
   else? ___Yes ___No

24. During your campaign, did you try to identify those voters who were favorable
   to your candidacy and/or undecided?

   Yes _____ No

25. In contacting voters, did you focus more attention upon certain voting units
   (e.g., wards, precincts, election districts, etc.) within your constituency
   than upon others?

   _____ Yes _____ No

26. Did you organize any type of drive to get voters to the polls?

   _____ Yes _____ No

   If YES: Was this drive focused on those voters who were likely to vote
   for you, or on all voters in general?

   _____ Those likely to vote for me.
   _____ All voters in general.
   _____ Other (PLEASE SPECIFY) _____

27. During your primary campaign, how much did you use each of the following public relations techniques?

	Used a great deal	Used some	Used a little	Didn't use
Television advertising	___	___	___	___
Radio advertising	___	___	___	___
Newspaper advertising	___	___	___	___
Brochures, cards, flyers, etc.	___	___	___	___
Bumperstickers, buttons, etc.	___	___	___	___
Other (PLEASE SPECIFY) _____	___	___	___	___

28. During your primary campaign, what particular issues did you emphasize as most important? _____

_____

29. During your campaign, did you at any time discuss any "women's issues"?

____ Yes   ____ No

If NO: Please skip to Question 33.

30. Which particular "women's issues" did you discuss? _____

_____

31. Did you initiate discussion of these women's issues, or did you discuss these only when asked for your position on these issues?

____ I initiated discussion of these issues.
____ I discussed these issues only when asked by others for my position.
____ I initiated discussion of some women's issues but discussed others only when asked for my position.

32. In deciding what positions to take on women's issues, did you get ideas from:

(a) other people? ___Yes ___No

If YES: Please specify the positions of these people or their relationship to you. _____

_____

(b) campaign manuals or other printed materials? ___Yes ___No

If YES: Please list the manuals and/or printed materials you consulted. _____

_____

(c) your experience from a previous campaign in which you ran? ___Yes ___No

(d) your experience from a previous campaign in which you worked for someone else? ___Yes ___No

33. In the future if you were to run again in a primary for the office you sought in 1976, how many changes would you make in the strategies which you followed in your 1976 campaign?

____ None   ____ Only a few   ____ Some   ____ Many

FINALLY, WE WOULD LIKE TO ASK A FEW BIOGRAPHICAL QUESTIONS. MAY WE REMIND YOU
THAT ALL INFORMATION WILL BE KEPT CONFIDENTIAL AND WILL ONLY BE USED WITHOUT
YOUR NAME IN STATISTICAL ANALYSES.

1. What is your date of birth? _____

2. What is your highest level of schooling?

____ Grade school or some high school   ____ College graduate
____ High school graduate   ____ Some post-graduate work
____ High school graduate plus other   ____ Advanced degree (PLEASE
     noncollege training   SPECIFY) _____
____ Some college

3. What is your current marital status?

____ Never married   ____ Divorced or separated
____ Currently married   ____ Widowed

4. How many children do you have? _____

How many of these children are presently living at home? _____

Please list the ages of those children living at home. _____

5. Are you currently employed? ____ Yes, full-time ____Yes, part time ____No

6. If you are currently employed or ever worked for an extended period of time,
what is (was) your occupation?

_____

7. What is your religious preference?

____ Catholic   ____ Other (PLEASE SPECIFY) _____
____ Jewish   ____ No religious preference
____ Protestant

8. What is your racial or ethnic heritage?

____ Black   ____ Oriental
____ White   ____ American Indian
____ Spanish-speaking   ____ Other (PLEASE SPECIFY) _____

9. Was any portion of this questionnaire filled out by someone other than the
candidate?

____ Yes   ____ No

If YES: It would be very helpful if you could list those portions which were
completed by someone else. _____

_____

THANK YOU FOR COMPLETING THE QUESTIONNAIRE AND HELPING TO MAKE THIS PROJECT A
SUCCESS! PLEASE ENCLOSE IT IN THE POSTAGE PAID ENVELOPE AND MAIL IT AS SOON AS
POSSIBLE.

NOTES

Chapter 1

1. See Susan C. Bourque and Jean Grossholtz, "Politics an Unnatural Practice: Political Science Looks at Female Participation," *Politics and Society*, 4 (Winter 1974): 225–266.

2. In referring here to "classical democratic theory" as though it were a readily identifiable and monolithic school of thought, I am following a convention which has been employed by a number of contemporary scholars, but a convention which nevertheless entails some degree of oversimplification. Perhaps the theorists whose works most frequently are considered to be within the classical democratic tradition are Jean-Jacques Rousseau, Jeremy Bentham, James Mill, and John Stuart Mill. Certainly, important differences exist among these theorists as well as among others who might be lumped into this category. See Carole Pateman, *Participation and Democratic Theory* (Cambridge: Cambridge University Press, 1970), pp. 17–20, for a discussion of some of these differences. Nevertheless, it seems that most of those who refer to a "classical" democratic theory or tradition have in mind a body of pre-twentieth-century thought which emphasized the general importance and desirability of widespread and extensive public participation in decision making; it is this common thread which seems to link together an otherwise diverse group of theorists. In referring to "classical democratic theory" throughout this chapter, I consider the emphasis on the desirability of widespread and extensive citizen participation to be the defining characteristic.

3. Pateman, p. 18, argues that among the so-called "classical democratic theorists," two different theories of democracy can be found. The main difference between these two subsets of classical democratic theorists is that theorists such as Rousseau and John Stuart Mill (whom Pateman labels "theorists of participatory democracy") viewed participation as important not only because of its protective function, but also because of its self-enrichment function of improving the capabilities of those who participate. Other theorists, such as Bentham and James Mill, viewed participation as serving only the protective function of ensuring that the interests of individual citizens were protected.

4. The influence of the pluralist and democratic elitist strains has been so pervasive that Pateman, p. 14, footnote 1, has noted, "Almost any recent piece of writing on democracy will furnish an example of the contemporary theory."

5. Bernard R. Berelson, Paul F. Lazarsfeld, and William N. McPhee, *Voting* (Chicago: University of Chicago Press, 1954), pp. 305–323.

6. See, for example, Ibid.; Angus Campbell et al., *The American Voter: An Abridgement* (New York: John Wiley & Sons, 1964); William H. Flanigan and

Nancy H. Zingale, *Political Behavior of the American Electorate*, 4th ed. (Boston: Allyn and Bacon, 1979), pp. 97–153.

7. Just as so-called "classical democratic theory" is not a monolithic school of thought, the revisionists' attempt to construct a contemporary theory of democracy grounded in empirical reality has not led to a consensus on what the precise tenets of such a theory should be. Contemporary democratic theory has numerous variants, although it is frequently discussed as though it were a single coherent body of thought. See, for example, Pateman, and Jack L. Walker, "A Critique of the Elitist Theory of Democracy," *American Political Science Review*, 60 (June 1966): pp. 285–295. Robert Dahl, "Further Reflections on 'The Elitist Theory of Democracy,' " *American Political Science Review*, 60 (June 1966): 298, has maintained that those theorists who frequently are grouped together under the general rubric "democratic elitists" uniformly agree on little except for the desirability of representative government. While I find the general thrust of Dahl's argument persuasive, I do think it is possible to characterize some broad differences between the very loosely defined school of thought called "classical democratic theory" with all its variants and the very loosely defined school of thought of the revisionists with all its variants. These differences stem largely from the normative nature of the classical theory as compared with the descriptive or empirical nature of the contemporary theory, and they are important for explaining the lack of attention to questions about the representation of women.

8. See, for example, Berelson et al., p. 312, and Robert A. Dahl, *A Preface to Democratic Theory* (Chicago: The University of Chicago Press, 1956), p. 132.

9. Peter Bachrach, *The Theory of Democratic Elitism: A Critique* (Boston: Little, Brown and Company, 1967), pp. 8–9.

10. James W. Prothro and Charles M. Grigg, "Fundamental Principles of Democracy: Bases of Agreement and Disagreement," *Journal of Politics*, 22 (May 1960): 276–294; Samuel A. Stouffer, *Communism, Conformity and Civil Liberties* (New York: John Wiley & Sons, 1955); Herbert McClosky, "Consensus and Ideology in American Politics," *American Political Science Review*, 58 (June 1964): 361–382. All of these studies documented the antidemocratic tendencies of the mass public on items involving specific applications of democratic principles. Moreover, the latter two studies showed elites to be far more democratic in their values.

11. Contemporary democratic theory is descriptive in the sense that it explains the operation of the democratic system in the United States. However, contemporary theory, although often presented as value-free, also is normative. As Pateman, p. 15, has noted, "The contemporary theory of democracy does not merely describe the operation of certain political systems, but implies that this is the kind of system that we should value and includes a set of standards or criteria by which a political system may be judged as 'democratic.' " Moreover, to the extent that revisionists present their theory as descriptive and fail to address explicitly normative questions, they are, in fact, endorsing the status quo. This is a point that Dahl seems to miss in his rejoinder to Walker. Dahl, "Further Reflections," p. 298, argues that contemporary theorists have attempted to describe and explain how the present system operates without prescribing how democracy ought to work. Yet, by failing to prescribe how democracy ought to work differently than it now

does, the work of the revisionists can be construed as an endorsement (even if unintentional) of the status quo.

12. Lane Davis, "The Cost of the New Realism," in *Frontiers of Democratic Theory*, ed. Henry S. Kariel (New York: Random House, Inc., 1970), p. 226.

13. That early studies found women in the general population to be even less tolerant of minorities (and thus even less committed to democratic values) than men in the general population makes it even more apparent why those working within the revisionist tradition were not likely to be concerned with stimulating greater participation by women. See, for example, Stouffer, pp. 131–155.

14. This is not to say that questions pertaining to the underrepresentation of women and/or other politically disadvantaged and unorganized interests have been totally ignored by revisionist theorists. Robert A. Dahl, *Democracy in the United States: Promise and Performance* (Chicago: Rand McNally & Company, 1972), p. 49, for example, showed some sensitivity to questions of nonrepresentation by arguing that much of what he said about the American polyarchy, while true for whites, was not true for blacks. Nevertheless, prior to recent years, problems relating to the representation of unorganized interests have not been a major, or even a significant, concern of those working within this framework.

15. William E. Connolly, *The Terms of Political Discourse* (Lexington: D.C. Heath and Company, 1974), p. 48.

16. Berelson et al., p. 73. Before 1980 and 1982, when pronounced differences between women and men were apparent in voting, only the elections of 1952 and 1972 showed sex differences in voting for the major parties' presidential candidates. Women showed 6% more support for Eisenhower in 1952 and 7% more support for McGovern in 1972. See Sandra Baxter and Marjorie Lansing, *Women and Politics: The Invisible Majority* (Ann Arbor: University of Michigan Press, 1980), pp. 61–64.

17. Judith Hole and Ellen Levine, *Rebirth of Feminism* (New York: Quadrangle Books, Inc., 1971), p. 78.

18. Bourque and Grossholtz, p. 252.

19. It should be noted in addition that there were so few women in policy-making positions that it rarely would have made a difference in policy outcomes if women had behaved differently from men.

20. Throughout this and subsequent chapters use of the term descriptive representation has been avoided intentionally. What is referred to here as numerical representation, like the conception of descriptive representation described by Hanna Fenichel Pitkin, *The Concept of Representation* (Berkeley: University of California Press, 1967), p. 61, "depends on the representative's characteristics, on what he *is* or is *like*." However, as Pitkin, p. 90, has noted, the view of representation known as descriptive representation "has no room for any kind of representing as acting for, or on the behalf of, others"; descriptive representation involves only resemblance of characteristics and has no relationship to behavior. Because I prefer to allow for the possibility that an increase in the number of women serving in office may be linked in some ways to different patterns of behavior and to policy outcomes, I have chosen to use the term numerical representation rather than descriptive representation.

21. While I believe that sex-role socialization and political opportunity variables are empirically distinct as I have defined them, nevertheless they often reinforce each other, may work to the advantage of the same group of people (i.e., an elite), may in many cases stem from the same sources, and may lead to the same outcomes. For example, voter prejudice against women candidates (which according to my definition is a political opportunity variable) may well have the same source as an individual woman politician's belief that women are less suited emotionally for politics than men (which I have defined as a sex-role socialization variable). Moreover, in both cases these variables work to the advantage of those presently in power, and they may lead to the same outcome since both would work to prevent a woman from gaining office. Nevertheless, one is subject to control and possible alteration by the individual woman while the other clearly is not.

22. Consistent with this definition, two distinct subsets of political opportunity variables can be identified. One subset consists of attitudinal factors and behavioral predispositions, such as voter prejudice against women candidates and party leaders' bias against women, which may have stemmed from societal socialization processes. Although these variables have a socialization component, they are considered to be political opportunity variables because they are *external* to individual women politicians and are thus beyond their direct control. The second set of political opportunity variables consists of certain features of the structure and operation of the political system, including incumbency, presence of open seats, and number of seats in the district. While these factors differ from the first subset of opportunity variables in some important ways, they too are external to women politicians and not subject to modification or alteration by individual women.

23. Naomi B. Lynn, "Sexual Politics: Research Note" (Paper presented at the Annual Meeting of the Midwest Political Science Association, Chicago, April 29–May 1, 1976), p 1

24. See, for example, Jeane J. Kirkpatrick, *Political Woman* (New York: Basic Books, 1974); Kirkpatrick, *The New Presidential Elite: Men and Women in National Politics* (New York: Russell Sage Foundation, 1976); Marilyn Johnson and Kathy Stanwick, *Profile of Women Holding Office* (New York: R. R. Bowker, 1976); Edmond Constantini and Kenneth H. Craik, "Women as Politicians: The Social Background, Personality, and Political Careers of Female Party Leaders," *Journal of Social Issues*, 28 (1972): 217–236; M. Kent Jennings and Norman Thomas, "Men and Women in Party Elites: Social Roles and Political Resources," *Midwest Journal of Political Science*, 12 (November 1968): 469–492; Susan Tolchin and Martin Tolchin, *Clout: Womanpower and Politics* (New York: G. P. Putnam's Sons, Capricorn Books, 1976); Emmy E. Werner, "Women in Congress: 1917–1964," *Western Political Quarterly*, 19 (March 1966): 16–30; Emmy E. Werner, "Women in the State Legislatures," *Western Political Quarterly*, 21 (March 1968): 40–50; Irene Diamond, *Sex Roles in the State House* (New Haven: Yale University Press, 1977); Marcia Manning Lee, "Why Few Women Hold Public Office: Democracy and Sexual Roles," *Political Science Quarterly*, 91 (Summer 1976): 297–324; Paula J. Dubeck, "Women and Access to Political Office: A Comparison

of Female and Male State Legislators," *The Sociological Quarterly*, 17 (Winter 1976): 42–52; Charles S. Bullock and Patricia Findley Heys, "Recruitment of Women for Congress: A Research Note," *Western Political Quarterly*, 25 (September 1972): 416–423; Naomi Lynn and Cornelia Butler Flora, "Societal Punishment and Aspects of Female Participation: 1972 National Convention Delegates," in *A Portrait of Marginality: The Political Behavior of the American Woman*, ed. Marianne Githens and Jewel L. Prestage (New York: David McKay Company, Inc., 1977), pp. 113–138; Marianne Githens, "Spectators, Agitators, or Lawmakers: Women in State Legislatures," in Githens and Prestage, pp. 196–209; Elizabeth G. King, "Women in Iowa Legislative Politics," in Githens and Prestage, pp. 284–303; Frieda L. Gehlen, "Women Members of Congress: A Distinctive Role," in Githens and Prestage, pp. 304–319.

25. Some works have included a cursory examination of women candidates or of campaigning by women candidates. See, for example, Kirkpatrick, *Political Woman*, ch. 4 and 5; Tolchin and Tolchin, ch. 7; Virginia Currey, "Campaign Theory and Practice—The Gender Variable," in Githens and Prestage, pp. 150–171. Moreover, there is a very valuable and informative study of women candidates based on journalists' observations of women's campaigns during the 1976 elections. See Ruth B. Mandel, *In the Running: The New Woman Candidate* (New York: Ticknor & Fields, 1981).

26. A full discussion of "interests" and "women's interests" appears in chapter 2.

27. The reasons for the lack of a comparison sample of male candidates in this study are twofold. First, with such a large number of women candidates, resources were not available to conduct a comparable study of males. Even if financial resources had been available, however, selection of a sample of male candidates comparable to the females in this study would have been extremely problematic. Since filing lists for primaries in some states were not available until early fall, a random sample of males could not have been selected and questionnaires mailed until several months after the primaries in many states. This delay would have resulted in some inaccuracy in response (particularly to questions about primary campaigns) reflecting both diminished recall and interference stemming from the general election campaign. A matched sample of males also would have been difficult to select since a woman often was running in a primary against several male candidates. Any means of determining which of several male candidates to select probably would have led to a sample not truly comparable to the females. Yet, the major factor, overshadowing all others, which made any attempt to select a comparable male sample infeasible was the lack of complete and accurate lists of candidates in many states. Given the difficulty of obtaining the names and addresses of female candidates (see Appendix A), any attempt to obtain the names and addresses of all male candidates, of whom there were thousands, certainly would have been a nearly impossible task. The lack of comprehensive and accurate lists of candidates in many areas of the country probably is one reason why political scientists in the past have not undertaken nationwide studies of candidates for public office.

Chapter 2

1. Thomas R. Dye, "What to Do About the Establishment: Prescription for Elites," in Thomas R. Dye and Harmon Zeigler, *The Irony of Democracy: An Uncommon Introduction to American Politics* (Belmont: Wadsworth Publishing Company, Duxbury Press, 1972), pp. 362–371; Joseph Schumpeter, *Capitalism, Socialism and Democracy* (London: Goerge Allen & Unwin, 1943); Giovanni Sartori, *Democratic Theory* (Detroit: Wayne State University Press, 1962); Bernard R. Berelson, Paul F. Lazarsfeld, and William N. McPhee, *Voting* (Chicago: University of Chicago Press, 1954), pp. 305–323.

2. Peter Bachrach, *The Theory of Democratic Elitism: A Critique* (Boston: Little, Brown and Company, 1967), p. 32.

3. Jack L. Walker, "A Critique of the Elitist Theory of Democracy," *American Political Science Review*, 60 (June 1966): 287.

4. Robert Dahl, "Further Reflections on 'The Elitist Theory of Democracy,' " *American Political Science Review*, 60 (June 1966): 299–300.

5. Dye, p. 369.

6. Bachrach; Walker; Carole Pateman, *Participation and Democratic Theory* (Cambridge: Cambridge University Press, 1970); and Dennis F. Thompson, *The Democratic Citizen: Social Science and Democratic Theory in the Twentieth Century* (Cambridge: Cambridge University Press, 1970).

7. See, for example, Bachrach and Pateman.

8. This is not to say that the political system bears full responsibility for the low participation rates of women or of its citizens generally. To some extent, less than maximum participation undoubtedly is inherent in a society like ours where there are numerous nonpolitical demands upon any individual's time (e.g., economic subsistence, professional responsibilities, family needs) and where the size of the polity is so large that the probability of one's participation having a major impact is very small. Nevertheless, the political system should bear some responsibility as one force which contributes to low participation rates by providing too few opportunities and too little stimulation for participation in the political realm.

9. See, for example, Sidney Verba and Norman H. Nie, *Participation in America: Political Democracy and Social Equality* (New York: Harper & Row, 1972), pp. 95–101, Susan Welch, "Women as Political Animals? A Test of Some Explanations for Male/Female Political Participation Differences," *American Journal of Political Science*, 4 (November 1977): 711–730; Susan B. Hansen, Linda M. Franz, and Margaret Netemeyer-Mays, "Women's Political Participation and Policy Preferences," *Social Science Quarterly*, 56 (March 1976): 576–590; Angus Campbell et al., *The American Voter: An Abridgement* (New York: John Wiley & Sons, 1964), pp. 483–493; Berelson et al., pp. 25, 163.

10. See Marianne Githens and Jewel L. Prestage, "Introduction," in *A Portrait of Marginality: The Political Behavior of the American Woman*, ed. Marianne Githens and Jewel L. Prestage (New York: David McKay Company, 1977), p. 4. For specific works that have stressed the importance of sex-role socialization, see

Irene Diamond, "Why Aren't They There? Women in the American State Legis-latures" (Paper presented at the Annual Meeting of the American Political Science Association, The Palmer House, Chicago, Illinois, September 2–5, 1976); and Marcia Manning Lee, "Why Few Women Hold Public Office," in *A Portrait of Marginality: The Political Behavior of the American Woman,* ed. Marianne Githens and Jewel L. Prestage (New York: David McKay Company, 1977), p. 291.

11. Louis Harris and Associates, *The 1972 Virginia Slims American Woman's Opinion Poll: A Survey of the Attitudes of Women on Their Role in Politics and the Economy* (Louis Harris and Associates, 1972), p. 16.

12. According to figures furnished by the National Information Bank on Women in Public Office, Center for the American Woman and Politics, Eagleton Institute of Politics, Rutgers University, women as of 1981 constituted only 12% of state legislators, 11% of statewide elective officials, 6% of members of county governing boards, and 10% of mayors and members of local councils.

13. John Stuart Mill, "The Subjection of Women," in *Essays on Sex Equality,* ed. Alice S. Rossi (Chicago: University of Chicago Press, 1970), p. 216.

14. Ibid., p. 217.

15. Ibid., pp. 220–221.

16. John Dewey, "Democracy as a Way of Life," in *Frontiers of Democratic Theory,* ed. Henry S. Kariel (New York: Random House, 1970), p. 14, while not referring explicitly to women, has made a similar argument, suggesting:

> The very fact of exclusion from participation is a subtle form of suppression. . . . It is part of the democratic conception that . . . individuals are not the only sufferers, but that the whole social body is deprived of the potential resources that should be at its service.

17. Kirsten Amundsen, *The Silenced Majority: Women and American De-mocracy* (Englewood Cliffs: Prentice-Hall, Inc., 1971), p. 133. This also should be clearly disastrous from the perspective of most of those who are referred to as pluralists or democratic elitists. All within this tradition share a concern with questions pertaining to the nature of political leadership. One effect of what Amundsen calls a "sexist ideology" is to ensure that most women, even though they may possess whatever other qualities are valued in those who govern, are excluded from consideration as possible governors on the basis of sex alone.

18. Many of those scholars who would locate themselves at other points along the mass participation continuum also would find increased numerical representa-tion of women of interest for this reason.

19. One must consider the immediate and direct impact because in the long run males may be affected as much by implementation of these policies as females. Although some men may benefit immediately and directly from im-plementation of these policies (e.g., divorced working fathers with children might benefit immediately from the provision of child care), much larger numbers of women are likely to receive immediate and direct benefits.

20. In recent years there has been a growing recognition that public policy decisions on everything from foreign aid to cuts in social services have a differen-tial impact upon women because of women's location in the social structure. In this sense, virtually all issues are "women's issues." However, I am defining

women's issues more narrowly for purposes of this study. Foreign aid and cuts in social services may have a *differential* impact on women, but they have an immediate and direct impact on both sexes. In contrast, policies on issues such as rape, child care, abortion, and sex discrimination have an immediate and direct impact on much larger numbers of women than men.

21. Kenneth Prewitt and Heinz Eulau, "Political Matrix and Political Representation: Prolegomenon to a New Departure from an Old Problem," *American Political Science Review*, 63 (June 1969): 428.

22. Hanna Pitkin, *The Concept of Representation* (Berkeley: University of California Press, 1967), pp. 221–222, also has employed this intergroup conception of representation, suggesting:

> Perhaps when we conventionally speak of political representation, representative government, and the like, we do not mean or require that the representative stand in the kind of one-to-one, person-to-person relationship to his constituency or to each constituent in which a private representative stands to his principal. . . . Political representation is primarily a public, institutionalized arrangement involving many people and groups, and operating in the complex ways of large-scale social arrangements. What makes it representation is not any single action by any one participant, but the over-all structure and functioning of the system, the patterns emerging from the multiple activities of many people.

23. Ibid., p. 145.

24. Ibid., pp. 160–161.

25. William E. Connolly, *The Terms of Political Discourse* (Lexington: D.C. Heath and Company, 1974), p. 48, has observed, "Most American political scientists, working largely within the confines of a pluralist theory of politics, do not explicitly define 'interests,' but tend to equate the notion in practice with the political pressure an individual or a group brings to bear on government; often, too, 'interests' so understood are located by the investigator by identifying the policy preferences of the agents involved."

26. Hazel Erskine, "The Polls: Women's Role," *Public Opinion Quarterly*, 25 (Summer 1971): 286.

27. Ibid.

28. *Gallup Opinion Index*, 113 (November 1974).

29. For example, *The Harris Survey*, May 19, 1974; *The Harris Survey*, May 28, 1977; *The Harris Survey*, February 13, 1978; "Opinion Roundup," *Public Opinion*, April/May 1982, p. 32; *Gallup Opinion Survey*, June 1982.

30. Robert Chandler, *Public Opinion: Changing Attitudes on Contemporary Political and Social Issues* (New York: R. R. Bowker Company, 1972), p. 47.

31. Governing bodies also have not responded to the sentiments of men in the general population on these issues, since a plurality of men have been found to favor all women's issues discussed above. Consequently, representatives have been unresponsive to public opinion generally on issues dealing with women.

32. Jeane J. Kirkpatrick, *The New Presidential Elite: Men and Women in National Politics* (New York: Russell Sage Foundation, 1976), p. 336, note 21.

33. Gerald D. Berreman, "Race, Caste, and Other Invidious Distinctions in Social Stratification," *Race*, 13 (April 1972): 386. See also Gerald Marwell, "Why

Ascription? Parts of a More or Less Formal Theory of the Functions and Dysfunctions of Sex Roles," *American Sociological Review*, 40 (August 1975): 445.

34. Kate Millett, *Sexual Politics* (New York: The Hearst Corporation, Avon Books, 1971), p. 44.

35. This, however, seems to be a recent development. Joan Acker, "Women and Social Stratification: A Case of Intellectual Sexism," *American Journal of Sociology*, 78 (January 1973): 936–945, has pointed out that until recent years sociologists largely overlooked sex as a basis for social ascription.

36. Theodore D. Kemper, "On the Naure and Purpose of Ascription," *American Sociological Review*, 39 (December 1974): 852.

37. Sandra L. Bem and Daryl J. Bem, "Case Study of a Nonconscious Ideology: Training the Woman to Know Her Place," in Daryl J. Bem, *Beliefs, Attitudes, and Human Affairs* (Belmont: Wadsworth Publishing Company, Brooks/Cole Publishing Company, 1970) p. 89. One could argue that women not only have been socialized to accept their inferior status, but that they in many cases have come to identify their own status and survival with that of the males upon whom they must depend for financial support. As Millett, p. 62, has noted, "women are a dependency class who live on surplus. And their marginal life frequently renders them conservative, for like all persons in their situation . . . they identify their own survival with the prosperity of those who feed them."

38. Connolly, p. 62.

39. See, for example, Isaac D. Balbus, "The Concept of Interest in Marxian and Pluralist Analysis," *Politics and Society*, 1 (1971): 151–177; Grenville Wall, "The Concept of Interest in Politics," *Politics and Society*, 5 (1975): 487–510; Brian Barry, *Political Argument* (New York: Humanities Press, 1965), ch. 10; S. I. Benn, "Interests in Politics," *Proceedings of Aristotelian Society*, 60 (1960): 123–140. A particularly good review of various theoretical conceptions of interests is offered by Connolly, ch. 2.

40. A further discussion of women's interests and the representation of those interests can be found in Virginia Sapiro, "When Are Interests Interesting? The Problem of Political Representation of Women," *American Political Science Review*, 75 (September 1981): 701–716.

41. See William A. Gamson, *Power and Discontent* (Homewood, Illinois: Dorsey Press, 1968), pp. 59–70, for a discussion of conceptual and operational difficulties associated with attempts to measure impact of interest groups.

42. See, for example, Joyce Gelb and Marian Lief Palley, "Women and Interest Group Politics: A Case Study of the Equal Credit Opportunity Act," *American Politics Quarterly*, 5 (July 1977): 331–352; Anne N. Costain, "Lobbying for Equal Credit" (unpublished manuscript, Department of Political Science, University of Colorado).

43. In 1980, women were notably less likely to vote for Ronald Reagan than were men. A CBS/*New York Times* exit poll showed that 54% of men but only 46% of women reported voting for Reagan. See "Opinion Roundup," *Public Opinion*, December/January 1981, p. 42. Similarly, election day polls conducted by the major networks in 1982 found sizable differences between women and men in voting in many statewide races and in races for U.S. House seats. See Adam Clymer, "Women's Election Role is Disturbing to G.O.P.," *The New York Times*,

November 18, 1982; and Gloria Steinem, "Losing a Battle But Winning the War?" *Ms.*, January 1983, pp. 35–36 + .

44. For example Bachrach, p. 91, has maintained, "To the extent . . . that elites more closely reflected the socioeconomic, racial, and other characteristics of the many, the latter's 'end product' interest would probably be better served." Similarly, Amundsen, p. 66, has argued that there might well be a:

> . . . politically significant relationship between the proportion of representative positions a group can claim for itself and the degree to which the needs and interests of that group are articulated and acted upon in political institutions. . . . The more group members are in decision-making positions, the better chance the group has of fair and effective representation.

Chapter 3

1. Kenneth Prewitt and Alan Stone, *The Ruling Elite: Elite Theory, Power, and American Democracy* (New York: Harper & Row, 1973), p. 168. Prewitt and Stone have not specified in a precise manner what they mean by "different *types* of persons" from those occupying positions of power. Gaetano Mosca, *The Ruling Class* (New York: McGraw-Hill, 1939), is somewhat clearer on this point; to Mosca, a different *type* of person would be one representing a "social force" different from that represented by existing elites. James T. Duke, *Conflict and Power in Social Life* (Provo, Utah: Brigham Young University Press, 1976), p. 127, has explained that a social force was to Mosca "any substantial subdivision or segment of society, for example, major institutional spheres such as religion or education, or major segments of economic life such as commerce, land, or labor, which by their organization and aggregation exert considerable influence over social life." Feminists have written extensively about the ways in which women and men differ in their experiences, perceptions, and values although perhaps none more eloquently than Simone de Beauvoir, *The Second Sex* (New York: Vintage Books, 1974), p. xix, who wrote of woman:

> She is defined and differentiated with reference to man and not he with reference to her; she is the incidental, the inessential as opposed to the essential. He is the Subject, he is the Absolute—she is the Other.

The work of de Beauvoir and other feminist scholars would certainly point to the conclusion that women constitute a distinct "social force" and are different *types* of persons from men.

2. Mosca.

3. Prewitt and Stone, pp. 164–165, have noted, "if the established elite does not make room for those who are giving leadership to new social interests, then the counter-elite will turn to extralegal, usually violent, methods of claiming the power which is their due."

4. Figures furnished by the National Information Bank on Women in Public Office, Center for the American Woman and Politics, Eagleton Institute of Politics, Rutgers University. Another key sign has been the increase in the proportion of women among national party convention delegates. Reforms in delegate selection procedures and intensive efforts by feminist organizations, particularly the National Women's Political Caucus, increased the proportion of women among

national party convention delegates from between 10% and 17% in the 1950s and 1960s to 39.9% for Democrats and 29.8% for Republicans in 1972. In 1976, 33.7% of Democratic delegates and 31.5% of Republican delegates were women; see Naomi Lynn, "American Women and the Political Process," in *Women: A Feminist Perspective*, 2nd ed., ed. Jo Freeman (Palo Alto: Mayfield Publishing Company, 1979), p. 414. In 1980 the Democratic rules required equal division of delegates between the sexes; as a result, half the delegates to the 1980 Democratic convention were women compared to 29% of delegates to the Republican convention (Karlyn Barker and Bill Peterson, "The Women Delegates: Substantial Clout But a Sense of Frustration, Division," *The Washington Post*, August 13, 1980, p. A14).

5. V. O. Key, Jr., *American State Politics* (New York: Knopf Publishers, 1956), p. 271, has noted, "perhaps the most important function that party leadership needs to perform is the development, grooming, and promotion of candidates for . . . offices."

6. See Robert Agranoff, *The New Style in Election Campaigns* (Boston: Holbrook Press, 1972), p. 8.

7. For example, Frank Sorauf *Party and Representation: Legislative Politics in Pennsylvania* (New York: Atherton Press, 1963), p. 53, observed that parties dominated and controlled the nominating process in Pennsylvania. John C. Wahlke, Heinz Eulau, William Buchanan, and LeRoy C. Ferguson, *The Legislative System: Explorations in Legislative Behavior* (New York: John Wiley and Sons, 1962), p. 100, in a comparative study of the recruitment of legislators in California, Tennessee, Ohio, and New Jersey, found parties play a dominant role in the recruitment process only in competitive states. Other studies of candidates in Wisconsin, Iowa, and Oregon have found parties less important than other agents in recruitment. See Leon Epstein, *Politics in Wisconsin* (Madison: University of Wisconsin Press, 1958); Samuel C. Patterson and G. R. Boynton, "Legislative Recruitment in a Civic Culture," *Social Science Quarterly*, 50 (September 1969): 243–263; Lester G. Seligman, et al., *Patterns of Recruitment: A State Chooses Its Lawmakers* (Chicago: Rand McNally College Publishing Company, 1974).

8. Malcolm E. Jewell and David M. Olson, *American State Political Parties and Elections* (Homewood, Illinois: The Dorsey Press, 1978), p. 87.

9. Frank Sorauf, *Political Parties in America*, 4th ed. (Boston: Little, Brown and Company, 1980), p. 216.

10. See Susan Tolchin and Martin Tolchin, *Clout: Womanpower and Politics* (New York: G. P. Putnam's Sons, Capricorn Books, 1976), pp. 71–78, for a more detailed description of these particular situations.

11. The McGovern-Fraser Commission, in developing guidelines for the selection of delegates to the Democratic convention in 1972, required "State Parties to overcome the effect of past discrimination by affirmative steps to encourage representation on the national convention delegation of . . . women in reasonable relationship to their presence in the population in the state." See *Mandate for Reform: A Report of the Commission on Party Structure and Delegate Selection to the Democrat National Committee*, George McGovern, chairman (Washington, D.C.: The Commission on Party Structure and Delegate Selection of the Demo-

crat National Committee, April 1970), p. 40. A later Commission memo, endorsed by Lawrence O'Brien, Chair of the Democratic National Committee, stated, "whenever the proportion of women . . . is less than the proportion . . . in the total population and the delegation is challenged . . . such a challenge will constitute a *prima facie* showing of violation of the guidelines, and the state party along with the challenged delegation, has the burden of showing that the state party took full and affirmative action to achieve such representation" (Penn Kimble and Josh Muravichik, "The New Politics and the Democrats," *Commentary,* December 1972, p. 79). While for the 1976 convention the Democrats did away with what became branded as the "quota system" and shifted the burden of proof from the state party to the group bringing the challenge, states still were required to establish affirmative action programs to "encourage full participation"; see F. Rhodes Cook, "National Conventions and Delegate Selection: An Overview," in *Parties and Elections in an Anti-Party Age,* ed. Jeff Fishel (Bloomington: Indiana University Press, 1978), p. 194. For both the 1980 and 1984 conventions, the Democrats have required "equal division" between women and men of the elected delegates from each state. Although Republican guidelines regarding representation of women have not been as strong, the Republican national party also has recommended, but not required, that states have equal numbers of women and men in their delegations.

12. For evidence of the decline in trust and confidence which has taken place during the 1960s and 1970s, see Arthur H. Miller, "Political Issues and Trust in Government: 1964–70," *American Political Science Review,* 68 (September 1974): 951–972; and Norman H. Nie, Sidney Verba, and John R. Petrocik, *The Changing American Voter,* enlarged ed. (Cambridge: Harvard University Press, 1979), pp. 277–280.

13. Quoted in Tolchin and Tolchin, p. 78.

14. John F. Bibby and Robert J. Huckshorn, "The Republican Party in American Politics," in *Parties and Elections in an Anti-Party Age,* ed. Jeff Fishel (Bloomington: Indiana University Press, 1978), p. 59.

15. Cynthia Fuchs Epstein, *Woman's Place: Options and Limits in Professional Careers* (Berkeley: University of California Press, 1970), p. 167.

16. See, for example, A. Lee Hunt, Jr. and Robert E. Pendley, "Community Gatekeepers: An Examination of Political Recruiters," *Midwest Journal of Political Science,* 16 (August 1972): 437, and Kenneth Prewitt, *The Recruitment of Political Leaders: A Study of Citizen-Politicians* (Indianapolis: The Bobbs-Merrill Company, Inc., 1970), p. 27.

17. Gunnar Myrdal, "Women, Servants, Mules, and Other Property," in *Masculine/Feminine: Readings in Sexual Mythology and the Liberation of Women,* ed. Betty Roszak and Theodore Roszak (New York: Harper & Row, Harper Colophon Books, 1969), p. 75.

18. Jeane J. Kirkpatrick, *Political Woman* (New York: Basic Books, 1974), p. 100.

19. Marilyn Johnson and Susan Carroll, "Profile of Women Holding Office, 1977," in *Women in Public Office: A Biographical Directory and Statistical Analysis,* 2nd ed., comp. Center for the American Woman and Politics (Metuchen, New Jersey: The Scarecrow Press, 1978), p. 43A, Table 57.

20. Polls traditionally have shown greater proportions of voters willing to vote for a woman candidate for lower-level than for higher-level offices. This pattern, however, is somewhat obscured by voters' greater willingness to view women as acceptable candidates for legislative than for executive offices. The most valid generalization probably is that for various types of executive offices, voter prejudice is more severe for higher-level than for lower-level offices: the same is true for various types of legislative offices. See chapter 4 for a discussion of some relevant poll results. See also, "Women Candidates: Many More Predicted for 1974," *Congressional Quarterly Weekly Reports*, 32 (April 13, 1974): 941, for a discussion of results of a poll conducted by the Eagleton Institute of Politics, Rutgers University, which showed this pattern.

21. Kirsten Amundsen, *The Silenced Majority: Woman and American Democracy* (Englewood Cliffs: Prentice-Hall, Inc., 1971), p. 133.

22. Statewide candidates include those who ran statewide for elective positions at the state level (e.g., governor, lieutenant governor). U.S. Senate candidates are included in the congressional category.

23. David A. Leuthold, *Electioneering in a Democracy: Campaigns for Congress* (New York: John Wiley & Sons, 1968), p. 15.

24. There also is evidence that family support may be more important for men than most research has led us to believe. Diane Kincaid Blair and Ann R. Henry, "The Family Factor in State Legislative Turnover," *Legislative Studies Quarterly*, 6 (February 1981): 55–68 have found that family problems are the major factor leading to retirement from office for male as well as female state legislators. Similarly, Virginia Sapiro, "Private Costs of Public Commitments or Public Costs of Private Commitments? Family Roles versus Political Ambition," *American Journal of Political Science*, 26 (May 1982): 265–279, found conflicts between family commitments and public commitments were common for male partisan elites.

25. The finding that women candidates frequently mentioned the encouragement of husbands and/or families as critical to their decisions to run for office is consistent with findings from a national study of women officeholders conducted at about the same time. Johnson and Carroll, pp. 13a–14a, 18a–19a, found very large majorities of women officeholders reported that their husbands approved and actively encouraged their holding office. Furthermore, the wives of male officeholders were proportionately far less supportive, leading Johnson and Carroll, p. 19a, to conclude that "family approval is a far more important selective criterion for the political participation of women than of men. It is likely that women whose families disapprove of their political activity fail to seek office in the first place, resulting in a high degree of family support among those who enter office."

26. Because the particular positions of people who can be considered "party leaders" may vary from one locale to another, respondents were allowed to assign their own subjective definition to the term. However, they were asked to list the positions held by those with whom they talked. While the data are not presented here, a range of party officials, elected officials, and candidates for office were perceived by the women as "party leaders." Although elected public officials at all levels of government were mentioned by a significant proportion of respondents,

local/district/county party officials were mentioned by far more candidates than any other category of official. State party officials also were mentioned with considerable frequency. Nevertheless, the wide array of officials considered by women to be party leaders demonstrates that a very lenient definition underlies this study. If allowing candidates to apply their own subjective definition of party leaders has any effect on the findings of this study, the effect undoubtedly is one of overstating the interaction between party representatives and women candidates.

27. N = 64 congressional, 20 statewide, 132 state senate, and 686 state house candidates.

28. Some readers may feel the proportion of candidates contacted by party leaders is surprisingly high; it is commonly believed that in many states, most party officials do not become involved in pre-primary recruitment. Yet, nationwide data on this question are lacking. Lewis Bowman and G. R. Boynton, "Recruitment Patterns among Local Party Officials: A Model and Some Preliminary Findings in Selected Locales," in *A Comparative Study of Party Organization*, ed. William E. Wright (Columbus, Ohio: Charles E. Merrill Publishing Company, 1971), p. 412, have suggested, "while the party organization as such may not be systematically involved in pre-primary recruitment, the local party officials may be active as individuals." Perhaps, at least in some states, the moderate level of involvement of party leaders in pre-primary recruitment stems from leaders approaching candidates not as official representatives of the party organization, but rather as individuals.

29. One cannot conclude from this evidence that party leaders rarely discouraged women from running for office in 1976. Respondents who received negative reactions from party leaders represent only those women who were discouraged from running but ran despite this discouragement. The finding that party leaders discouraged few of the women who became candidates in 1976 could have occurred for any of three reasons. First, it is possible that the parties did not, in fact, actively discourage women from running for office. Second, it may be that most women whom party leaders discouraged ultimately decided not to run. Third, those women who anticipated negative reactions simply may have avoided discussing their candidacies with party representatives; their numbers may be reflected among those candidates who indicated they had no interaction with party leaders.

30. L. Sandy Maisel, "Congressional Elections in 1978: The Road to Nomination, the Road to Election," *American Politics Quarterly* 9 (January 1981): 38–41, has suggested that parties are weakly organized at the congressional district level, and for this reason, often are not actively involved in seeking out congressional candidates.

31. Bowman and Boynton, p. 412.

32. Incumbents are excluded from the analysis of party recruitment because incumbents cannot be said to be recruited in any meaningful sense. An incumbent, by virtue of having served in office, was recruited at an earlier time.

33. It has often been suggested that parties frequently nominate women to run in hopeless situations where it is virtually predetermined that the candidate of the opposing party will win. Moreover, recent studies, limited to small geographic areas, have provided some evidence indicating that women often are recruited to

serve as sacrificial lambs. See, for example, Lynn, p. 416; Nikki R. Van Hightower, "The Recruitment of Women for Public Office," *American Politics Quarterly,* 5 (July 1977): 301–314; Nancy Hammond and Glenda Belote, "From Deviance to Legitimacy: Women as Political Candidates," *The University of Michigan Papers in Women's Studies,* 1 (June 1974): 58–72; Elizabeth G. King, "Women in Iowa Legislative Politics," in *A Portrait of Marginality: The Political Behavior of the American Woman,* ed. Marianne Githens and Jewel L. Prestage (New York: David McKay Company, Inc., 1977), pp. 284–303.

34. A single-member district was considered to have no open seat if an incumbent of the opposing party was seeking re-election. The definition of open seat is worded in a more general form because many candidates ran in multimember districts. Of the 27 definite party recruits for the state senate, 3 were in multimember districts; 51 of the 158 definite party recruits for the state house were in multimember districts. Among total party recruits, 5 of the 58 state senate recruits and 90 of the 300 state house recruits were in multimember districts.

35. See Robert J. Huckshorn and Robert C. Spencer, *The Politics of Defeat: Campaigning for Congress* (Amherst: The University of Massachusetts Press, 1971), p. 52; and Sorauf, *Party Politics in America,* pp. 218–219.

36. The preferred method to ascertain whether a candidate was recruited by her party to serve as a sacrificial lamb would involve an examination of election returns in her district for several previous elections. Unfortunately, these data are not readily available. Nevertheless, the measures employed probably would correlate highly with measures derived from election returns and serve as alternative methods to measure whether a district is safe for the opposing party.

37. In the case of a multimember district, a candidate was considered unopposed as long as the number of competitors in her primary did not exceed the number of seats.

38. The recruitment of women as sacrificial lambs may have little to do with the candidate's sex *per se.* Previous studies of recruitment in some states have found that party officials are most active in recruiting candidates in areas safe for the other party and least active in recruiting where the seats are safe for their own party. See, for example, Lester Seligman, "Political Recruitment and Party Structure: A Case Study," *American Political Science Review* 55 (March 1961): 77–86. However, Bowman and Boynton, p. 415, have noted that studies in other states have found greater recruiting efforts by parties in safe or competitive districts than in hopeless districts. Unfortunately, since nationwide data are not available, it is impossible to compare the proportion of women and men across the country recruited by the parties as sacrificial lambs. Nevertheless, regardless of the corresponding proportion for men, the important point is that the larger the proportion of female party recruits who are sacrificial lambs, the less the parties are facilitating the movement of women into elite positions.

39. There were too few party recruits at the state senate level (N = 53) to provide a meaningful analysis of party differences. However, like the findings for state house party recruits, Republicans appear to have recruited larger proportions of sacrificial lambs.

40. Table 3, "Apportionment of Legislatures: House," *The Book of States, 1976–1977* (Lexington, Kentucky: The Council of State Governments, 1976), p.

43, shows 1,996, or 35.8%, of a nationwide total of 5,581 state house seats to be in multimember districts. It is not possible with existing data to develop an exact measure of the proportion of seats up for election in 1976 in multimember districts. In several of the states, only a portion of all state legislative districts held elections in 1976, and it is not known how many of these were multimember versus single-member districts, since some states have a mixture of both. However, in the absence of an exact measure of the proportion of seats in 1976 in multimember districts, this figure of 35.8% based on the nationwide distribution of seats seems a reasonable estimate.

41. A sizable number of women recruited in multimember districts were in New Hampshire (among definite party recruits, 19 Democrats and 6 Republicans; among total party recruits, 28 Democrats and 8 Republicans). However, the greater tendency of Democrats relative to Republicans to recruit women in multimember districts persists even if candidates from New Hampshire are excluded.

42. Throughout this chapter I have suggested that party leaders tended to recruit women more actively for less prestigious than for more prestigious offices, to recruit sizable numbers of women as sacrificial lambs, and to recruit women disproportionately in multimember districts in response to the conflicting pressures they faced during elite circulation in the 1970s. I do not mean to imply that these practices did not characterize the recruitment of women prior to the development of the contemporary feminist movement. While no studies focused specifically on the recruitment of the relatively few women who ran for office before the 1970s, occasional hints in earlier studies of political elites suggest that party leaders did engage in recruiting women to run as sacrificial lambs or to help fill the ticket in multimember districts. See M. Kent Jennings and Norman Thomas, "Men and Women in Party Elites: Social Roles and Political Resources," *Midwest Journal of Political Science,* 7 (November 1968): 483, and Heinz Eulau et al., "Career Perspectives of State Legislators," in *Political Decision-makers,* ed. Dwaine Marwick (New York: The Free Press of Glencoe, 1961), p. 234. For many years, parties probably have recruited a few women in those situations where pressures which might work against the recruitment of women were so minimal that little risk was involved or where they just desperately needed a candidate— any candidate. Intensified pressures to recruit women during the 1970s probably meant more party leaders were affected, but probably did not result in different *types* of responses by party leaders.

43. Even if the patterns uncovered here are true for any emerging social group, the patterns may be more resistant to change for women than for other disadvantaged groups. The reason has to do with larger group size, i.e., the fact that women constitute a majority of the population. Robert N. Stern, Walter R. Gove, and Omer R. Galle, "Equality for Blacks and Women: An Essay on Relative Progress," *Social Science Quarterly,* 56 (March 1976): 666–668, have suggested, "the larger the minority group, the more incentive the majority will have to maintain discrimination and prejudice. . . . The larger a disadvantaged group relative to a dominant group, the more difficult will be any attempt at attaining equality."

44. Information was not available on the incumbency status of those running in the opposing party's primary for 13 of the 300 nonincumbent total party recruits

for the state house and for 5 of the 58 nonincumbent total party recruits for the state senate. To give the parties the full benefit of the doubt, I assumed that all women with missing data were recruited to run for open seats. With this assumption, a maximum of 25.8% of all nonincumbent respondents among candidates for the state house and 24.2% of all nonincumbent respondents among candidates for the state senate were recruited by party leaders to run in districts where there was a reasonable chance of general election victory.

45. There were 4,778 state house seats and 1,168 state senate seats up for election in 1976. These figures are drawn from a chart, distributed by the AFL-CIO, which provided a state-by-state summary of the number of seats contested in 1976.

46. Herbert L. Wiltsee, "The State Legislatures," in *The Book of States, 1976–1977* (Lexington, Kentucky: The Council of State Governments, 1976), p. 32.

47. See Judy Mann, "Strength," *The Washington Post*, August 13, 1982.

Chapter 4

1. The figure for 1972 is drawn from Irene Diamond, "Female Candidates in the 1974 Primaries" (paper presented at the Adelphi University Symposium on Women in Politics, September 1975), p. 1. Figures for other years were furnished by the National Women's Education Fund.

2. Proportions of winning candidates are based on election outcomes for the entire female candidate population, not just respondents. N = 113 congressional, 35 statewide, 239 state senate, and 1,426 state house candidates.

3. While these percentages are all well below 50%, the readers should consider that a large number of these races involved more than one other contender for the seat. N = 81 congressional, 30 statewide, 118 state senate, and 771 state house candidates.

4. Naomi Lynn, "Women in American Politics: An Overview," in *Women: A Feminist Perspective*, ed. Jo Freeman (Palo Alto: Mayfield Publishing Company, 1975), p. 373.

5. N = 52 congressional, 19 statewide, 177 state senate, and 1,078 state house candidates.

6. Christopher Buchanan, "Why Aren't There More Women in Congress?" *Congressional Quarterly Weekly Reports*, 36 (August 12, 1978): 2110.

7. The number of candidates running in primaries varies greatly (unlike the general election), and thus no estimate of the *proportion* of male candidates who emerge victorious from primaries can be made.

8. N = 50 congressional, 17 statewide, 75 state senate, and 462 state house candidates who ran in contested primaries.

9. For a discussion of some of the many advantages that accrue from incumbency, see Alan L. Clem, *The Making of Congressmen: Seven Campaigns of 1974* (North Scituate, Massachusetts: Duxbury Press, 1976), p. 9; Robert Agranoff, *The New Style in Election Campaigns* (Boston: Holbrook Press, 1972), p. 97; Dan Nimmo, *The Political Persuaders: The Techniques of Modern Election Campaigns* (Englewood Cliffs: Prentice-Hall, 1970), p. 48; John Kingdon, *Candidates for Office: Beliefs and Strategies* (New York: Random House, 1968), pp. 110–111.

10. Among state senate candidates, 77.8% of incumbents who ran in contested

primaries (N = 9) compared with 90.9% of nonincumbents opposed in primaries (N = 66) reported one or more problems (tau$_b$ = .14). The corresponding figures for state assembly candidates were 54.9% of incumbents (N = 82) in contrast to 85.0% of nonincumbents (N = 380) with tau$_b$ = .29.

11. Among state senate candidates in competitive primaries, 77.8% of the incumbents (N = 9) listed one or more assets in comparison with 65.2% of nonincumbents (N = 66) with tau$_b$ = .09. At the state house level, 64.6% of incumbents (N = 82) and 63.9% of nonincumbents (N = 380) mentioned at least one advantage (tau$_b$ = .005).

12. Irene Diamond, *Sex Roles in the State House* (New Haven: Yale University Press, 1977), chapter 2.

13. See Citizens Conference on State Legislatures, *The Sometime Governments: A Critical Study of the 50 American Legislatures* (Kansas City: Citizens Conference on State Legislatures, 1971). This index is similar to schemes that rate legislatures on the basis of professionalism. See, for example, John G. Grumm, "Structural Determinants of Legislative Output," in *Legislatures in Developmental Perspective*, ed. Allan Kornberg and Lloyd D. Musolf (Durham: Duke University Press, 1970), pp. 447–451. However, the Citizens Conference's index considers more factors that would seem to contribute to making a legislative seat desirable.

14. No index has been designed specifically to measure the desirability of, or prestige associated with, serving in various state legislatures. Desirability perhaps could have been measured in terms of size of legislative body, or salary, or days in session. However, the desirability of serving in a particular legislature is likely to be a function of many, rather than merely a few, factors. Although the FAIRR index was developed by the Citizens Conference to measure overall legislative performance, not desirability of serving in a legislature, performance and desirability seem highly interrelated conceptually, and most of the criteria used to create the FAIRR index seem relevant to measuring seat desirability. Although the FAIRR index is somewhat dated, this is not likely to present a major problem. Undoubtedly between 1970 (when the FAIRR index was constructed) and 1976 (when the data for this study were collected) some changes took place in some legislatures which may have altered the relative rankings of the states from 1 to 50 on overall legislative performance. For this reason, exact state values were not used; rather states were grouped into three broad categories. Given the incremental nature of most governmental reform, it is highly unlikely that many states between 1970 and 1976 underwent sufficient change along a large enough number of the dimensions to move them from one broad category to another.

15. States with seats of high desirability are California, New York, Illinois, Florida, Wisconsin, Iowa, Hawaii, Michigan, Nebraska, Minnesota, New Mexico, Alaska, Nevada, Oklahoma, Utah, Ohio, and South Dakota. States with seats of moderate desirability are Idaho, Washington, Maryland, Pennsylvania, North Dakota, Kansas, Connecticut, West Virginia, Tennessee, Oregon, Colorado, Massachusetts, Maine, Kentucky, New Jersey, Louisiana, Virginia, Missouri, Rhode Island, and Vermont. States with seats of low desirability are Texas, New Hampshire, Indiana, Montana, Mississippi, Arizona, South Carolina, Georgia, Arkansas, North Carolina, Delaware, Wyoming, and Alabama.

16. N = 150 candidates in states with seats of high desirability, 161 in states with seats of moderate desirability, and 151 in states with low desirability who ran in contested primaries.

17. Numerous studies examining the campaigns of mostly male candidates have highlighted fund raising as a major problem. See, for example, David A. Leuthold, *Electioneering in a Democracy: Campaigns for Congress* (New York: John Wiley & Sons, 1968), p. 84 and Agranoff, p. 244. Unfortunately, there are no studies that directly compare the severity of fund-raising problems of women and men.

18. Suzanne Paizis, *Getting Her Elected: A Political Woman's Handbook* (Sacramento: Creative Editions, 1977), pp. 8–9.

19. Tina Rosenberg, "Running on Empty," *Savvy*, November 1982, p. 44.

20. Paizis, pp. 22–23.

21. Kingdon, pp. 112–113, has referred to time, money, and human energy as the three "costs" of campaigning.

22. Male candidates may be more likely than female candidates to be concentrated in flexible careers, such as law, where they can take time off from work to campaign (see chapter 5). Male candidates also are not as likely to have as many household/family maintenance responsibilities as female candidates. Both of these factors might work to place women at a disadvantage relative to men with regard to time as a campaign resource. However, there probably are other factors that place men at a disadvantage relative to women. For example, female candidates may be less likely than male candidates to be employed in full-time jobs. Because some factors work to the advantage while others work to the disadvantage of women, there is no reason to suspect that, in the aggregate, lack of time poses a substantially bigger problem for women than for men. Similarly, it may well be the case that women candidates attract campaign workers from different sources than men (for example, from the League of Women Voters rather than from Kiwanis), but there is no reason to expect that women generally have greater difficulty attracting volunteers than do men.

23. Problems included in the "people" category consist largely of responses which mentioned a lack of help or workers. However, also included here are references to problems such as inexperienced or undependable staff members, infighting among workers, and complacency or overconfidence among staff. Problems involving lack of time include both references to a lack of time due to entering the race late and to a lack of time due to other commitments (for example, employment or family obligations). Because most candidates made only a general reference to time as a problem, it was impossible to separate those who mentioned time for one reason from those who mentioned time for the other reason.

24. Past research (on predominantly male samples) has indicated that incumbents have an easier time acquiring resources. Leuthold, for example, noted that incumbents had less difficulty raising funds (p. 84) and were able to attract more workers (p. 91).

25. There were too few incumbents for state senate, statewide, and congressional seats who faced primary opposition to allow for meaningful analysis. Consequently, only state house candidates are examined here.

26. N = 148 candidates in states with high desirability seats, 158 candidates in states with moderate desirability seats, and 150 candidates in states with low desirability seats.

27. N = 298 Democrats and 164 Republicans.

28. N = 82 incumbents and 380 nonincumbents.

29. All responses that referred explicitly to the candidate's gender were grouped into one general category. A large majority of respondents who gave answers which were coded into this category simply mentioned "being a woman" without defining more explicitly the nature of the specific problems encountered as a result of gender. It is important to note here that some of the other factors women mentioned as problems in their campaigns (for example, lack of money, lack of party support) may have stemmed, in part, from the fact that they were women. In particular, I have suggested that fund raising is perceived as a major problem by female candidates in part because of the specific difficulties *women* have in raising money. However, what is of interest here is not an objective assessment of the extent to which gender affected the campaigns of women candidates but rather an analysis of the extent to which women candidates *perceived* their gender as a handicap.

30. N = 380 nonincumbents and 82 incumbents.

31. N = 82 incumbents and 380 nonincumbents.

32. Only 5, or 9.1%, of all candidates for all offices who mentioned "being a woman" as a disadvantage also mentioned it as an advantage.

33. Responses in this category included, for example, references to false ads about their campaigns, opponents who conducted smear campaigns, discrimination in ballot designation, and threatening phone calls.

34. N = 9 incumbents and 66 nonincumbents among candidates for the state senate. N = 82 incumbents and 380 nonincumbents for the state house.

35. There is another possible explanation for the findings of differences between winners and losers. Previous studies have shown that the mere fact of winning or losing may affect a candidate's perceptions of his/her campaign. The best-known effect of this type is, of course, the "congratulation-rationalization effect," first documented by John W. Kingdon, "Politicians' Beliefs About Voters," *American Political Science Review*, 61 (March 1967): 139–140. Kingdon found that winners believed voters made informed decisions based on issues and the personal characteristics of the candidates. Losers, on the other hand, "rationalized" their losses by blaming the voters for relying on party labels, rather than on issues or candidate characteristics. Findings from this study might reflect, at least in part, a similar rationalization process. Losers may have magnified problems in order to rationalize their losses. If so, their perceptions would not serve as valid indicators of political reality. Nevertheless, they would still serve as indicators of the factors candidates considered critical in accounting for their defeats, thereby suggesting a hypothesis about factors that may affect election outcomes to be tested in the next chapter.

36. Again, statewide and congressional candidates are not examined because of the small number of candidates for these offices who were victorious in contested primaries.

Chapter 5

1. See Jo Freeman, *The Politics of Women's Liberation* (New York: David McKay Company, 1975), p. 206; *The New York Times,* December 21, 1976, pp. 1 and 6; Myra MacPherson, "Catch 22 for Women," *The Washington Post,* January 16, 1977, p. 1.

2. Kenneth Prewitt, *The Recruitment of Political Leaders: A Study of Citizen-Politicians* (Indianapolis: Bobbs-Merrill Company, 1970), p. 31.

3. Debra Leff, "Survey Shows Women 'Political Novices,' " *Women's Political Times,* Summer 1978, p. 7.

4. Among the numerous studies which document the high educational and occupational levels of candidates and officeholders are Prewitt; David A. Leuthold, *Electioneering in a Democracy: Campaigns for Congress* (New York: John Wiley & Sons, 1968); Frank Sorauf, *Party and Representation: Legislative Politics in Pennsylvania* (New York: Atherton Press, 1963); Lester G. Seligman, Michael R. King, Chong Lim Kim, and Roland E. Smith, *Patterns of Recruitment: A State Chooses Its Lawmakers* (Chicago: Rand McNally College Publishing Company, 1974); Heinz Eulau, William Buchanan, LeRoy C. Ferguson, and John C. Wahlke, "Career Perspectives of State Legislators," in *Political Decision-makers,* ed. by Dwaine Marwick (New York: The Free Press of Glencoe, 1961); Jeff Fishel, *Party and Opposition: Congressional Challengers in American Politics* (New York: David McKay Company, 1973); Jerome M. Mileur and George T. Sulzner, *Campaigning for the Massachusetts Senate: Electioneering Outside the Political Limelight* (Amherst: The University of Massachusetts Press, 1974).

5. For example, Prewitt, p. 27, found the median years of education completed by congressional candidates to be 17 years. Heinz Eulau et al., p. 489, found more than 46% of legislators in each of four states to have completed college. Jerome Mileur and George Sulzner, p. 61, found about three-fourths of all candidates for the state senate in Massachusetts had a college degree. More than 85% of candidates for the Oregon state legislature in the study conducted by Lester Seligman et al., p. 121, had at least some college education.

6. Jeane J. Kirkpatrick, *Political Woman* (New York: Basic Books, 1974), p. 61.

7. At the time of this study, 27.4% of congressional, 20.0% of statewide, 36.9% of state senate, and 37.6% of state house candidates were not employed outside the home. Perhaps these candidates could have been considered homemakers, even though they had held other occupations previously. However, since unemployed males generally are not described as househusbands but rather in terms of their former occupations outside the home, I have followed the same convention in classifying women candidates.

8. For example, Eulau et al., p. 489, found a large majority of state legislators to be professionals or proprietors, managers, and officials. Mileur and Sulzner, p. 61, found one-half of state senate candidates in Massachusetts to be professionals, with business the second most frequent occupation. Seligman et al., p. 122, found 69% of legislative candidates in Oregon to have professional or managerial occupations.

9. For documentation of the large proportion of lawyers found among public

officeholders, see, for example, Eulau et al., p. 490; Mileur and Sulzner, p. 61; Sorauf, p. 70; Fishel, p. 26 (although Fishel finds a decline in the number of lawyers in Congress); Heinz Eulau and John D. Sprague, *Lawyers in Politics: A Study in Professional Convergence* (Indianapolis: The Bobbs-Merrill Company, Inc., 1964), pp. 11–12.

10. Leuthold, p. 24.

11. There is good reason to suspect that the proportions of candidates who have held appointive governmental positions is considerably understated. Respondents were asked if they had held appointive governmental positions and what these positions were. Unfortunately, there clearly was confusion about the definition of an appointive governmental position. I had intended respondents to list boards and commissions as well as administrative positions. Although some respondents interpreted this question to include appointments to boards and commissions, others clearly did not. Because of the inconsistency in responses to this question, it is omitted from all subsequent analysis in this chapter.

12. For example, most of the candidates in Mileur and Sulzner, p. 65, had held at least one public office, and 13 of the 20 congressional candidates in Leuthold, p. 27, had previously been elected to office. Fishel, p. 50, found 50% of Democratic congressional challengers and 40% of Republicans had held public office.

13. Only bits and pieces of evidence exist about the partisan and organizational experience of candidates. Nevertheless, the levels of activity among women seem very comparable to those for men. Sorauf, p. 86, found 69.8% of Pennsylvania legislative candidates had held party office and that they were, p. 79, "with few exceptions 'joiners' par excellence." Candidates for the Massachusetts state senate in Mileur's and Sulzner's study, p. 68, almost all had some party experience and one-half had a lengthy record. Fishel, p. 50, found only about one-third of congressional challengers lacked party office experience.

14. The data are not presented, but 26.0% of congressional candidates belonged to two or fewer organizations.

15. It is not possible to say with certainty why congressional candidates had no more political experience on the average than state legislative candidates. However, the electoral situations in the districts where women ran for congressional seats may provide a clue. The common wisdom among those in Washington who followed women's campaigns in 1976 was that there were no more than "half a dozen" or a "handful" of nonincumbent women running for Congress who had any chance of victory. While I have no empirical "proof" of this statement, a large proportion of congressional candidates (60.0%), relative to state legislative candidates (41.1% for state senate, 40.6% for state house), ran in general elections in districts where an incumbent sought re-election. Thus, many congressional candidacies probably were hopeless from the start. Since few congressional candidates were recruited by the parties, women must have voluntarily chosen to run in these districts. One would suspect that a "hopeless" race would be most attractive to a woman relatively lacking in political experience and name recognition, who could benefit either professionally or politically from the visibility a congressional campaign would provide. Consequently, the major reason female congressional candidates were deficient in political experience may be that many were political novices running primarily to gain name recognition and publicity.

16. For an introductory discussion of this technique, see William R. Klecka, "Discriminant Analysis," in *Statistical Package for the Social Sciences,* ed. by Norman A. Nie et al. (New York: McGraw-Hill, 1975), pp. 434–467; Donald G. Morrison, "On the Interpretation of Discriminant Analysis," *Journal of Marketing Research,* 6 (May 1969): 153–163; John H. Aldridge and Charles F. Cnudde, "Probing the Bounds of Conventional Wisdom: A Comparison of Regression, Probit and Discriminant Analysis," *American Journal of Political Science,* 19 (August 1975): 571–608. For a more mathematical and advanced discussion, see William W. Cooley and Paul R. Lohnes, *Multivariate Data Analysis* (New York: John Wiley & Sons, 1971). Discriminant analysis is used here, rather than regression analysis, because the dependent variable is dichotomous. Since multicollinearity is a potential problem with any multivariate technique, the intercorrelations among independent variables in all discriminant analyses throughout this chapter have been carefully checked. While these intercorrelations are not presented, all are below .5 and most are much lower.

17. The specific classification procedure used is that described in Klecka, p. 445.

18. For a description of the specific mathematical basis used for determining which variables are included and which are excluded in the analysis, see Klecka, p. 448. The eight variables included in the analyses are education, occupation, elective officeholding experience, party activity, experience in elective or appointive party positions, experience as a delegate to a national party convention, experience as a delegate to a state party convention, and number of organizational memberships. Experience in an appointive governmental position was not included because of the suspected unreliability of the answers (see note 11 above). Also, experience in running for public office was excluded, for a very different reason. Experience in running for office and holding previous elective office were highly intercorrelated both conceptually and empirically. As a result, only one could be used in subsequent analysis, and officeholding experience proved more robust in preliminary computer runs.

19. A caveat is in order here. The finding that women with more organizational memberships were more likely to lose may be spurious. More specifically, it may be the product of a small N and missing data. Only 11 of the 46 congressional/statewide candidates in general elections won. The question on organizations required candidates to list memberships; when a respondent listed no memberships, it was not possible to determine whether she belonged to zero organizations or simply skipped the question, perhaps because she belonged to too many organizations to list quickly. Some candidates also may have listed only a couple of organizations when they belonged to many. Because the number of congressional/statewide winners was so small, the failure of a few of these candidates to provide complete data could have led to the unanticipated negative relationship.

20. Lewis A. Froman, Jr., *Congressmen and Their Constituencies* (Chicago: Rand McNally & Company, 1963), p. 58.

21. Dan Nimmo, *The Political Persuaders: The Techniques of Modern Election Campaigns* (Englewood Cliffs: Prentice-Hall, 1970), p. 79.

22. *The New York Times,* March 6, 1978.

23. Leff, p. 7.

24. Robert Agranoff, *The Management of Election Campaigns* (Boston: Holbrook Press, 1976), p. 462.

25. Joseph Napolitan, *The Election Game and How to Win It* (Garden City: Doubleday & Company, 1972), p. 17.

26. Candidates were asked to specify the previous campaign experience of their managers. In some cases, managers may have had experience which the candidate was unaware of or did not list. If so, the actual proportions of inexperienced campaign managers may have been somewhat lower than they appear in table 5.7.

27. Agranoff, p. 12. So few studies have asked similar questions of male candidates for comparable offices that it is almost impossible to determine whether women's campaigns are more poorly run than men's. However, it seems unlikely that men's campaigns are significantly better.

28. Froman, p. 11.

29. See chapter 4 for a discussion of this index.

30. See David W. Adamany, *Campaign Finance in America* (North Scituate, Massachusetts: Duxbury Press, 1972), pp. 24–50.

Chapter 6

1. According to the criteria I am using as defined in chapter 1, voter prejudice is most appropriately considered a political opportunity variable. However, I am including it here in the discussion of gender because it is so frequently cited as a reason, related to sex, for why women are not more successful.

2. See "Opinion Roundup," *Public Opinion*, 2 (January/February 1979): 36, for a summary of poll results on this question over the years.

3. *Gallup Opinion Index*, September 1975.

4. Jeane J. Kirkpatrick, *Political Woman* (New York: Basic Books, Inc., 1974), p. 86.

5. See Ruth B. Mandel, *In the Running: The New Woman Candidate* (New York: Ticknor & Fields, 1981), chapter 3, for a particularly insightful and more extensive discussion of the need for women candidates to cultivate an acceptable image.

6. Suzanne Paizis, *Getting Her Elected: A Political Woman's Handbook* (Sacramento: Creative Editions, 1977), p. 86.

7. While not directly assessed in this study, some research has suggested that women candidates do not get fewer votes than male candidates simply because of their gender. R. Darcy and Sarah Slavin Schramm, "When Women Run Against Men," *Public Opinion Quarterly*, 41 (Spring 1977): 1–12, concluded that candidate sex had little or no effect on the outcome of congressional elections in 1970, 1972, and 1974, once incumbency and party were controlled. They suggested, p. 10, "If there are some voters who would favor or oppose women candidates they are balanced neatly by voters with opposing tendencies; or, more likely, such people either do not vote, are unaware of the candidates at all, or both." Albert K. Karnig and B. Oliver Walter, "Election of Women to City Councils," *Social Science Quarterly*, 56 (March 1976): 608, also concluded that "female candidates for council office are not victimized by insurmountable prejudice at the polls."

8. An individual with a very traditional sex-role identity may have very non-

traditional sex-role attitudes; similarly, a person with very traditional sex-role attitudes may be androgynous or sex-reversed in her or his sex-role identity. Moreover, sex-role attitudes and identities correlate to different degrees with other measures (e.g., political attitudes). See Marjorie Randon Hershey and John L. Sullivan, "Sex Role Attitudes, Identities, and Political Ideology," *Sex Roles*, 3 (February 1977): 37–57.

9. Sandra L. Bem, "The Measurement of Psychological Androgyny," *Journal of Consulting and Clinical Psychology*, 42 (April 1974): 155.

10. Sandra L. Bem, "Sex Role Adaptability: One Consequence of Psychological Androgyny," *Journal of Personality and Social Psychology*, 31 (April 1975): 634–643.

11. See Bem, 1974, pp. 155–162.

12. Ibid., p. 160.

13. Dropping of unreliable items is consistent with the procedure followed by other researchers who have used the BSRI. See, for example, Marjorie Randon Hershey, "Racial Differences in Sex-Role Identities and Sex Stereotyping: Evidence Against a Common Assumption," *Social Science Quarterly*, 58 (March 1978): 583–596. Item-to-total correlations for the excluded items were as follows:

Athletic .17	Flatterable .15	Does not use
Masculine .008	Gullible .02	harsh lan-
Shy .04	Childlike .008	guage .16

Item-to-total correlations for all other items were greater than .25.

14. Respondents were excluded from the analysis if they left more than two of the 33 remaining items in the two scales blank.

15. Janet T. Spence, Robert Helmreich, and Joy Stapp, "Ratings of Self and Peers on Sex Role Attributes and Their Relation to Self-Esteem and Conceptions of Masculinity and Femininity," *Journal of Personality and Social Psychology*, 32 (July 1975): 29–39; Sandra Lipsitz Bem, "On the Utility of Alternative Procedures for Assessing Psychological Androgyny," *Journal of Consulting and Clinical Psychology*, 45 (April 1977): 196–205.

16. See Bem, 1977, p. 198, for precise values of these medians. While it might have been preferable to use medians from a study of a representative sample of the general population, the BSRI has not been tested on such a sample, as far as I know. Consequently, Bem's sample was as representative as any available. Since Bem's sample consists of students enrolled in an elite institution, one would suspect that the females in her sample are less traditional in their sex-role identities than the general population. If so, then women candidates may be even more atypical in their sex-role identities than they appear here.

17. Unlike many earlier efforts to measure sex roles, the BSRI does not assume that masculinity and femininity are bipolar and unidimensional. For this reason, it generally has been recognized as superior to previous measures. In recent years, however, the BSRI has been attacked as atheoretical and psychometrically unsound. See, for example, Elazar J. Pedhazur and Toby J. Tetenbaum, "Bem Sex Role Inventory: A Theoretical and Methodological Critique," *Journal of Personality and Social Psychology*, 37 (June 1979): 996–1016, and Anne Locksley and Mary Ellen Colten, "Psychological Androgyny: A Case of Mistaken Identity?" *Journal*

of Personality and Social Psychology, 37 (June 1979): 1017–1031. Sandra Lipsitz Bem, "Theory and Measurement of Androgyny: A Reply to the Pedhazur-Tetenbaum and Locksley-Colten Critiques," *Journal of Personality and Social Psychology,* 37 (June 1979): 1047–1054, has responded to these criticisms, defending both the theoretical rationale underlying the BSRI and its empirical derivation. While I find much of Bem's defense convincing, there is no doubt that psychologists are divided as to the validity of the BSRI, and that the concept of psychological androgyny itself, as well as the best means for measuring it, is subject to debate—a debate that probably will continue for some time.

18. N = 44 congressional, 17 statewide, 64 state senate, and 404 state house candidates.

19. Before combining these items into a single scale, the three items were factor analyzed, using principal components analysis. Only one factor with an eigenvalue greater than 1.00 emerged. The eigenvalue was 1.99, and the factor accounted for 66.2% of the variance in the items. Loadings for the items on this factor were .67 for the first item in table 6.1, .83 for the second item, and .61 for the third.

20. Bem's original scheme for classifying individuals into sex-role identity groupings was used, instead of the more recently developed method, for a number of reasons. First, it shows greater variation among candidates. Second, the major advantage of the newer method is that it separates out undifferentiated from androgynous individuals; however, there were so few candidates with undifferentiated sex-role identities that leaving them in the ranks of the androgynous individuals could produce no meaningful differences in results. Third, the original method results in an ordinal measure while the more recently developed method yields a nominal measure, and an ordinal measure was preferable. The five categories were collapsed into three because the literature leads to the prediction that androgynous individuals would be most adaptable and thus the best campaigners. Those who are sex-typed (i.e., feminine) and those who are sex-reversed (i.e., masculine) should make the worst campaigners since they would be able to respond *only* with masculine behavior or *only* with feminine behavior across all situations. Unlike androgynous individuals, they would not be able to display both types of behavior, depending on the situation.

21. See, for example, Mileur and Sulzner, p. 69; A. D. Cover, "One Good Term Deserves Another: The Advantage of Incumbency in Congressional Elections," *American Journal of Political Science,* 21 (August 1977): 523–541; James F. Sheffield, Jr., and Lawrence K. Goering, "Winning and Losing: Candidate Advantage in Local Elections," *American Politics Quarterly,* 6 (October 1978): 453–468.

22. N = 73 congressional, 22 statewide, 165 state senate, and 952 state house candidates.

23. N = 66 congressional/statewide, 69 state senate, and 446 state house candidates.

24. N = 45 congressional/statewide, 112 state senate, and 693 state house candidates.

25. See Irene Diamond, *Sex Roles in the State House* (New Haven: Yale University Press, 1977), pp. 8–30.

26. N = 165 state senate candidates and 952 state house candidates.

27. N = 952 candidates.

28. Only 3.0% of all congressional/statewide candidates, 12.0% of state senate candidates, and 17.7% of state house candidates in contested primaries were incumbents, compared with 17.4% of congressional/statewide candidates, 25.0% of state senate candidates, and 33.5% of state house candidates in general elections.

29. Variables in tables 5.5, 5.11, 6.6, and 6.9 were included in this final set of discriminant analyses.

Chapter 7

1. As of 1977, only 5 of the 675 U.S. Circuit and District Court judges were women. At the state level, only about 2% of the judges in appellate and trial courts of general jurisdiction were women. Before the appointment of Sandra Day O'Connor in 1981, there were no women on the United States Supreme Court. See Marilyn Johnson and Susan Carroll, "Profile of Women Holding Office, 1977," in *Women in Public Office: A Biographical Directory and Statistical Analysis*, 2nd ed., comp. Center for the American Woman and Politics (Metuchen, New Jersey: The Scarecrow Press, 1978), p. 4A. See also Susan Ness and Fredrica Wechsler, "Women Judges—Why So Few?" *Graduate Woman*, 73 (November/December 1979): 10–12+ for a fine discussion of the underrepresentation of women in the judiciary and why the Omnibus Judgeship Act of 1978 did not remedy the situation.

2. In the late 1970s, two women—Dixy Lee Ray of Washington and Ella Grasso of Connecticut—served simultaneously as governors for the first time.

3. Joseph A. Schlesinger, *Ambition and Politics: Political Careers in the United States* (Chicago: Rand McNally & Company, 1966), p. 195.

4. Ibid., p. 8.

5. N = 73 congressional candidates, 20 statewide candidates, 161 state senate candidates, and 916 state house candidates.

6. Of those who expressed a desire to serve in office for a period of twelve or fewer years, 32.6% of congressional candidates (N = 46), 50.0% of statewide candidates (N = 12), 33.0% of state senate candidates (N = 112), and 38.2% of state house candidates (N = 610) had held elective office before 1976.

7. N = 44 congressional candidates, 96 state senate candidates, and 519 state house candidates. Figures are not presented for statewide candidates because the number of cases is small.

8. Schlesinger, p. 10.

9. Heinz Eulau, William Buchanan, LeRoy C. Ferguson, and John C. Wahlke, "Career Perspectives of State Legislators," in *Political Decision-Makers*, ed. Dwaine Marwick (New York: The Free Press of Glencoe, 1961), p. 219.

10. There are clear and obvious exceptions to this generalization. For example, it is undoubtedly more prestigious to be mayor of New York City than to be a New York state legislator. Similarly, there are probably many local and county offices less prestigious than the New Hampshire General Court, which, because it consists of 400 members and pays only $200 biennially, certainly is among the least prestigious offices in the United States. Nevertheless, of the thousands of local

offices in this country, relatively few are in major metropolitan areas. Similarly, of the several thousand state legislative seats nationwide, most are far more competitive and have higher salaries than the lower house of the New Hampshire legislature.

11. N = 31 congressional candidates, 62 state senate candidates, and 399 state house candidates.

12. Barbara G. Farah, "Climbing the Political Ladder: The Aspirations and Expectations of Partisan Elites," in *New Research on Women and Sex Roles at the University of Michigan*, ed. Dorothy G. McGuigan (Ann Arbor: University of Michigan Center for the Continuing Education of Women, 1976), p. 242. Johnson and Carroll, p. 52A, also found that larger proportions of women than men aspired ultimately to lower-level offices.

13. See, for example, Edmond Costantini and Kenneth Craik, "Women as Politicians: The Social Background, Personality, and Political Careers of Female Party Leaders," *Journal of Social Issues*, 28 (1972): 217–236; Jeane J. Kirkpatrick, *Political Woman* (New York: Basic Books, 1974), p. 152; Irene Diamond, *Sex Roles in the State House* (New Haven: Yale University Press, 1977); Naomi Lynn and Cornelia Butler Flora, "Societal Punishment and Aspects of Female Political Participation: 1972 National Convention Delegates," in *A Portrait of Marginality: The Political Behavior of the American Woman*, ed. Marianne Githens and Jewel L. Prestage (New York: David McKay Company, Inc., 1977), pp. 118–138; Jeane J. Kirkpatrick, *The New Presidential Elite: Men and Women in National Politics* (New York: Russell Sage Foundation, 1976), pp. 410–413.

14. It is important to note here that Eulau et al., p. 258, found this was frequently mentioned by legislators as a reason for lack of aspiration to other offices; 23% gave this response. Thus, this reason clearly is not always a product of sex-role socialization, although in some cases it may be.

15. Age as a reason for lack of ambition may be related to sex-role socialization; many women may wait until their children are grown before running for office, thus beginning their political careers at a later age than men. While this may be true, age is not considered primarily as a sex-related impediment to ambition, because it consistently has been an important factor inhibiting ambition among men.

16. See, for example, Schlesinger, pp. 172–193; Kenneth Prewitt and William Nowlin, "Political Ambitions and the Behavior of Incumbent Politicians," *Western Political Quarterly*, 22 (June 1969): 305; Johnson and Carroll, p. 46; William II. Dutton, "The Political Ambitions of Local Legislators: A Comparative Perspective," *Polity*, 7 (Summer 1975): 513; Jeff Fishel, *Party and Opposition: Congressional Challengers in American Politics* (New York: David McKay Company, 1973), p. 45.

17. See, for example, Johnson and Carroll, p. 47, and John W. Soule, "Future Political Ambitions and the Behavior of Incumbent State Legislators," *Midwest Journal of Political Science*, 13 (August 1969): 447.

18. Fishel, pp. 48–50, found a relationship between ambition and both party and public officeholding.

19. Soule, p. 453.

20. Johnson and Carroll, p. 49A.

21. Farah, p. 239.

22. The Bem Sex Role Inventory (BSRI) is used to measure sex-role identities. See chapter 6 for a full discussion of the BSRI.

23. While it might be preferable to develop an ordinal measure, with several gradients of levels of ambition, for use as a dependent variable, the complexity of the ambition structures of women candidates made this an impossible task. Therefore, I opted to isolate those women who unquestionably had the highest levels of ambition, both in terms of projected tenure in office and in terms of future offices desired, and to compare them with all other candidates. Any variable critical to the nurturance of political ambition should produce differences between these two groups.

24. Among state legislative candidates age fifty or under, 39.8% of ambitious candidates compared with 35.2% of their less-ambitious counterparts (tau_b = $-.04$) had children of age twelve or under. Among state legislative candidates over fifty, none of the ambitious candidates, compared with 2.6% of their less-ambitious counterparts (tau_b = $-.04$), had children of age twelve or under. Thus, the presence or absence of young children has little or no effect on ambition, independent of age.

25. See chapter 5 for a description of this procedure.

26. The classification function correctly classified only 1.69% of the ambitious candidates as ambitious; it misclassified .1% of the less-ambitious candidates as ambitious.

27. For example, Eulau et al., p. 247, in writing about the state legislators they studied, concluded, "for most, the state legislature is likely to be a terminal point in their political career."

Chapter 8

1. For a discussion of women's interests on policy issues dealing with women, the failure of governing bodies in the past to represent adequately these interests, and the possible linkage between greater numerical representation and representation of interests, see chapter 2.

2. See, for example, Shelah Gilbert Leader, "The Policy Impact of Elected Women Officials," in *The Impact of the Electoral Process*, ed. Louis Maisel and Joseph Cooper (Beverly Hills: Sage Publications, 1977), and Kathleen A. Frankovic, "Sex and Voting in the U.S. House of Representatives 1961–1975," *American Politics Quarterly*, 5 (July 1977): 315–330.

3. Past research has generated very little evidence bearing on the question of whether female candidates and officeholders are attitudinal and behavioral feminists. Nevertheless, the scant evidence that does exist, drawn mainly from studies of small and geographically limited samples of women officeholders and candidates, tends to support the overall pattern of mixed feminist and nonfeminist tendencies found in the present study. See, for example, Jeane J. Kirkpatrick, *Political Woman* (New York: Basic Books, Inc., 1974); Susan Gluck Mezey, "Women and Representation: The Case of Hawaii," *Journal of Politics*, 40 (May 1978): 369–385; and Susan Gluck Mezey, "Support for Women's Rights Policy: An Analysis of Local Politicians," *American Politics Quarterly*, 6 (October 1978): 485–497.

4. Alison Jaggar, "Political Philosophies of Women's Liberation," in *Feminism and Philosophy*, ed. Mary Vetterling-Braggin, Frederick A. Elliston, and Jane English (Totowa, New Jersey: Littlefield, Adams & Co., 1977), p. 5.

5. Ibid., pp. 5–21.

6. Jo Freeman, "Introduction," in *Women: A Feminist Perspective*, 2nd ed., ed. Jo Freeman (Palo Alto: Mayfield Publishing Company, 1979), p. xxi.

7. Jaggar, p. 7, has noted that contemporary liberal feminists not only believe that laws that discriminate against women should be eliminated, but also that laws should be used to ensure that such discrimination cannot take place. Moreover, she has suggested, p. 8, that the modern liberal feminist advocates some laws that discriminate *in favor* of women—e.g., affirmative action—as temporary measures to remedy past inequities and to ensure equality of opportunity in the future.

8. Ibid., p. 6.

9. An exception here may be lesbian separatists who wish to establish a matriarchal society excluding men as full members.

10. Feminist organizations included National Organization for Women (NOW), Women's Political Caucus (WPC), Women's Equity Action League (WEAL), National Abortion Rights Action League (NARAL), and other pro-ERA and pro-choice groups.

11. A total of 36.4% of statewide candidates (N = 22), 24.7% of congressional candidates (N = 73), 25.5% of state senate candidates (N = 165), and 18.9% of state house candidates (N = 952) belonged to at least one feminist organization.

12. The antifeminist organizations listed by respondents were primarily anti-ERA and pro-life groups such as Stop ERA and Right-to-Life. Right-wing groups with broad, multi-issue agendas, such as the John Birch Society, were not included in this category.

13. N = 46 congressional, 16 statewide, 69 state senate, and 436 state house candidates.

14. Of course, those who discussed women's issues were not *necessarily* espousing feminist views. However, most of the women who did discuss women's issues during their campaigns viewed the feminist movement favorably. Among all candidates who discussed women's issues, 82.0% of congressional candidates, 100.0% of statewide candidates, 87.5% of candidates for the state senate, and 88.1% of candidates for the state house expressed positive sentiments toward the women's movement. Of those candidates who discussed women's issues, 72.5% of congressional candidates, 100.0% of statewide candidates, 86.6% of candidates for the state senate, and 85.9% of candidates for the state house also favored ratification of the ERA. Given the distribution of candidates' views on the women's movement and the ERA, it seems reasonable to assume that most of the women who discussed women's issues in their primary campaigns were expressing feminist views.

15. Candidates were asked to list the issues they emphasized as most important during their primary campaigns. They could list as many as they wished.

16. N = 44 congressional, 17 statewide, 64 state senate, and 404 state house candidates.

17. Jeff Fishel, "American Political Parties and Elections: An Overview," in *Parties and Elections in an Anti-Party Age*, ed. Jeff Fishel (Bloomington: Indiana University Press, 1978), p. xxiii.

18. For a discussion of the major parties' coalitions and the differences between the parties, see Herbert McClosky, Paul J. Hoffman, and Rosemary O'Hara, "Issue Conflict and Consensus Among Party Leaders and Followers," *American Political Science Review*, 54 (June 1960): 417; Everett Carl Ladd, Jr., and Charles D. Hadley, *Transformations of the American Party System*, 2nd ed. (New York: W. W. Norton, 1978); James L. Sundquist, *Dynamics of the Party System* (Washington, D.C.: Brookings, 1973); Robert Huckshorn, *Political Parties in America* (North Scituate, Massachusetts: Duxbury Press, 1980); Hugh LeBlanc, *American Political Parties* (New York: St. Martin's Press, 1982).

19. See Kirkpatrick, p. 164; Mezey, "Women and Representation: The Case of Hawaii." It is important to note that neither of these studies included a representative sample of women officeholders nationwide. Thus, the lack of support for the women's movement may have been a function of the particular women sampled.

20. The two child care items which resulted in higher levels of support for the feminist position than the one examined were:

(a) I oppose federal income tax deductions for child care services.

(b) The national and/or state government should provide child care services for those low income families in need of such services.

The two abortion items which resulted in higher levels of support for the feminist position than the one examined were:

(a) If a woman wants to have an abortion, that is a matter for her and her doctor to decide, and the government should have nothing to do with it.

(b) I would favor a constitutional amendment which would return the authority to legislate abortion to the states.

Because the two ERA items yielded similar levels of support, there was no clear reason to choose one over the other.

21. In the candidate population as a whole, 66.4% of congressional candidates, 62.2% of statewide candidates, 58.2% of candidates for the state senate, and 58.0% of candidates for the state house were Democrats.

22. While there were moderate to strong relationships between party affiliation and ideology (tau$_c$ = .70 for congressional candidates, .33 for statewide candidates, .54 for state senate candidates, and .54 for state house candidates), a majority of Republicans did not consider themselves conservatives. Moreover, some Democrats classified themselves as conservatives. Among Republicans, only 65.0% of congressional candidates (N = 20), 28.6% of statewide candidates (N = 7), 32.1% of state senate candidates (N = 56), and 46.9% of state house candidates (N = 341) considered themselves conservatives. For Democrats, the proportion of conservatives was 7.9% among congressional candidates (N = 38), 10.0% among statewide candidates (N = 10), 6.9% among state senate candidates (N = 87), and 11.7% among state house candidates (N = 505).

23. Forty-eight and three-tenths percent of congressional candidates, 27.8% of statewide candidates, 43.2% of state senate candidates, and 43.0% of state house candidates considered themselves liberals. In contrast, only 27.6% of congressional candidates, 16.7% of statewide candidates, 17.1% of state senate candi-

dates, and 25.9% of state house candidates identified as conservatives. N = 58 congressional, 18 statewide, 146 state senate, and 846 state house candidates.

24. Only state legislative candidates were examined, because of the very small number of general election victors among congressional and statewide candidates. While the data are not presented here, the relationships between election outcomes and atitudes on the women's issues presented in table 8.3 ranged between $tau_c = -.07$ and $tau_c = .09$ for both state senate and state house candidates.

25. Unratified states in 1976 included Alabama, Arkansas, Arizona, Florida, Georgia, Illinois, Indiana, Louisiana, Mississippi, Missouri, Nevada, North Carolina, Oklahoma, South Carolina, Utah, and Virginia.

26. N = 51 state senate and 202 state house candidates.

27. A much smaller proportion appeared antifeminist on all three atittudinal measures—4.7% of congressional candidates (N = 64), no statewide candidates (N = 15), 2.8% of state senate candidates (N = 142), and 1.8% of state house candidates (N = 812). Even smaller proportions were attitudinal *and* behavioral antifeminists.

28. If some women do perceive that discussing women's issues could cost them votes, this study suggests that their perceptions may be reinforced by the actual outcomes of primary elections. For whatever reasons, and the reasons may well *not* be related to discussion of women's issues, those candidates who did not discuss women's issues at any time during their campaigns fared somewhat better than those who did. Among candidates for the state senate in competitive primaries, 53.3% of those who *never* discussed women's issues (N = 15) won, while only 35.7% of those who discussed women's issues (N = 56) were successful. Similarly, among candidates for the state house who faced primary opposition, 56.0% of those who never discussed women's issues (N = 125) were victorious compared with 44.9% of those who did (N = 316).

29. Leader.

30. Some previous research suggests it is not unreasonable to assume that elected officials will, in fact, vote in congruence with their attitudes. For example, John L. Sullivan and Robert E. O'Connor, "Electoral Choice and Popular Control of Public Policy: The Case of the 1966 House Elections," *American Political Science Review,* 66 (December 1972): 1256–1265, found that congressional candidates elected to office in 1966 voted consistently with attitudes they expressed on a pre-election questionnaire.

31. Marilyn Johnson and Susan Carroll, "Profile of Women Holding Office, 1977," in *Women in Public Office: A Biographical Directory and Statistical Analysis,* 2nd ed., comp. Center for the American Woman and Politics (Metuchen, N.J.: Scarecrow Press, 1978); Mezey, "Support for Women's Rights Policies."

32. The Congressional Caucus for Women's Issues was formed in 1977 as the "Congresswomen's Caucus" with only congresswomen as members. In 1981, the group changed its name to the Congressional Caucus for Women's Issues and admitted congressmen as members. However, men cannot hold Caucus office, serve on the Executive Committee, vote on policy matters, or elect officers. See Irwin Gertzog, *Congressional Women* (New York: Praeger Publishers, 1984).

33. I feel on safe ground in drawing this conclusion with one qualification. As this analysis shows, very few women with a conservative ideology choose to run

for office. I suspect, in large part, this is because most women with conservative ideologies probably have very traditional views of the role that they and other women should play in society. As a result, their ideology in most cases probably inhibits them from running for office—a very unconventional act for a woman. If this explanation is valid, then women who run for office are likely to continue to be disproportionately nonconservative for many years to come. Thus, as long as the self-selection process now in operation is not disrupted, an increase in the number of women elected to office should enhance prospects for increased representation of the interests of women. Only if large numbers of conservative women were somehow mobilized to run for office would the election of more women to office not *necessarily* enhance prospects for increased representation of women's interests. (I would argue that prospects for increased representation still *might* be enhanced even if large numbers of conservative women ran for office. Many of those women who engage in political activity, even conservative women, may be resocialized by direct experience into attitudes more supportive of women's issues and changes in sex-role conceptions. Susan B. Hansen, Linda M. Franz, and Margaret Netemeyer-Mays, "Women's Political Participation and Policy Preferences," *Social Science Quarterly*, 56 [March 1976]: 585–586, found that women whose participation requires interaction with others are more supportive of women's issues than either their male counterparts or women in the general population. The authors suggested, p. 586,

> Through work with others in campaigns and through informal politicking, women may obtain information concerning women's problems and may meet other women actively working on these issues. They might also experience some subtle or not-so-subtle forms of sexism. . . . Participation that required interaction, then, may function as a consciousness-raising activity for many women.

Thus, even if sizable numbers of conservative women were mobilized to run, prospects for increased representation of the interests of women still *might* exist.) It seems highly unlikely, however, that conservative women will be mobilized in large numbers; it is much more likely that the present self-selection process that favors women of liberal and moderate ideologies will continue.

34. N = 73 congressional, 19 statewide, 163 state senate, and 920 state house candidates.

Chapter 9

1. See Council of State Governments, *The Book of the States 1980–1981*, Volume 23 (Lexington, Kentucky: Council of State Governments, 1980), p. 170.

2. Samuel Kernell, "Toward Understanding 19th Century Congressional Careers: Ambition, Competition, and Rotation," *American Journal of Political Science*, 21 (November 1977): 669–693.

3. Morris P. Fiorina, *Congress: Keystone of the Washington Establishment* (New Haven: Yale University, 1977), p. 20, has argued that members of Congress do try to make use of these "perks" to improve their re-election chances, but that they may not profit much from them, at least not in terms of name recognition.

4. Gary C. Jacobson, "The Effects of Campaign Spending in Congressional Elections," *American Political Science Review*, 72 (June 1978): 489.

5. For discussions of the gender gap, see Ruth B. Mandel, "How Women

Vote: The New Gender Gap," *Working Woman*, September 1982, pp. 128–131; Ruth B. Mandel, "The Power of the Women's Vote," *Working Woman*, April 1983, pp. 107–110; Gloria Steinem, "Losing a Battle But Winning the War?" *Ms.*, January 1983, pp. 35–36+.

6. Dom Bonafede, "Women's Movement Broadens the Scope of Its Role in American Politics," *National Journal*, December 11, 1982, p. 2109.

7. Robert Benenson, "Women and Politics," *Editorial Research Reports*, 2 (September 17, 1982), p. 715.

8. W. Dale Nelson, "GOP Looks for Women to Run for Senate," *Home News*, September 7, 1983, p. B8.

9. Susan Carroll, "Women's Rights and Political Parties: Issue Development, the 1972 Conventions, and the National Women's Political Caucus" (unpublished M.A. thesis, Indiana University, 1975), p. 53.

10. Kathy Wilson, "Mr. President, One Term is Enough," *Women's Political Times*, July/August 1983, p. 4.

11. Joan Walsh, "Gender Gap Gives NOW New Power," *In These Times*, October 12–18, 1983, p. 5.

12. Katherine E. Kleeman, *Women's PACs* (New Brunswick, N.J.: Center for the American Woman and Politics, Rutgers University, 1983), p. 20.

13. Bonafede, p. 2109. The figures for NOW and NWPC reflect contributions to candidates of both sexes.

14. See Kleeman.

15. For information about Johnson and her campaign, see *Women's Political Times*, December 1982, p. 3; *Congressional Quarterly Weekly Reports*, January 8, 1983, p. 23; Rob Gurwitt, "Connecticut Primary Will Be a Quiet Affair," *Congressional Quarterly Weekly Reports*, August 21, 1982, p. 2087; *The New York Times*, October 29, 1982; *The New York Times*, November 4, 1982; *Congressional Quarterly Weekly Reports*, October 9, 1982, p. 2503.

16. Harriett Woods, "Woods: Beaten But Not Defeated," *Women's Political Times*, December 1982, p. 3.

17. For information about Woods and her campaign, see Ibid.; Judy Mann, "Strength," *The Washington Post*, September 13, 1982; *St. Louis Globe—Democrat*, October 15, 1982; *The New York Times*, October 25, 1982; *The New York Times*, October 13, 1982; Tina Rosenberg, "Running on Empty," *Savvy*, November 1982, pp. 40–44; *Women's Political Times*, September 1982, p. 4.

18. For information about Molina and her campaign, see *Women's Political Times*, September 1982, p. 5; Tony Castro, "Secrets of the Golden Palominos," *Los Angeles Herald Examiner*, February 1982; "Will Gloria Molina Lead Us Into Decade of the Hispanic?" *Los Angeles Times*, November 11, 1982; *Los Angeles Times*, April 4, 1982; *Los Angeles Times*, June 7, 1982; *Los Angeles Times*, May 23, 1982; Kathy A. Stanwick, *Political Women Tell What It Takes* (New Brunswick, N.J.: Center for the American Woman and Politics, Rutgers University, 1983), p. 9.

19. National Women's Political Caucus, "Women and the 1982 Election: A Post-Election Summary and Analysis," November 1982.

20. Kathy A. Stanwick and Katherine E. Kleeman, *Women Make A Difference* (New Brunswick, N.J.: Center for the American Woman and Politics, Rutgers University 1983).

BIBLIOGRAPHY

Acker, Joan. "Women and Social Stratification: A Case of Intellectual Sexism." *American Journal of Sociology* 78 (January 1973): 936–945.

Adamany, David W. *Campaign Finance in America*. North Scituate, Massachusetts: Duxbury Press, 1972.

Agranoff, Robert. *The New Style in Election Campaigns*. Boston: Holbrook Press, 1972.

———. *The Management of Election Campaigns*. Boston: Holbrook Press, 1976.

Aldridge, John H., and Charles F. Cnudde. "Probing the Bounds of Conventional Wisdom: A Comparison of Regression, Probit and Discriminant Analysis." *American Journal of Political Science* 19 (August 1975): 571–608.

Amundsen, Kirsten. *The Silenced Majority: Women and American Democracy*. Englewood Cliffs: Prentice-Hall, 1971.

Bachrach, Peter. *The Theory of Democratic Elitism: A Critique*. Boston: Little, Brown and Company, 1967.

Balbus, Isaac D. "The Concept of Interest in Marxian and Pluralist Analysis." *Politics and Society* 1 (1971): 151–177.

Barry, Brian. *Political Argument*. New York: Humanities Press, 1965.

Baxter, Sandra, and Marjorie Lansing. *Women and Politics: The Invisible Majority*. Ann Arbor: University of Michigan Press, 1980.

Beauvoir, Simone de. *The Second Sex*. New York: Vintage Books, 1974.

Bem, Sandra Lipsitz. "The Measurement of Psychological Androgyny." *Journal of Consulting and Clinical Psychology* 42 (April 1972): 155–162.

———. "Sex Role Adaptability: One Consequence of Psychological Androgyny." *Journal of Personality and Social Psychology* 31 (April 1975): 634–643.

———. "On the Utility of Alternative Procedures for Assessing Psychological Androgyny." *Journal of Consulting and Clinical Psychology* 45 (April 1977): 196–205.

———. "Theory and Measurement of Androgyny: A Reply to the Pedhazur-Tetenbaum and Locksley-Colten Critiques." *Journal of Personality and Social Psychology* 37 (June 1979): 1047–1054.

Bem, Sandra Lipsitz, and Daryl J. Bem. "Case Study of a Nonconscious Ideology: Training the Woman to Know Her Place." In *Beliefs, Attitudes, and Human Affairs*, edited by Daryl J. Bem. Belmont, California: Brooks/Cole Publishing Company, 1970.

Benenson, Robert. "Women and Politics." *Editorial Research Reports* 2 (September 17, 1982): 695–716.

Benn, S. I. "Interests in Politics." *Proceedings of Aristotelian Society* 60 (1960): 123–140.

Berelson, Bernard R., Paul F. Lazarsfeld, and William N. McPhee. *Voting*. Chicago: University of Chicago Press, 1954.

Berreman, Gerald D. "Race, Caste, and Other Invidious Distinctions in Social Stratification." *Race* 13 (April 1972): 385–414.

Bibby, John F., and Robert J. Huckshorn. "The Republican Party in American Politics." In *Parties and Elections in an Anti-Party Age*, edited by Jeff Fishel. Bloomington: Indiana University Press, 1978.

Blair, Diane Kincaid, and Ann R. Henry. "The Family Factor in State Legislative Turnover." *Legislative Studies Quarterly* 6 (February 1981): 55–68.

Bonafede, Dom. "Women's Movement Broadens the Scope of Its Role in American Politics." *National Journal*, December 11, 1982, 2108–2111.

Bourque, Susan C., and Jean Grossholtz. "Politics an Unnatural Practice: Political Science Looks at Female Participation." *Politics and Society* 4 (Winter 1974): 225–266.

Bowman, Lewis, and G. R. Boynton. "Recruitment Patterns Among Local Party Officials: A Model and Some Preliminary Findings in Selected Locales." In *A Comparative Study of Party Organization*, edited by William E. Wright. Columbus, Ohio: Charles E. Merrill Publishing Company, 1971.

Buchanan, Christopher, "Why Aren't There More Women in Congress?" *Congressional Quarterly Weekly Reports* 36 (August 12, 1978): 2108–2110.

Bullock, Charles S., and Patricia Findley Heys. "Recruitment of Women for Congress: A Research Note." *Western Political Quarterly* 25 (September 1972): 416–423.

Campbell, Angus, Philip E. Converse, Warren E. Miller, and Donald E. Stokes. *The American Voter: An Abridgement*. New York: John Wiley & Sons, 1964.

Carroll, Susan. "Women's Rights and Political Parties: Issue Development, the 1972 Conventions, and the National Women's Political Caucus." Master's thesis, Indiana University, 1975.

Chandler, Robert. *Public Opinion: Changing Attitudes on Contemporary Political and Social Issues*. New York: R. R. Bowker Company, 1972.

Citizens Conference on State Legislatures. *The Sometime Governments: A Critical Study of the 50 American Legislatures*. Kansas City: Citizens Conference on State Legislatures, 1971.

Clem, Alan L. *The Making of Congressmen: Seven Campaigns of 1974*. North Scituate, Massachusetts: Duxbury Press, 1976.

Congressional Quarterly Weekly Reports, January 8, 1983.

———, October 9, 1982.

Connolly, William E. *The Terms of Political Discourse*. Lexington: D. C. Heath and Company, 1974.

Cook, F. Rhodes. "National Conventions and Delegate Selection: An Overview." In *Parties and Elections in an Anti-Party Age*, edited by Jeff Fishel. Bloomington: Indiana University Press, 1978.

Cooley, William W., and Paul R. Lohnes. *Multivariate Data Analysis*. New York: John Wiley & Sons, 1971.

Costain, Anne N. "Lobbying for Equal Credit." Department of Political Science, University of Colorado. Photocopy.

Costantini, Edmond, and Kenneth H. Craik. "Women as Politicians: The Social Background, Personality, and Political Careers of Female Party Leaders." *Journal of Social Issues* 28 (1972): 217–236.

The Council of State Governments. *The Book of States, 1976–1977*. Lexington, Kentucky: The Council of State Governments, 1976.

———. *The Book of the States, 1980–1981*. Lexington, Kentucky: The Council of State Governments, 1980.

Cover, A. D. "One Good Term Deserves Another: The Advantage of Incumbency in Congressional Elections." *American Journal of Political Science* 21 (August 1977): 523–541.

Currey, Virginia. "Campaign Theory and Practice—The Gender Variable." In *A Portrait of Marginality: The Political Behavior of the American Woman*, edited by Marianne Githens and Jewel L. Prestage. New York: David McKay Company, 1977.

Dahl, Robert A. *A Preface to Democratic Theory*. Chicago: The University of Chicago Press, 1956.

————. "Further Reflections on 'The Elitist Theory of Democracy.'" *American Political Science Review* 60 (June 1966): 296–305.

————. *Democracy in the United States: Promise and Performance*. Chicago: Rand McNally & Company, 1972.

Darcy, R., and Sarah Slavin Schramm. "When Women Run Against Men." *Public Opinion Quarterly* 41 (Spring 1977): 1–12.

Davis, Lane. "The Cost of the New Realism." In *Frontiers of Democratic Theory*, edited by Henry S. Kariel. New York: Random House, 1970.

Democratic National Committee. *Mandate for Reform: A Report of the Commission on Party Structure and Delegate Selection to the Democratic National Committee*. George McGovern, Chairman. Washington, D.C.: The Commission on Party Structure and Delegate Selection of the Democratic National Committee, April 1970.

Dewey, John. "Democracy as a Way of Life." In *Frontiers of Democratic Theory*, edited by Henry S. Kariel. New York: Random House, 1970.

Diamond, Irene. "Female Candidates in the 1974 Primaries." Paper presented at the Adelphi University Symposium on Women in Politics, September 1975.

————. "Why Aren't They There? Women in the American State Legislatures." Paper presented at the annual meeting of the American Political Science Association, The Palmer House, Chicago, September 2–5, 1976.

————. *Sex Roles in the State House*. New Haven: Yale University Press, 1977.

Dubeck, Paula J. "Women and Access to Political Office: A Comparison of Female and Male State Legislators." *The Sociological Quarterly* 17 (Winter 1976): 42–52.

Duke, James T. *Conflict and Power in Social Life*. Provo, Utah: Brigham Young University Press, 1976.

Dutton, William H. "The Political Ambitions of Local Legislators: A Comparative Perspective." *Polity* 7 (Summer 1975): 504–522.

Dye, Thomas R. "What to Do About the Establishment: Prescription for Elites." In *The Irony of Democracy: An Uncommon Introduction to American Politics*, by Thomas R. Dye and L. Harmon Zeigler. Belmont, California: Wadsworth Publishing Company, Duxbury Press, 1972.

Epstein, Cynthia Fuchs. *Women's Place: Options and Limits in Professional Careers*. Berkeley: University of California Press, 1970.

Epstein, Leon. *Politics in Wisconsin*. Madison: University of Wisconsin Press, 1958.

Erskine, Hazel. "The Polls: Women's Role." *Public Opinion Quarterly* 25 (Summer 1971): 275–290.

Eulau, Heinz, William Buchanan, LeRoy C. Ferguson, and John C. Wahlke. "Career Perspectives of State Legislators." In *Political Decisionmakers*, edited by Dwaine Marwick. New York: The Free Press of Glencoe, 1961.

Eulau, Heinz, and John D. Sprague. *Lawyers in Politics: A Study in Professional Convergence*. Indianapolis: The Bobbs-Merrill Company, 1964.

Farah, Barbara. "Climbing the Political Ladder: The Aspirations and Expectations of Partisan Elites." In *New Research on Women and Sex Roles at the University of Michigan*, edited by Dorothy G. McGuigan. Ann Arbor: University of Michigan Center for the Continuing Education of Women, 1976.

Fiorina, Morris P. *Congress: Keystone of the Washington Establishment*. New Haven: Yale University Press, 1977.

Fishel, Jeff. *Party and Opposition: Congressional Challengers in American Politics*. New York: David McKay Company, 1973.

―――. "American Political Parties and Elections: An Overview." In *Parties and Elections in an Anti-Party Age*, edited by Jeff Fishel. Bloomington: Indiana University Press, 1978.

Flanigan, William H., and Nancy H. Zingale. *Political Behavior of the American Electorate*. 4th ed. Boston: Allyn and Bacon, 1979.

Frankovic, Kathleen A. "Sex and Voting in the U.S. House of Representatives 1961–1975." *American Politics Quarterly* 5 (July 1977): 315–330.

Freeman, Jo. *The Politics of Women's Liberation*. New York: David McKay Company, 1975.

―――. "Introduction." In *Women: A Feminist Perspective*, edited by Jo Freeman. Palo Alto: Mayfield Publishing Company, 1979.

Froman, Lewis A., Jr. *Congressmen and Their Constituencies*. Chicago: Rand McNally & Company, 1963.

Gallup Opinion Index, November 1974.

―――, September 1975.

Gallup Opinion Survey, June 1982.

Gamson, William A. *Power and Discontent*. Homewood, Illinois: Dorsey Press, 1968.

Gehlen, Frieda L. "Women Members of Congress: A Distinctive Role." In *A Portrait of Marginality: The Political Behavior of the American Woman*, edited by Marianne Githens and Jewel L. Prestage. New York: David McKay Company, 1977.

Gelb, Joyce, and Marian Lief Palley. "Women and Interest Group Politics: A Case Study of the Equal Credit Opportunity Act." *American Politics Quarterly* 4 (July 1977): 331–352.

Gertzog, Irwin. *Congressional Women*. New York: Praeger Publishers, 1984.

Githens, Marianne. "Spectators, Agitators, or Lawmakers: Women in State Legislatures." In *A Portrait of Marginality: The Political Behavior of the American Woman*, edited by Marianne Githens and Jewel L. Prestage. New York: David McKay Company, 1977.

Githens, Marianne, and Jewel L. Prestage. "Introduction." In *A Portrait of Marginality: The Political Behavior of the American Woman*, edited by Marianne Githens and Jewel L. Prestage. New York: David McKay Company, 1977.

Grumm, John G. "Structural Determinants of Legislative Output." In *Legislatures in Developmental Perspective*, edited by Allan Kornberg and Lloyd D. Musolf. Durham: Duke University Press, 1970.

Gurwitt, Rob. "Connecticut Primary Will Be a Quiet Affair." *Congressional Quarterly Weekly Reports*, August 21, 1982, 2087.

Hammond, Nancy, and Glenda Belote. "From Deviance to Legitimacy: Women

as Political Candidates." *The University of Michigan Papers in Women's Studies*
1 (June 1974): 58–72.

Hansen, Susan B., Linda M. Franz, and Margaret Netemeyer-Mays. "Women's
Political Participation and Policy Preferences." *Social Science Quarterly* 56
(March 1976): 576–590.

Harris, Louis, and Associates. *The 1972 Virginia Slims American Women's Opinion Poll: A Survey of the Attitudes of Women on Their Role in Politics and the
Economy*. Louis Harris and Associates, 1972.

The Harris Survey. May 19, 1974.

———. May 28, 1977.

———. February 13, 1978.

Hershey, Marjorie Randon. "Racial Differences in Sex-Role Identities and Sex
Stereotyping: Evidence Against a Common Assumption." *Social Science Quarterly* 58 (March 1978): 583–596.

Hershey, Marjorie Randon, and Sullivan, John L. "Sex Role Attitudes, Identities
and Political Ideology." *Sex Roles*. 3 (February 1977): 37–57.

Hole, Judith, and Ellen Levine. *Rebirth of Feminism*. New York: Quadrangle
Books, 1971.

Huckshorn, Robert. *Political Parties in America*. North Scituate, Massachusetts:
Duxbury Press, 1980.

Huckshorn, Robert J., and Robert C. Spencer. *The Politics of Defeat: Campaigning for Congress*. Amherst: The University of Massachusetts Press, 1971.

Hunt, A. Lee, and Robert E. Pendley. "Community Gatekeepers: An Examination of Political Recruiters." *Midwest Journal of Political Science* 16 (August
1972): 411–438.

In These Times, October 12–18, 1983.

Jacobson, Gary C. "The Effects of Campaign Spending in Congressional Elections." *American Political Science Review* 72 (June 1978): 469–491.

Jaggar, Alison. "Political Philosophies of Women's Liberation." In *Feminism and
Philosophy*, edited by Mary Vetterling-Braggin, Frederick A. Elliston, and
Jane English. Totowa, New Jersey: Littlefield, Adams & Co., 1977.

Jennings, M. Kent, and Norman Thomas. "Men and Women in Party Elites:
Social Roles and Political Resources." *Midwest Journal of Political Science* 12
(November 1968): 469–492.

Jewell, Malcolm E., and David M. Olson. *American State Political Parties and
Elections*. Homewood, Illinois: The Dorsey Press, 1978.

Johnson, Marilyn, and Susan Carroll. "Profile of Women Holding Office, 1977."
In *Women in Public Office: A Biographical Directory and Statistical Analysis*,
compiled by the Center for the American Woman and Politics. Metuchen, New
Jersey: The Scarecrow Press, 1978.

Karnig, Albert K., and B. Oliver Walter. "Election of Women to City Councils."
Social Science Quarterly 56 (March 1976): 605–613.

Kemper, Theodore D. "On the Nature and Purpose of Ascription." *American
Sociological Review* 39 (December 1974): 844–853.

Kernell, Samuel. "Toward Understanding 19th Century Congressional Careers:
Ambition, Competition, and Rotation." *American Journal of Political Science*
21 (November 1977): 669–693.

Key, V. O., Jr. *American State Politics*. New York: Knopf Publishers, 1956.

Kimble, Penn, and Josh Muravichik. "The New Politics and the Democrats."
Commentary, December 1972, 78–84.

King, Elizabeth G. "Women in Iowa Legislative Politics." In *A Portrait of Marginality: The Political Behavior of the American Woman*, edited by Marianne Githens and Jewel L. Prestage. New York: David McKay Company, 1977.

Kingdon, John W. *Candidates for Office: Beliefs and Strategies*. New York: Random House, 1968.

———. "Politicians' Beliefs About Voters." *American Political Science Review* 61 (March 1967): 137–145.

Kirkpatrick, Jeane J. *Political Woman*. New York: Basic Books, 1974.

———. *The New Presidential Elite: Men and Women in National Politics*. New York: Russell Sage Foundation, 1976.

Klecka, William R. "Discriminant Analysis." In *Statistical Package for the Social Sciences*, edited by Norman H. Nie, C. Hadlai Hull, Jean G. Jenkins, Karin Steinbrenner, and Dale H. Bent. New York: McGraw-Hill, 1975.

Kleeman, Katherine E. *Women's PACs*. New Brunswick, N.J.: Center for the American Woman and Politics, Rutgers University, 1983.

Ladd, Everett Carl, Jr., and Charles D. Hadley. *Transformations of the American Party System*. 2nd ed. New York: W. W. Norton, 1978.

Leader, Shelah Gilbert. "The Policy Impact of Elected Women Officials." In *The Impact of the Electoral Process*, edited by Louis Maisel and Joseph Cooper. Beverly Hills: Sage Publications, 1977.

LeBlanc, Hugh. *American Political Parties*. New York: St. Martin's Press, 1982.

Lee, Marcia Manning. "Why Few Women Hold Public Office: Democracy and Sexual Roles." *Political Science Quarterly* 91 (Summer 1976): 297–324.

———. "Why Few Women Hold Public Office." In *A Portrait of Marginality: The Political Behavior of the American Woman*, edited by Marianne Githens and Jewel L. Prestage. New York: David McKay Company, 1977.

Leuthold, David A. *Electioneering in a Democracy: Campaigns for Congress*. New York: John Wiley & Sons, 1968.

Locksley, Anne, and Mary Ellen Colten. "Psychological Androgyny: A Case of Mistaken Identity?" *Journal of Personality and Social Psychology* 37 (June 1979): 1017–1031.

Los Angeles Herald Examiner, February 1982.

Los Angeles Times, April 4, 1982.

———, May 23, 1982.

———, June 7, 1982.

———, November 11, 1982.

Lynn, Naomi. "Women in American Politics: An Overview." In *Women: A Feminist Perspective*, edited by Jo Freeman. Palo Alto: Mayfield Publishing Company, 1975.

———. "Sexual Politics: Research Note." Paper presented at the annual meeting of the Midwest Political Science Association, Chicago, April 29–May 1, 1976.

———. "American Women and the Political Process." In *Women: A Feminist Perspective*. 2nd ed., edited by Jo Freeman. Palo Alto: Mayfield Publishing Company, 1979.

Lynn, Naomi, and Cornelia Butler Flora. "Societal Punishment and Aspects of Female Participation: 1972 National Convention Delegates." In *A Portrait of Marginality: The Political Behavior of the American Woman*, edited by Marianne Githens and Jewel L. Prestage. New York: David McKay Company, 1977.

Maisel, L. Sandy. "Congressional Elections in 1978: The Road to Nomination, the Road to Election." *American Politics Quarterly* 9 (January 1981): 38–41.

Mandel, Ruth B. *In the Running: Women as Political Candidates*. New York: Ticknor & Fields, 1981.

———. "How Women Vote: The New Gender Gap." *Working Woman*, September 1982, 128–131.

———. "The Power of the Women's Vote." *Working Woman*, April 1983, 107–110.

Marwell, Gerald. "Why Ascription? Parts of a More or Less Formal Theory of the Functions and Dysfunctions of Sex Roles." *American Sociological Review* 40 (August 1975): 445–455.

McClosky, Herbert. "Consensus and Ideology in American Politics." *American Political Science Review* 58 (June 1964): 361–382.

McClosky, Herbert, Paul J. Hoffman, and Rosemary O'Hara. "Issue Conflict and Consensus among Party Leaders and Followers." *American Political Science Review* 54 (June 1960): 406–427.

Mezey, Susan Gluck. "Women and Representation: The Case of Hawaii." *Journal of Politics* 40 (May 1978): 369–385.

———. "Support for Women's Rights Policy: An Analysis of Local Politicians." *American Politics Quarterly* 6 (October 1978): 485–497.

Mileur, Jerome M., and George T. Sulzner. *Campaigning for the Massachusetts Senate: Electioneering Outside the Political Limelight*. Amherst: The University of Massachusetts Press, 1974.

Mill, John Stuart. "The Subjection of Women." In *Essays on Sex Equality*, edited by Alice S. Rossi. Chicago: University of Chicago Press, 1970.

Miller, Arthur H. "Political Issues and Trust in Government: 1964–70." *American Political Science Review* 68 (September 1974): 951–972.

Millett, Kate. *Sexual Politics*. New York: The Hearst Corporation, Avon Books, 1971.

Morrison, Donald G. "On the Interpretation of Discriminant Analysis." *Journal of Marketing Research* 6 (May 1969): 153–163.

Mosca, Gaetano. *The Ruling Class*. New York: McGraw-Hill, 1939.

Myrdal, Gunnar. "Women, Servants, Mules, and Other Property." In *Masculine/Feminine: Readings in Sexual Mythology and the Liberation of Women*, edited by Betty Roszak and Theodore Roszak. New York: Harper & Row, Harper Colophon Books, 1969.

Napolitan, Joseph. *The Election Game and How to Win It*. Garden City, New York: Doubleday & Company, 1972.

National Women's Political Caucus. "Women and the 1982 Election: A Post-Election Summary and Analysis." November 1982.

Ness, Susan, and Fredrica Wechsler. "Women Judges—Why So Few?" *Graduate Woman*, November/December, 1979.

The New York Times, December 21, 1976.

———, March 6, 1978.

———, October 13, 1982.

———, October 25, 1982.

———, October 29, 1982.

———, November 4, 1982.

———, November 18, 1982.

Nie, Norman H., Sidney Verba, and John R. Petrocik. *The Changing American Voter*. enl. ed. Cambridge: Harvard University Press, 1979.

Nimmo, Dan. *The Political Persuaders: The Techniques of Modern Election Campaigns*. Englewood Cliffs: Prentice-Hall, 1970.

"Opinion Roundup." *Public Opinion,* January/February 1979, 36.
———. *Public Opinion,* December/January 1981, 42.
———. *Public Opinion,* April/May 1982, 32.
Paizis, Suzanne. *Getting Her Elected: A Political Woman's Handbook.* Sacramento: Creative Editions, 1977.
Pateman, Carole. *Participation and Democratic Theory.* Cambridge: Cambridge University Press, 1970.
Patterson, Samuel C., and G. R. Boynton. "Legislative Recruitment in a Civic Culture." *Social Science Quarterly* 50 (September 1969): 243–263.
Pedhazur, Elazar, and Toby J. Tetenbaum. "Bem Sex Role Inventory: A Theoretical and Methodological Critique." *Journal of Personality and Social Psychology* 37 (June 1979): 996–1016.
Pitkin, Hanna Fenichel. *The Concept of Representation.* Berkeley: University of California Press, 1967.
Prewitt, Kenneth. *The Recruitment of Political Leaders: A Study of Citizen-Politicians.* Indianapolis: Bobbs-Merrill Company, 1970.
Prewitt, Kenneth, and Heinz Eulau. "Political Matrix and Political Representation: Prolegomenon to a New Departure from an Old Problem." *American Political Science Review* 63 (June 1969): 427–441.
Prewitt, Kenneth, and William Nowlin. "Political Ambitions and the Behavior of Incumbent Politicians." *Western Political Quarterly* 22 (June 1969): 298–308.
Prewitt, Kenneth, and Alan Stone. *The Ruling Elites: Elite Theory, Power, and American Democracy.* New York: Harper & Row, 1973.
Prothro, James W., and Charles M. Grigg. "Fundamental Principles of Democracy: Bases of Agreement and Disagreement." *Journal of Politics* 22 (May 1960): 276–294.

Rosenberg, Tina. "Running on Empty." *Savvy,* November 1982, 40–44.

Sapiro, Virginia. "When Are Interests Interesting? The Problem of Political Representation of Women," *American Political Science Review* 75 (September 1981): 701–716.
———. "Private Costs of Public Commitments or Public Costs of Private Commitments? Family Roles versus Political Ambition." *American Journal of Political Science* 26 (May 1982): 265–279.
Sartori, Giovanni. *Democratic Theory.* Detroit: Wayne State University Press, 1962.
Schlesinger, Joseph A. *Ambition and Politics: Political Careers in the United States.* Chicago: Rand McNally & Company, 1966.
Schumpeter, Joseph. *Capitalism, Socialism and Democracy.* London: George Allen & Unwin, 1943.
Seligman, Lester. "Political Recruitment and Party Structure: A Case Study." *American Political Science Review* 55 (March 1961): 77–86.
Seligman, Lester, Michael R. King, Chong Lim Kim, and Roland E. Smith. *Patterns of Recruitment: A State Choses Its Lawmakers.* Chicago: Rand McNally College Publishing Company, 1974.
Sheffield, James F., Jr., and Lawrence K. Goering. "Winning and Losing: Candidate Advantage in Local Elections." *American Politics Quarterly* 6 (October 1978): 453–468.
Sorauf, Frank. *Party and Representation: Legislative Politics in Pennsylvania.* New York: Atherton Press, 1963.
———. *Political Parties in America.* 4th ed. Boston: Little, Brown and Company, 1980.

Soule, John W. "Future Political Ambitions and the Behavior of Incumbent State Legislators." *Midwest Journal of Political Science* 13 (August 1969): 439–454.

Stanwick, Kathy A. *Political Women Tell What It Takes*. New Brunswick, N.J.: Center for the American Woman and Politics, Rutgers University, 1983.

Stanwick, Kathy A. and Katherine E. Kleeman. *Women Make a Difference*. New Brunswick, N.J.: Center for the American Woman and Politics, Rutgers University, 1983.

Steinem, Gloria. "Losing a Battle But Winning the War?" *Ms.*, January 1983.

St. Louis Globe-Democrat, October 15, 1982.

Stouffer, Samuel A. *Communism, Conformity and Civil Liberties*. New York: John Wiley & Sons, 1955.

Sullivan, John L., and Robert E. O'Connor. "Electoral Choice and Popular Control of Public Policy: The Case of the 1966 House Elections." *American Political Science Review* 66 (December 1972): 1256–1265.

Sundquist, James L. *Dynamics of the Party System*. Washington, D.C.: Brookings, 1973.

Thompson, Dennis F. *The Democratic Citizen: Social Science and Democratic Theory in the Twentieth Century*. Cambridge: Cambridge University Press, 1970.

Tolchin, Susan, and Martin Tolchin. *Clout: Womanpower and Politics*. New York: G. P. Putnam's Sons, Capricorn Books, 1976.

Van Hightower, Nikki R. "The Recruitment of Women for Public Office." *American Politics Quarterly* 5 (July 1977): 301–314.

Verba, Sidney, and Norman H. Nie. *Participation in America: Political Democracy and Social Equality*. New York: Harper & Row, 1972.

Wahlke, John C., Heinz Eulau, William Buchanan, and LeRoy C. Ferguson. *The Legislative System: Explorations in Legislative Behavior*. New York: John Wiley & Sons, 1962.

Walker, Jack L. "A Critique of the Elitist Theory of Democracy." *American Political Science Review* 60 (June 1966): 285–295.

Wall, Grenville. "The Concept of Interest in Politics." *Politics and Society* 5 (1975): 487–510.

The Washington Post, January 16, 1977.

———, August 13, 1980.

———, August 13, 1982.

———, September 13, 1982.

Welch, Susan. "Women as Political Animals? A Test of Some Explanations for Male-Female Participation Differences." *American Journal of Political Science* 4 (November 1977): 711–730.

Werner, Emmy E. "Women in Congress: 1917–1964." *Western Political Quarterly* 19 (March 1966): 16–30.

———. "Women in the State Legislatures." *Western Political Quarterly* 21 (March 1968): 40–50.

Wiltsee, Herbert L. "The State Legislatures." *The Book of States, 1976–1977*. Lexington, Kentucky: The Council of State Governments, 1976.

Women's Political Times, Summer 1978.

———, June 1979.

———, September 1982.

———, December 1982.

———, July/August 1983.

INDEX

(Italicized numbers indicate reference to a table.)